Praise for *Michael Jackson, Inc.*

"A fascinating, fresh, detailed account of how Michael Jackson changed the game for artists in the entertainment industry, packed with new angles and insights. Greenburg avoids cheap sensationalism in favor of real, research-based reporting. The result is at once a story of Jackson's remarkable business acumen, as well as a cautionary tale about the price of the ticket. While Jackson's success came at a great cost, reading this book makes clear how he paved the way for generations of artists to come."

— Joseph Vogel, author of *Man in the Music: The Creative Life and Work of Michael Jackson*

"Jackson was crazy like a fox, and could be as cold in business as he was hot onstage and in the studio. I'm crazy for this gripping, beautifully reported book."

—Michael Gross, author of *House of Outrageous Fortune*

"We know the circus that Michael Jackson's personal life became in the media, yet Zack found the stories of who he became in the business world, which was starkly different and industry influencing. Jackson went hard in the vocal booth and even harder in the boardroom. Artist-entrepreneurs like Jay Z, Diddy, and Lady Gaga owe him the world; we're indebted to Zack for shedding light on Jackson's business acumen."

—Datwon Thomas, contributing editor at Ozy.com and former executive editor of *VIBE*

"The King of Pop is perfectly captured by Zack O'Malley Greenburg, who has a journalist's eye for detail with *Michael Jackson, Inc.* The words dance across the page, the mark of a writer with vivid, natural storytelling talent. Bravo, Zack!"

—Chuck Leavell, keyboardist for the Rolling Stones and author of *Growing a Better America*

ALSO BY ZACK O'MALLEY GREENBURG

*Empire State of Mind: How Jay-Z Went
from Street Corner to Corner Office*

MICHAEL JACKSON, INC.

THE RISE, FALL, AND REBIRTH
OF A BILLION-DOLLAR EMPIRE

Zack O'Malley Greenburg

ATRIA BOOKS

NEW YORK   LONDON   TORONTO   SYDNEY   NEW DELHI

ATRIA BOOKS

A Division of Simon & Schuster, Inc.
1230 Avenue of the Americas
New York, NY 10020

First Atria Books hardcover edition June 2014

ATRIA BOOKS and colophon are trademarks of Simon & Schuster, Inc.

For information about special discounts for bulk purchases, please contact Simon & Schuster Special Sales at 1-866-506-1949 or business@simonandschuster.com.

The Simon & Schuster Speakers Bureau can bring authors to your live event. For more information or to book an event contact the Simon & Schuster Speakers Bureau at 1-866-248-3049 or visit our website at www.simonspeakers.com.

Interior design by Paul Dippolito
Jacket design by Anna Dorfman
Jacket painting by Borbay

Manufactured in the United States of America

10   9   8   7   6   5   4   3   2   1

Library of Congress Cataloging-in-Publication Data

Greenburg, Zack O'Malley.
   Michael Jackson, Inc.: the rise, fall, and rebirth of a billion-dollar empire /
   Zack O'Malley Greenburg.
      pages   cm
   Includes bibliographical references and index.
   1. Jackson, Michael, 1958–2009—Finance, Personal. 2. Popular music—
Economic aspects—United States. I. Title.
   ML420.J175G75 2014
   782.42166092—dc23   2013045449
   [B]
ISBN 978-1-4767-0596-5
ISBN 978-1-4767-0638-2 (ebook)

For Cousin Andrew, another star gone too soon—
and for Danielle, who rocks my world

CONTENTS

Introduction 1

1 Steeltown Dreaming 11

2 Motown University 24

3 Epic Changes 39

4 Empire Building 52

5 Kissing the Monster 63

6 The Business of Victory 80

7 Buying the Beatles 96

8 Dancing with the Stars 110

9 Good and Bad 120

10 Off to Neverland 135

11 New Shoes 144

12 Dangerous Ventures 153

13 History Lesson 169

14 Invincible? 183

15 The Prodigal King 199

16 This Is It 210

17 Postmortem Payday 223

18 Immortal 234

Acknowledgments 245

Books for Food 249

Appendix: Michael Jackson's Career Earnings 250

Appendix: Michael Jackson's ATV Memo 252

Notes 253

Index 279

INTRODUCTION

Once every few months during the mid-1980s, a handful of America's savviest businessmen gathered to plot financial strategy for a billion-dollar entertainment conglomerate.

This informal investment committee included David Geffen, who'd launched multiple record labels and would go on to become one of Hollywood's richest men after founding DreamWorks Studios; John Johnson, who started *Ebony* magazine and would become the first black man to appear in the Forbes 400 list of wealthiest Americans; John Branca, who has since handled finances for dozens of Rock and Roll Hall of Famers including the Beach Boys and the Rolling Stones; and Michael Jackson, the King of Pop and chairman of the board, inscrutable in his customary sunglasses.

Shares of the entertainment company in question were never traded on the New York Stock Exchange or the NASDAQ. Though few would even consider it to actually be a company, this multinational's products have been consumed by billions of people over the past few decades. Had the organization been officially incorporated, it might have been called Michael Jackson, Inc.

In 1985, this conglomerate made its most substantial acquisition: ATV, the company that housed the prized music publishing catalogue of the Beatles. Included were copyrights to most of the band's biggest hits, including "Yesterday," "Come Together," "Hey Jude," and hundreds of others.

At an investment committee meeting months before the deal was consummated, however, the acquisition was looking unlikely. Michael Jackson, Inc. was deep into negotiations with Australian billionaire Robert Holmes à Court, whose asking price for ATV had soared past $40 million—prompting disagreement among Jackson's inner circle over how to proceed.

CBS Records chief Walter Yetnikoff, a confidant who wasn't on the committee, found the price to be exorbitant, and he had plenty of company.[1] Even Geffen seemed to think the bidding had gotten too high. Johnson thought differently. "This is something you believe in and want to get," he told the singer. "Don't blow it over price."[2]

Not wanting to upset anyone, Jackson remained silent—as he often did in meetings—but he'd already made his decision. He scrawled a note on the back of a financial statement and passed it to Branca beneath the table.

"John please let's not bargain," it read. "I don't want to lose the deal . . . IT'S MY CATALOGUE."[3]

A few months later, Jackson purchased ATV for $47.5 million. Today, that investment alone is worth about $1 billion.

———

As evidenced by the size of the empire he left behind when he died suddenly in 2009, Michael Jackson was effectively a corporation in and of himself. He was not only the founder and creative force behind this empire, but also its most important product. By the middle of the 1980s, he chaired an organization that included Branca (Jackson's chief executive officer, if you will), manager Frank Dileo (his chief marketing officer), and a handful of others.

Jackson and his team made many game-changing moves beyond acquiring ATV. Among them: creating and promoting *Thriller*, the bestselling album of all time (roughly 100 million units sold), landing unprecedented endorsement deals with Pepsi ($5.2 million in 1983, $10 million in 1987, $15 million in 1990), and launching record-setting excursions like the Bad Tour ($125 million in gross ticket sales). The latter drew 4.4 million people, who each paid about $28 per ticket. With a modern price of $130, it would have grossed nearly $600 million, making it the second most lucrative tour of all time. At $200 per ticket, it would have been number one.

"I got to witness the divinity in him every night," says Sheryl Crow, who served as one of Jackson's backup singers on the Bad Tour. "[He had] that thing that is not quantifiable—that thing that you watch, and you cannot figure out why it is that you feel the molecules in the room change, but you are aware of it."[4]

Perhaps most significantly, Jackson fundamentally changed the formula for monetizing fame forever. In addition to making the most successful music video of all time, starring in movies and penning a bestselling autobiography, he launched an eponymous clothing line, teamed up with Sega to place himself in a video game, and scored a deal for his own LA Gear sneaker, unbelievably earning a bigger initial guarantee than Michael Jordan did with Nike. All in all, he earned $1.1 billion in his career—$1.9 billion, adjusted for inflation (see appendix for a year-by-year breakdown).

"He had good instincts . . . more, more, more; better, better, better," says Sandy Gallin, who served as Jackson's manager for the first half of the 1990s. "He would, in his mind, negotiate the same way. No matter what anybody would offer, he wanted more."[5]

Jackson helped flip the paradigm of entertainer as contractor on its head, offering a new path: entertainer as owner. On top of the ATV deal, he secured the rights to his own master recordings and compositions, and launched his music imprint as a joint venture under the Sony umbrella. Not all of his gambits turned out as well as Jackson might have hoped; some failed altogether (for example, an attempt to buy a bankrupt Marvel Comics a decade before Disney purchased it for $4 billion), but most still earned him double-digit millions—and paved the way for the modern celebrity mogul.

"Michael Jackson was so much bigger than Jay Z or 50 Cent or anybody else who did it, in comparison," says 50 Cent, who completed the shoes-clothes-label trifecta years later. Jackson, he adds, is "why music is the way it is now . . . you've seen a shift in an area [previously] reserved for professional athletes."[6]

For that reason and others, plenty of megastars still look up to the King of Pop as a trailblazer on and off the stage despite the moves that didn't work out. "He was extremely smart," explains fellow actor-musician-entrepreneur Ludacris. "From my perspective, because I'm business-oriented and savvy, I noticed and even read up on everything that he did."[7] Adds superproducer Pharrell Williams: "He was so far advanced in the way he thought about things."[8]

———

The tale of Michael Jackson, Inc. begins with its namesake's early days as part of the Jackson 5, touring the "chitlin circuit." At gigs, Jackson met famous musicians like Smokey Robinson, Gladys Knight, and Jackie Wilson. Even at age seven, he'd ask question after question not only about their performances, but about how the music industry worked.

Along the way, Jackson developed a sense of perfectionism, something his violent father pounded into his son with his fists after miscues in rehearsal. At age nine, Jackson gained a comparatively kinder, gentler mentor in Berry Gordy—who founded his own entertainment conglomerate, Motown Records, and signed the Jackson 5 to the label in 1968. Under Gordy's tutelage, Jackson eagerly absorbed lessons on how to write, record, market, and profit from a song.

"I was a person that had a lot of rules and sayings," says Gordy. "Stuff like . . . 'You have to capture your audience in the first twenty seconds; if you don't, then you can't release it' [and] 'It's not in how much you promote it, it's not about that, it's what's in the groove.'"[9]

Jackson's early experience paved the way for the monster deals he made as an adult with the help of advisors like his longtime attorney Branca, whom he handpicked at age twenty-one. The lawyer set a new industry high with Jackson's royalty rate ahead of *Thriller*, which still stands as the bestselling album in history. On top of

ATV, Branca was able to help Jackson land the catalogues of Bread, Sly and the Family Stone, and a handful of songs made famous by Elvis Presley.

"Michael Jackson had the mindset of being a businessman the whole time by acquiring businesses," says Kevin Liles, former president of Def Jam Records. "[It was like] the Michael Jackson private equity firm."[10] Even his Neverland Ranch, purchased for $17.5 million in 1988, has soared in value—some real estate veterans say it could fetch as much as $75 million[11] to $100 million on the open market.[12]

With some help from his team, Jackson also revolutionized the modern music video after overcoming fierce resistance from MTV, which had largely avoided airing music by black artists before caving on Jackson's "Billie Jean." His subsequent "short films," as he liked to call them—namely, "Beat It" and "Thriller"—shattered the notion of what a video could be, both artistically and commercially. Today, there's only one music video in the Library of Congress's exclusive National Film Registry: "Thriller."[13]

"That was the beginning, in my estimation, of music videos becoming the chief promotional tool to sell music," says Fred "Fab 5 Freddy" Brathwaite, longtime host of the show *Yo! MTV Raps*. "Radio play was important, but seeing the artist—and the artist being able to give you a good performance—solidified and became indelible along with the sounds."[14]

Jackson also aimed to instill a sense of marketing in everyone on his team. In 1986, he gave them copies of *Humbug*, a biography of circus impresario P. T. Barnum; he wanted his life to be the greatest show on earth. At his insistence, lieutenants planted fantastical stories about him in mainstream publications and the tabloids.

But Barnum was a complicated role model. Though the aforementioned book describes him as perhaps the greatest showman in American history, it also reveals him to be "a hardheaded businessman [who] followed no battle plan to victory," someone who thought all publicity was good, and was at the same time "self-conscious, and anxious for a claim on national gratitude."[15] At times, the same could be said about the King of Pop.

When Jackson stopped supplying fresh story fodder in the late 1980s, the press started doing it for him. Outrageous headlines followed him throughout his life ("Michael Jackson: Prince Using ESP to Drive My Chimp Crazy") and after his death ("MJ Is Alive— And Running for President"). After he was accused of child molestation in 1993, his image took a hit that would last the rest of his life. His ever-changing physical appearance, altered both by voluntary cosmetic surgery and by the onset of vitiligo, didn't enhance his reputation.

Even so, Jackson had his share of triumphs during the final decade and a half of his life. On the business end, he and his team convinced Sony to pay $115 million for the privilege of merging its publishing arm with his catalogue, creating Sony/ATV, a joint venture now worth about $2 billion. He played to millions of fans abroad in support of his double album *HIStory*. On the personal side, he started a family of his own and set a Guinness World Record for the most charities supported by a pop star.[16]

But he didn't launch a full-scale tour in the United States or earn another endorsement deal after 1993, and his legal troubles sank a budding film career on both sides of the camera. Jackson became deeply distrustful of many of his closest advisors, sometimes with good reason, sometimes not. As a consequence, he disbanded his original business team and replaced it with a carousel of sycophants.

Without a consistent group of advisors to help refine and execute ideas—and to tether his creative genius to reality—the financial prospects of Michael Jackson, Inc. dimmed considerably. After Jackson's annual income stream reached twin peaks of $125 million in 1988 and $118 million in 1995, it declined to $18 million by 1998 and hovered in that vicinity for the rest of his life. But his expenditures remained high as ever. "He did have a business head," says Walter Yetnikoff, Jackson's longtime boss at CBS Records. "His problem was that he overspent."[17]

The perfectionistic impulses that had helped him create *Thriller* drove Jackson to spend increasingly outrageous quantities of time and money trying to top it. For *Invincible*, released in 2001, he ran up recording costs of $30 million to $40 million in an era where $1 million was considered a fairly large budget. He never released another studio album. By 2009, though he was still rich on paper thanks to his Sony/ATV stake and personal publishing holdings, he was running out of cash and nearing the point where he'd have to sell those assets to pay back his loans.

"All people who become legends overnight, especially when they're very young, people do not tell them no," says film director Joel Schumacher, who first worked with Michael Jackson on the 1978 film *The Wiz*. "So they actually learn to become a person that cannot take no. And they make sure there's no one around them that says no. And many times the entourage can [lead] you to your demise."[18]

Jackson died on June 25, 2009, of a drug overdose administered by a member of that retinue—his personal doctor, Conrad Murray, who was later convicted of involuntary manslaughter and sentenced to four years in prison. But when the news of Jackson's death broke, something fascinating happened. The public's tattered memories of his later years seemed to fade as *Thriller* returned to heavy rotation on radio stations around the world.

Indeed, the music video medium that Jackson had reinvented was suddenly securing his legacy. By the morning after his death, a new generation of fans had watched a young, handsome Jackson resolve conflict through dance in the short film for "Beat It" on YouTube. In twenty-four hours, the singer's music racked up 3 million spins on MySpace alone.[19] Jackson sold a record 8 million albums in the US that year—nearly twice as many as the runner-up, Taylor Swift.[20]

Within just a few months, a resurrected Michael Jackson, Inc.—

led by coexecutors John Branca and music industry veteran John McClain—was flourishing once again. Deals included a $60 million advance for *This Is It* (a film based on the concert series for which Jackson was rehearsing when he died), a record deal with Sony worth $250 million (the largest in history), and an agreement with Cirque du Soleil to produce a roving spectacle based on Jackson's music. The show would make him the top touring act in North America— and help wipe away his personal debts—just three years after he passed away. All in all, Jackson's estate has earned over $700 million in the five years since his death, more than any musician dead or alive during that period.

———

Covering this ongoing story for *Forbes* made me aware of the magnitude of Michael Jackson's postmortem business—and of the fascinating story behind the assets he accumulated and cultivated during his life. The realization that his most important moves were not simply executed by savvy handlers, but in many cases driven by Jackson's own intelligence and intuition, gave me the idea for *Michael Jackson, Inc.*

My first book, *Empire State of Mind*, was a business-focused biography of Jay Z, someone widely lauded for his skills as a mogul. I saw that I could approach Jackson's career from a similar angle. But I also identified with Jackson in a way that few others likely do: I was, briefly, a child actor. And though my experience constituted perhaps a single note when compared to the double album of childhood pain and pressure that Jackson experienced, I did get a taste of the delicious, terrible, reality-bending world of show business.

At around the same age Jackson started performing, I played the title role in *Lorenzo's Oil* alongside Susan Sarandon and Nick Nolte. I began to notice a change in the way people perceived me not long after my sixth birthday, when I found myself signing autographs for a pair of girls one year my senior. Stranger still, after months playing a very sick child, donning a bald cap every morning and sometimes wearing an earpiece designed to make me slur my speech, I began to wonder if I might be ill myself.

Eventually, I decided on "early retirement" and shifted my focus to more meaningful pursuits like winning a middle school intramural basketball championship. My parents were more than willing to let me leave show business, a luxury that Michael Jackson never had. That's not to say he wouldn't have chosen to be an entertainer; Jackson brought unparalleled electricity to his performances, something that could only have been generated by an inner drive as prodigious as his outsized talent.

"Onstage for me was home," Jackson told Oprah Winfrey in 1993. "I was most comfortable, and still am most comfortable, onstage. But once I got off stage, I was very sad . . . I used to always cry from loneliness."[21]

The struggles of his childhood bred in him a combination of perfectionism and insecurity—one that fed his desire to constantly break new ground in the fields of music, dance, and film—but also resulted in negative consequences both for his personal happiness and the success of his business empire.

In the coming pages, I retrace the steps of Jackson's journey from impoverished child to international superstar, notebook in hand as I travel to his birthplace of Gary, Indiana; the Apollo Theater in New York; his adopted hometown of Los Angeles and the rolling hills of Neverland; even the lush midlands of Ireland and the blazing neon lights of Las Vegas.

Along the way, I draw on interviews with more than a hundred people who witnessed Jackson's rise as a musician—and as a business—including members of his immediate and extended family, industry executives who helped him build his empire, and various entertainers and Hollywood veterans who came to know and work with him over the years. My reporting relies on firsthand interviews with many of the key players in Jackson's life, and I have avoided the use of press clippings and secondary sources as much as possible. In the instances where I've used these, they're mostly limited to color (album reviews, honorifics, times, and dates).

This is a book about Michael Jackson's business and everything that went into it. That includes the bundle of contradictions that could be used to describe him: a supremely confident visionary occasionally crippled by insecurity, a warm and generous human being capable of stonewalling colleagues to get his way, an ambitious long-term planner who sometimes left his side of multimillion-dollar agreements unfinished, a showbiz revolutionary who eventually lost control of his personal finances.

His highs were as high as anyone's, if not higher, and even his lows offer valuable lessons. The story of how Jackson transformed himself from a poor kid in a hardscrabble steel town into the world's most successful superstar—and a business unto himself—makes him a remarkable case study for generations of entertainers to come, both on the stage and in the boardroom.

"He had a kid's heart, but a mind of a genius," says Berry Gordy. "He was so loving and soft-spoken, and a thinker. . . . He wanted to do everything, and he was capable. You can only do so much in a lifetime."[22]

Chapter 1

STEELTOWN DREAMING

Jackson Street isn't the sort of place where houses have grounds-keepers. The few inhabited homes on the rutted strip of asphalt in Gary, Indiana, sport overgrown yards and heavily fortified doors; the empty ones are marked by boarded or broken windows and crumbling roofs.

That's not the case at 2300 Jackson Street, Michael Jackson's childhood home—a squat box that looks more like an oversize Monopoly piece than a structure capable of housing a family of eleven. In the twilight of a summer Sunday, a middle-aged man in baggy black jeans and a sleeveless denim vest patrols the tidy front yard, gently brooming stray leaves into a bag on the walkway to the front door.

The house is surrounded by a wrought iron fence, its bars decked with roses, candles, and teddy bears left by years of visits by mourners from around the world. In one corner of the yard, a gleaming black monument towers over the greenery, looking like a monolith dreamed up by Stanley Kubrick, save for the inscription:

KING OF POP

MICHAEL J. JACKSON

AUGUST 29, 1958

JUNE 25, 2009

HOME TOWN OF MICHAEL JACKSON – GARY, IN.

"Never can say good bye"[1]

The groundskeeper looks up from his sweeping and ambles over to the gate. He extends his hand, introducing himself as Greg Campbell.

"That's one hump, not two," he says, letting out a deep guffaw. "You know, camels have humps."[2]

When I ask Campbell how he came to be sweeping up in front of this particular house, he informs me that he grew up just four blocks away. He went to grade school nearby with Jermaine and La Toya Jackson, and spent many afternoons in front of 2300 Jackson Street singing with the brothers.

"We all started on the corner singing Temptations songs," he says, and suddenly erupts into one of them—"*I've got sun-shiiiiiiine!*"— his pure tone ringing through the empty street. "It's a lot of history."

He looks back at the house.

"This is the beginning right here. Everybody got whupped, everybody played instruments."

As it turns out, Campbell isn't the only childhood acquaintance of Michael Jackson on the premises. Another man bounds out of the gated door of the house, thick braids coiled neatly into a ponytail behind him. He rushes up to greet me, identifying himself as Keith Jackson—Michael's first cousin—and asks if I'd like to buy a T-shirt for twenty dollars. I decline.

Keith was only a toddler when the young King of Pop actually lived at the house, but he swears he remembers everything that happened in 1965 as though it occurred last Tuesday.

"For me, it was the music, man; just to sit there and watch them rehearse," he recalls. "We had the privilege of being there inside the house while other kids was just trying to peek through the window. So that was a moment in time that I really enjoyed, just watching them when they first started. Right here. I mean, I was like two or three years old, but I still remember."[3]

Nearly half a century later, though, Keith Jackson offers something else about his cousin—something having little to do with his well-documented musical prowess.

"Mike was very smart, man," he says. "Outside of being an entertainer, he was definitely a great businessman as well."

————

Michael Jackson's father doesn't do phone interviews, or at least that's what I was told when I first tried to contact him. If I wanted to talk to Joe Jackson, I would have to come to Las Vegas—alone—and meet him at the Orleans Hotel and Casino, a sprawling faux-Cajun complex on the wrong side of Interstate 15.

When I arrived in the lobby, it wasn't hard to spot the Jackson family patriarch. He was clad all in black—alligator loafers, slacks, dress shirt—with a lone red feather in his fedora. Bulky rings clung to his fingers like gilded barnacles. He removed his black-and-gold Prada sunglasses to reveal a pair of squinty eyes set toward the outer edges of his face, giving him the look of a nefarious disco piranha. Then he motioned me to a couch and we sat down. I asked if I could record our conversation; he nodded, but then reached for my device.

"Let me put this right here like this," he said in a high, hushed voice, looking across the lobby at a middle-aged stranger. "I don't want her to be hearing what I'm saying."[4]

Joe Jackson has long been a suspicious man, but he hasn't always lived gaudily. He and his wife Katherine bought their house at 2300 Jackson Street for $9,000 in 1949, with the help of loans from her parents. The couple's first child, Maureen (nicknamed Rebbie), arrived the next year. She was followed by Jackie, Tito, Jermaine, La Toya, and Marlon (whose twin, Brandon, died shortly after birth), with barely nine months between each. And then, on August 29, 1958, came Michael Jackson.

"He was very hyperactive, couldn't be still," recalls Joe. "Those things made me think that he would be good in performing."

The Jacksons would add two more children, Randy and Janet, and as their home's purchase price suggests, accommodations were far from luxurious: the minuscule abode measures 24 by 36 feet.[5]

"When you look at the house and see how small it is, it's like, 'Where did you guys sleep?'" says Gary's mayor, Karen Freeman-Wilson, who grew up in the city at the same time as the Jacksons. "There was a daybed in one of the rooms, along with maybe a dresser or some other piece of furniture, and it was crowded."[6]

Still, a toddler's imagination can make even the tiniest house seem spacious. "I had remembered it as being large," Jackson wrote of his childhood dwelling. "When you're that young, the whole world seems so huge that a little room can seem four times its size."[7]

Michael's mother worked part-time at Sears but mostly stayed home with the children, while his father earned $30 per day as a crane operator at nearby Inland Steel.[8] Whenever the mill cut back on Joe's shifts, he'd work in the fields harvesting crops. He never told his children when he'd lost work; their only clue was an uptick in potato-based meals.[9]

Michael Jackson's musical talents can be traced in part to his parents. His mother grew up singing spirituals in church, while Joe played guitar in a Gary band called the Falcons as an adult.[10] The Jackson boys absorbed their parents' hobby, singing while washing the dishes every evening.[11] Joe figured music could help keep his kids off the dangerous streets of Gary; if they were inside watching the Falcons, they couldn't be outside getting involved with gangs.

Joe's guitar was not to be played by anyone else, and he made this especially clear to his children. That, of course, only made them more eager to try. When Joe worked late shifts at the mill, the oldest brothers—Jackie, Tito, and Jermaine—would sneak into his closet and take turns strumming while a young Michael watched. They'd play the scales they were learning in music class at school, branching out to the soulful tunes they heard on the radio. Katherine eventually found them out, but in an effort to encourage her sons' musical development, she said she wouldn't tell Joe as long as they were cautious.

One day, Tito did the unthinkable while performing a song by the Four Tops with his brothers: he broke a string on the guitar.

With their father due home any minute, the boys panicked—there wasn't time to replace it. Joe was an avid practitioner of corporal punishment, and they knew this was just the sort of transgression that would result in a sound beating. Unable to come up with a plan, they placed the guitar back in Joe's closet and hoped for leniency.

They got their wish, though not quite in the form they'd been expecting. When Joe noticed the broken string, he stormed into the boys' room holding his guitar and demanded to know who was responsible. Tito confessed, but just as Joe grabbed him to begin administering his punishment, the youngster protested.

"I can play!"

"Play, then!" Joe thundered. "Let me see what you can do."

Tito composed himself and started playing "The Jerk" by the Larks, with Jackie and Jermaine singing harmony while fighting back tears. When they'd finished, Joe left the room without saying a word—or lifting a finger. Two days later he returned from work with a red guitar for Tito and instructions for the other brothers to get ready to start rehearsing. And so the Jackson 5 was born.[12]

Though Jermaine started out as the group's lead singer, the family already knew there was something remarkable about Michael. Even as a toddler, he moved and sang with the grace and fluidity of a veteran entertainer. "Michael was so talented," recalls his father. "I don't think he even knew his own talents . . . he didn't know because everything he tried came out perfect."[13]

Shortly after the boys started practicing as a band, they were playing for their grandmother when a curious thing happened: five-year-old Michael, who'd been playing the bongos and studying his older brothers, jumped in and started singing Jermaine's part. His brothers complained, and Joe stopped the song. But Michael's grandmother had heard something. She asked him to sing again, anything he wanted, and he launched into a rendition of "Jingle Bells." Jermaine still remembers "the wide-eyed look on Joseph's face."[14]

Michael clinched his status as the group's frontman shortly thereafter with a school performance of "Climb Ev'ry Mountain." The famous tune from Rodgers and Hammerstein's *The Sound of Music* was his first solo in front of a big crowd, but that wasn't apparent to those in the gymnasium watching him. "When I finished that song, the reaction in the auditorium overwhelmed me," he wrote. "My teachers were crying and I just couldn't believe it. I had made them all happy. It was such a great feeling."[15]

Jackson's business career had a less auspicious beginning. The singer's childhood compatriots remember his ill-fated attempt to become a candy distributor—and his failure to grasp the concept of profit. "There was a store down the street somewhere up there," says Campbell. "He'd go get them little malt balls for a nickel, and sell 'em for a nickel."[16]

Indeed, Michael's earliest years offer few clues that, within two decades, he'd become the visionary behind a billion-dollar empire. But there were hints he might one day be the sort of entertainer who'd donate millions to charity.

"Mike was always the giving type of guy," says Keith Jackson. "I remember when he used to get his allowance from my uncle and my aunty Katherine, that he would actually go buy a bunch of candy and would give it to other kids. He'd just give it away, man."[17]

As a youngster, Jackson was so fixated on giving that he'd sometimes take. He developed a habit of swiping pieces from his mother's modest jewelry collection and presenting them to teachers as gifts. Eventually she found out what was going on and quietly put a stop to it.[18] But the incident foreshadowed a trait that would later prove destructive to Jackson. Says his father: "He could never say no."[19]

————

These days, there's not much about Mister Lucky's Lounge that looks lucky. It sits abandoned on the corner of Grant Street and West Eleventh Avenue in Gary, Indiana, windows covered with plywood, mismatched bricks slowly disintegrating at the edges.

The only recent additions to the building are two incongruously fresh-looking canvas signs. Each proclaims the onetime nightspot's name in black and green letters atop a four-leaf clover. "Welcome Michael Jackson Fans!" the sign reads. "Mr. Lucky's Lounge: the Jackson 5's first performance venue!"

The second sign is dominated by an illustration of what appears to be a brick. "*Everybody Needs a Little Luck*," it suggests gently, before erupting into an all-out exhortation: "BUY YOUR LUCKY BRICK *at* www.MISTERLUCKYSLOUNGE.com."[20] [21]

In addition to becoming the first venue to host a proper Jackson 5 concert, Mister Lucky's was also the first place Michael Jackson earned money as a musician. He and his brothers took home a combined $11 for that initial paid performance in 1964. As usual, six-year-old Michael used his share to buy candy, which he then gave away to other neighborhood children.[22]

Building off the boys' success at Mister Lucky's, Joe booked the Jackson 5 at nearby venues, entered them in talent shows in neighboring towns, and ran a schedule of practices and performances that seemed as rigorous and time-consuming as that of a Broadway production. "Rehearsing with them, that's what led to them being so talented," says Joe. "I rehearsed them *a lot*. They'll tell you."[23]

Of course, there were no understudies. Michael remembers performing all night after spending days sick in bed. "As players, Jermaine, Tito, and the rest of us were under tremendous pressure," Jackson wrote in his autobiography. "Our manager was the kind who reminded us that James Brown would *fine* his Famous Flames if they missed a cue or bent a note during a performance. As lead singer, I felt I—more than the others—couldn't afford an 'off night.'"[24]

When Michael was eight years old, he and his brothers faced their biggest test yet: a citywide talent show at Gary's Roosevelt High. They rose to the occasion, delivering a sparkling rendition of "My Girl" by the Temptations, one of the top acts signed to Motown Records. The performance ignited a dream of Joe's that would soon become an obsession. "I realized that it would be good to [get a] deal with Motown," he recalls. "Most of the talent shows they won, they was singing Motown songs."[25]

It wasn't long before Joe left the Falcons, opting instead to focus on managing the Jackson 5. He and Katherine had saved $300 to build an additional room onto their house; much to his wife's chagrin, Joe used the bulk of it to buy musical equipment. Then he traded his Buick sedan for a Volkswagen van that could accommodate the boys and their gear.[26]

The Jacksons would get their new room soon enough. By 1966, Michael and his brothers were performing five sets a night, six nights a week, in Gary or anywhere Joe could find a gig. Often that led to concerts at strip joints. Michael's mother, a member of the Jehovah's Witnesses—a Christian sect that forbids the celebration of holidays and birthdays—insisted she didn't learn this until reading his autobiography (a claim that strains credulity). For Michael, the gigs meant learning, and earning, in ways unfamiliar to most middle-schoolers.

"I'd go out into the audience, crawl under the tables, and pull up the ladies' skirts to look under," he wrote. "People would throw money as I scurried by, and when I began to dance, I'd scoop up all the dollars and coins that had hit the floor earlier and push them into the pockets of my jacket."[27]

Though Michael has said he mostly enjoyed the performances, the rigor of the Jackson 5's touring schedule left the boys exhausted. When they weren't on the road, they practiced at home and took lessons with Shirley Cartman, a music teacher at their school who also ran her own studio.[28]

Joe pushed them to hone their craft at the expense of all other activities, including having a social life appropriate for children their age. "They couldn't talk to nobody, couldn't do nothing," says Catherine Sinclair, who grew up in Gary and lived near the Jacksons when Michael was young. "[Joe] wouldn't allow it."[29]

The brothers did get to socialize with kids outside of school by playing sports, particularly baseball. While his siblings practiced, Michael would sit in the dugout, studying his music.[30] Jackie was such a good pitcher that pro scouts sometimes attended his high school games. But when Jermaine collided with another player while chasing a fly ball—ending up with a black eye and fourteen stitches—Joe made his boys stop playing sports so as to avoid injuries that could derail their musical careers.[31]

He didn't seem quite as concerned about potential injuries doled out by his own fists. Keith Jackson remembers Joe putting on boxing gloves "to toughen us up, just boxing with each other and stuff like that."[32] Behind the scenes, the blows were more severe. Joe delivered regular beatings for missteps in rehearsal and household infractions alike.

"If you messed up, you got hit, sometimes with a belt, sometimes with a switch," Michael later wrote. He'd occasionally retaliate, throwing fists—or, at least once, a shoe—at his father, but that only made things worse. "That's why I got it more than all my brothers combined. I would fight back and my father would kill me, just tear me up."[33]

Joe seemed unremorseful when I asked him why he employed corporal punishment. "Everybody that I knew of, especially black people, they whupped their kids," he said. "I never beat the kids . . . I never beat nobody. But my wife whupped those kids more than I did because I was working jobs, and she was at home with them all the time. So, yeah I whupped them some, but I got a lot of whupping myself when I was a kid."[34]

When he wasn't at home disciplining his children or working long shifts at the mill, Joe was busy landing agreements with a range of regional music power brokers. Two such players were Pervis Spann and E. Rodney Jones, DJs for Chicago's WVON. They were so impressed by hearing the Jackson 5 at Chicago's Regal Theatre during the winter of 1966 that they offered to manage the group.[35]

Though the DJs spent $40,000 on polishing, promoting, and

otherwise preparing the Jackson 5 for the big time, all of the major labels passed on the group—including Berry Gordy's Motown, which turned down the boys as many as eight times.[36] Yet Joe remained defiantly optimistic, often telling Katherine, "I'm going to take these boys to Motown if it's the last thing I do!"[37]

Michael and his brothers had one suitor—a local label called Steeltown Records. The fledgling company had been founded in 1966 by aspiring music executive Ben Brown and songwriter Gordon Keith, a Gary steelworker. The latter had discovered the Jackson 5 thanks to gig advertisements tacked to local telephone poles. When he saw the boys play in person, he was hooked.

"I could not understand for the life of me why they had been turned down by so many people in the business," says Keith, then a very religious man. "My belief system provided for thinking that, if I wanted to, I could probably fly. So I think the good Lord meant for me to be the one to take them forward."[38]

By 1967, Keith was eager to sign the Jackson 5 to a long-term deal, but Joe refused, insisting on something that would give his boys the option of leaving if Motown ever called. Eventually Keith caved to Joe's demands. "I only had a six-month contract signed with [Steeltown]," says the elder Jackson. "I didn't want to be hung up in no long-term contract."[39]

Joe signed the deal because he figured it would enable his boys to cut a few songs and gain some valuable exposure. He was right. The Jackson 5 recorded a track called "Big Boy," written by saxophonist Eddie Silvers (a onetime member of Fats Domino's band) in Chicago. Thanks in part to Keith's help getting local radio play, the single started selling by the Volkswagen mini-busload—about 50,000 copies, according to Jermaine.[40]

"When that record with its killer bass line began to get radio play in Gary, we became a big deal in our neighborhood," Michael recalled. "No one could believe we had our own record. *We* had a hard time believing it."[41]

Soon the boys were scoring bigger gigs. They traveled along the chitlin circuit, piling into Joe's van to play 2,000-seat theaters in Rust Belt cities like Cleveland and Baltimore, earning $500 per night. Along the way, Michael continued to learn by peppering the musicians he met with questions, as Smokey Robinson recalls in his autobiography.

"Michael was a strange and lovely child," he writes. "I always saw him as an old soul in the body of a boy. . . . He was also an astute student. He'd be listening and watching the other acts like a hawk, always learning."[42]

Jackson also accumulated knowledge at school, often on only a few hours of sleep after driving back from a weeknight gig with his brothers. He was perhaps the strongest student of the bunch, in part because of an intellectual curiosity that manifested itself both backstage and in the classroom. "His thirst for knowledge was far greater than any of ours," Jermaine wrote. "He was *that* curious kid who asked, 'Why? Why? Why?' and he listened to and logged every detail."[43]

Joe continued to find sadistically creative ways to keep his children in line. When conventional methods couldn't convince them to keep their bedroom window closed, he donned a scary mask one night and climbed in; the boys awoke and, upon seeing the dark figure in their room, shrieked in terror. Then Joe turned on the lights, removed the mask, and said, "I could have been someone else. Now, keep the window closed!"[44]

Despite the boys' frightening home life, their musical momentum continued. In 1967, Joe entered Michael and his brothers in another talent show at the Regal Theatre. They won the contest—and a paid gig at the venue as an opener for Gladys Knight. The songstress and her Pips had just been signed to Motown and were soaring up the charts thanks to their hit "I Heard It Through the Grapevine."

When Knight heard the Jackson 5, she immediately summoned

the brothers to her dressing room and offered encouragement: "You boys should be at Motown!" Knight was the first of many who tried to get them to come to the label. At the time, Joe recalls, Motown "wasn't ready."[45]

The Jackson 5 would have to wait. But their success at Chicago's premier concert venue had earned them something else: a call from the Apollo Theater in Harlem, New York City.

————

There's a tree stump sitting on a golden pedestal in the middle of the stage at the Apollo, and Tito Jackson can't keep his hands off of it. It's the summer of 2012, and he and his brothers are set to return to the legendary stage nearly half a century after their first appearance. "It's been here forever," Tito says of the charmed stump. "That was like a good-luck piece; rub it down and take the stage."[46]

As legend has it, the slab of wood was part of the Tree of Hope, a stately plant that once stood outside the Harlem Lafayette Theatre on Seventh Avenue between 131st and 132nd Streets. For many years, performers would rub the tree before hitting the stage. Shortly after the Apollo opened in 1934 just a few blocks away, the Tree of Hope was felled to make room for the widening of Seventh Avenue. A thick piece of the trunk ended up at the Apollo, where the legend continued to grow long after the tree itself had ceased to do so.[47]

Jermaine Jackson insists he isn't one for indulging in superstition or maudlin sentiment. "I didn't touch the tree stump because I'm very picky about germs," he says. "Tito touched it."[48]

But in August of 1967, when members of the Jackson 5 arrived in Harlem for their Apollo debut, they all rubbed the tree before taking the stage—even Jermaine. "He didn't know any better then," pipes Marlon.[49] "Not too many people had touched the tree," says Jermaine, somberly. "At that time."

They felt they needed every bit of luck they could get at the theater's Super Top Dog Amateur Finals Night, where they'd face a squadron of other talented acts. They'd also have to contend with an audience known for booing musicians off the stage—and, in some cases, throwing food at them.

As soon as they walked through the front door, the brothers found themselves surrounded by photos of artists who'd played the Apollo, including Michael's idols Jackie Wilson and James Brown. Even the dressing rooms were grander than anything they'd experienced before. Jermaine recalls fancy coasters and meat patties;[50] Jackie reminisces about playing basketball in the schoolyard across the street.[51] But more than the perks, the brothers remember the Apollo's crowd.

"There was an act on before us, and they got booed and [pelted] with eggs," says Jermaine. "We were coming on next. Michael got scared because he thought maybe they were going to do us the same way."[52]

As the eight-year-old Michael started to cry, his brothers rushed to comfort their frontman.

"Just do your best, just do your thing," Jermaine remembers saying.

Tito wasn't quite so gentle: "Get in shape, boy!"[53]

Michael collected himself and, after a stop at the Tree of Hope, the brothers took the stage. The Jackson 5 didn't need the extra boost—they quickly turned the audience to their side and cruised to victory in the competition.

"We put a great performance together and people loved us," says Jermaine. "That's how it all started." Adds Tito: "We never got booed."

The Apollo's management seemed to enjoy the Jackson 5 as much as the crowd did, inviting them back many times over the next few years to open for acts such as James Brown, Jackie Wilson, and Etta James.

Michael Jackson and his brothers had conquered the Apollo and communed with its most notable talisman, but a major-label deal continued to elude them.

Chapter 2

MOTOWN UNIVERSITY

When it comes to role models in the music business, it's hard to beat Berry Gordy. The former boxer founded Motown Records, a label that defined and delivered the sound of a generation, in 1960. A dozen years later, he supercharged his company with a move from Detroit to Los Angeles, opening up opportunities in the broader entertainment world. And in 1988—after launching the careers of Michael Jackson, Diana Ross, Stevie Wonder, and countless others— he sold his record company for $61 million.

The octogenarian Gordy has gotten used to the trappings of success, but age hasn't slowed his ambition. Today he's having lunch at the Lobby Lounge on the thirty-fifth floor of the Mandarin Oriental hotel in New York, where he's been staying for the months leading up to the debut of his latest venture, *Motown: The Musical*. For a man whose Detroit mansion once contained an oil portrait of him dressed as Napoleon, the eatery is fittingly grand: orchid blossoms at every table, Dom Pérignon on the menu ($85 per glass), and floor-to-ceiling windows overlooking Central Park and Columbus Circle, where cars swirl like multicolored gears of an asphalt clock far below.

Gordy's own appearance is a tad more understated. He sports neat black slacks and a brown button-down beneath a dark blazer. When a waitress sidles up to take his order, he settles on carrot juice. These are the kinds of details that Michael Jackson used to notice when he and his brothers first joined Motown.

"Michael would stare at everything I was doing," says Gordy, easing into his chair. "It was a little unnerving because I would look away, and then I'd look back, and Michael was studying [my] every move."[1]

He pauses.

"Everything, you know," he continues. "And I could never figure that out . . . he was just so focused on me. Everybody else would be playing, and he'd just be looking at me and watching, and I'd always feel his eyes on me."

———————

By 1968, the Jackson 5 had released its debut single on Gary's Steeltown Records and wowed the tough crowd at New York's Apollo Theater. The boys returned to Chicago's Regal Theatre that summer, the same night as Bobby Taylor and the Vancouvers, one of Motown's top acts.

The lead singer was so impressed with what he saw that he insisted on bringing the Jackson 5 to his label's attention.[2] It was Suzanne de Passe, one of Gordy's lieutenants, who heard the group's recording and decided to lobby her boss on their behalf. Despite their obvious talent, the boys from Gary would be a hard sell.[3]

"I was doing extremely well in so many areas in my company, and the last kind of group I wanted was a kids' group," recalls Gordy. "Because I had Stevie Wonder . . . he was underage, they were close to the same age, and he had to have tutors and chaperones and this and that."[4]

Despite Joe Jackson's repeated attempts get Motown's attention, Gordy doesn't recall any of the Jackson 5's music making it to his ears before de Passe strong-armed him into seeing the group's Detroit audition during the summer of 1968.[5] Says Gordy: "First time I saw them, met them, heard of them, is when she dragged me into their thing."[6]

He immediately understood why de Passe was so excited. The

brothers were disciplined and played their parts well, but there was something about the tiny frontman. Gordy saw a child who could wring more feeling from "Who's Loving You" than Smokey Robinson himself. The effect was almost supernatural.

"That delighted me and kind of scared me at the same time," says Gordy. "Because I was saying, 'Wow, how could he do that? Has he been here before?'" From Michael Jackson's viewpoint onstage, though, it didn't seem like he and his brothers were on the verge of a record deal with Motown. "People stared through us like we were ghosts," he recalled.[7]

Yet Gordy was already laying out a plan for their repertoire. The bluesy songs that Michael sang were beyond impressive, but the Motown chief felt that something more carefree would be a better fit—and as he looked at the future King of Pop, the notes of "I Want You Back" started to coalesce in his brain (a memory so powerful that, upon relating it to me, Gordy bursts out in song: "*Ooooob* baby, dot da dee a dee, da da da . . .").[8]

Whether or not Gordy composed the song on the spot is another matter. Michael was under the impression that Gordy and his team of songwriters had originally written "I Want You Back" with Gladys Knight in mind and titled it "I Want to Be Free," but that hearing the Jackson 5's audition changed Gordy's mind.[9]

At any rate, there was some business to settle before the group's first major hit could be recorded. Gordy signed the Jackson 5 to a deal that gave the group 6 percent of 90 percent of the wholesale price of each album sold, a standard Motown royalty rate. That sum would then be split five ways, leaving Michael with about two cents per album (wholesale prices back then were roughly $2 per record)[10]—not much by today's standards, which generally call for rates in the 10 percent to 15 percent range for up-and-coming acts.[11]

Joe Jackson had been so eager to get his boys to Motown that he neglected to tie up certain loose ends. Gordy discovered this when he got a call from his legal department saying that somebody named Richard Arons had shown up and claimed he owned half of the Jackson 5 through a previous agreement. Annoyed, the Motown boss told Jackson that such attachments weren't part of the deal they'd made—and that he and his children were free to leave if they couldn't honor it.[12]

Then there was the matter of Steeltown Records. Label co-founder Gordon Keith claims that nobody ever bought the Jackson 5 out of their contract with him, and that he's now owed "millions and millions of dollars" as a result.[13] Gordy says he knew nothing of any such deal, and that Joe Jackson (who insists the Steeltown pact had already expired)[14] was able to resolve the group's legal issues to Motown's satisfaction. Says Gordy: "They came back to us clear with no attachments."[15]

Once the wrangling came to a close and the Jackson 5 officially joined Motown's roster, Gordy went to work with his team of producers and songwriters—Freddie Perren, Alphonso Mizell, and Deke Richards—collectively known as the Corporation. Michael remembers the Motown boss sitting the boys down and telling them that not only would their first single become the biggest hit in the country, but that their second and third records would make it to number 1 on the charts as well. "I'm gonna make you the biggest thing in the world," he told them. "And you're gonna be written about in the history books."[16]

———

The distance from Gary, Indiana, to Los Angeles, California, is 2,030 miles—farther apart than Rome and Baghdad. For Michael Jackson, the gulf between the way he experienced his birthplace and his adopted hometown was just as vast. That first became apparent when he and his brothers moved west in 1969 at the behest of Gordy, who was about to relocate his label's headquarters to Tinseltown.

"When we flew to California from Chicago, it was like being in another country, another world," Jackson wrote. "To come from our part of Indiana, which is so urban and often bleak, and to land in Southern California was like having the world transformed into a wonderful dream . . . trees had oranges and leaves on them in the middle of winter."

There, Jackson was able to continue studying Gordy up close—and, from afar, stars like Fred Astaire, Marcel Marceau, and Katharine Hepburn. But he was perhaps most enamored of Diana Ross. She and Gordy lived on the same street in Beverly Hills, and Jackson stayed frequently with both of them during his first year and a half in California while his parents closed up their house in Gary and looked for a new one in Los Angeles.

Ross encouraged Jackson's growth as a visual artist as well as a musical one, often buying him pencils and paints. She took him to museums, where she introduced him to the works of Degas and Michelangelo. Though few know it, Jackson went on to become a skilled draftsman, in part because of Ross's influence.

"Michael was a person that really loved her," says Gordy. "And they got to be really, really close friends. . . . Michael was a big, big fan of hers and probably a lot of other stars [but] ended up doing his own thing. He would take it a step further. Just like I might spend one million dollars on something that he would spend five million dollars on it when he got there."[17]

Money wasn't a concern for Gordy when the Jackson 5 hit the studio to start recording "I Want You Back." Jackson often sang his parts close to flawlessly the first time around ("He could hear a song and just go in and record it," recalls his father[18]), but Gordy wanted the group's Motown debut to be perfect. Whenever Gordy asked him for another take, Jackson was happy to oblige—and always managed to learn something from the experience.

"Why you doing that?" Jackson would ask when Gordy demanded a do-over.[19]

"We got to do it again," his mentor would reply.

"Why? It seems okay."

"No, it's not okay, because right here you took a breath and you should have been, you know, coming down. Or coming out with it full, and in the meantime you were breathing. So you just got to do that over."

"Oh, my goodness!"

Jackson's patience, Gordy's persistence, and an outsized recording budget all helped the boys craft a memorable debut, but they also benefited from the help of some classic Hollywood stagecraft. Their album was titled *Diana Ross Presents the Jackson 5*, an attempt to connect them to their famous label mate. Although Suzanne de Passe was the one who actually had brought the group to Berry Gordy's attention, Ross made for a better story. That led to some amusingly hypocritical pronouncements.

"Honesty has always been a very special word for me," Ross wrote in the album's liner notes. "A very special idea. . . . When I think of my personal idea of honesty, I think of something being straight out, all there on the table. . . . That's how I feel about the Jackson 5—five brothers by the name of Jackson who I discovered in Gary, Indiana."[20]

Joe Jackson believes that the packaging of his sons as Diana Ross's discovery was not only a bid to prop them up, but to deflect attention from the songstress's impending departure from the Supremes. "Berry had to come up with some type of gimmick to fill that in to make it look good," he says.[21] At any rate, Jackson had just learned an important lesson about show business: there was a difference between public relations and truth.

Ross introduced the boys in front of a national television audience on an episode of ABC's variety show *The Hollywood Palace* that aired in October of 1969. "I Want You Back" debuted that same month, and by the end of January it had soared to the top spot on the *Billboard* charts. The single sold more than 4 million copies worldwide in its first year and pushed the group's initial album past the 1 million mark.[22]

When the brothers released two more chart toppers, "ABC" (February 1970) and "The Love You Save" (May 1970), Gordy's prophecy was realized. They followed with "I'll Be There," which became the group's fourth consecutive number 1 single. The mainstream press quickly took note.

"Supplied with some good arrangements and instrumental backing from the Motown assembly line, the boys from Gary, Indiana, perform with an exuberance and flair which many of the older groups on the same label rarely achieve these days," wrote *Rolling Stone*, which heaped additional praise on "the magnificent lead singer."[23]

A year later, Jackson found himself on the magazine's cover, accompanied by the headline "Why does this eleven-year-old stay up past his bedtime?" Thanks to another Motown publicity trick, his listed age was incorrect—Jackson was just months from becoming a teenager—but nobody seemed to notice. The Jacksons were well on their way to becoming American icons.

Michael understood his family's newfound fame as well as anyone. Keith Jackson remembers seeing it firsthand while joining his cousins on the road just as they were exploding onto the national stage. One morning after waking up in an eleventh-floor hotel room, the boys noticed a group of mostly female fans congregating on the street below. Keith and a few of Michael's brothers had a mischievous plan, much to the chagrin of the eventual King of Pop.[24]

"We had these balloons, we filled them with water and we just dropped them on the people," Keith Jackson recalls. "So Michael saw and he was like, 'Keith, what you doing, *no*! Don't do that to my fans!' I was like, 'Oh, sorry, cuz.'"

Keith was struck not only by Michael's concern for these total strangers, but by the intensity of the fans themselves. A few moments later, when he and his cousins walked into the hallway outside of their room, they discovered the fans had used the balloon-tossing incident to triangulate the boys' location.

"Next thing I know I heard this stampede, I'm thinking the building is falling down, I look to my left—and of course, back then, we all had afros, so of course they all thought I was one of them—and we all looked and, man, it's like two hundred girls running our way, screaming," says Keith. "So all the brothers and everybody, Mike and them, they run in the room and shut the door. Guess who got left out? Me. I got beat up, scratched up. All that, man. They kept calling me 'Mike'. . . . I'm like, 'I'm not him, I'm not him!' So I got beat up by these girls."

————

When the Jacksons weren't on the road, they settled into an increasingly cushy life in California. Flush with new cash from Motown, Joe bought his family a sprawling estate at 4641 Hayvenhurst Avenue in Encino, twelve miles from the heart of Hollywood. Though Joe and Gordy didn't always see eye to eye, their children grew closer as the years went on (particularly Jermaine and Hazel, Berry's daughter). And while schoolwork, recording sessions, and tours gobbled up most of the brothers' waking hours, Gordy also made a bit of time for regular-kid fun—something unfamiliar to the boys' father—scheduling baseball games every week.

Michael usually played catcher in the Jackson vs. Gordy contests and didn't exhibit anything close to the hand-eye coordination he displayed onstage ("He missed a lot of balls," Gordy recalls). But Tito generally hit more than enough home runs to make up for his younger brother's miscues, and Jackie pitched like a young Bob Gibson. Michael was still a cheerful participant despite his athletic flaws.

"He was an old man in a kid's body, but he had the childlike qualities about him that were so beautiful and so pure," says Gordy. "And all the stuff that he did for the world and was trying to do for the world and for kids was so sincere. And he wanted to be a kid, and I gave him the opportunity to be a kid."[25]

At the same time, Jackson's musical education continued in the studio. Gordy was prone to aphorisms, many of which his young charge would carry well into his solo career: the ideas that competition breeds champions and that songwriters should write semi-autobiographically. Once your audience was hooked on a song, according to Gordy, you had to spend the next three minutes telling a story with a beginning, middle, and end. The chorus should summarize the arc of the story, and the dynamics should swell steadily until the grand finale, closing with one final mention of the song's name so that people would remember it (as they most certainly did when a young Michael Jackson yelled, "I want you back!" during the fade-out of the Jackson 5's first number 1 single).[26]

Gordy doesn't recall spending a great deal of time consciously teaching Jackson about the business of music, but he believes that osmosis accounted for the basis of the future King of Pop's acumen. He frequently took business calls in the studio, rarely lowering his voice or trying to disguise his dealings, and Jackson was all ears.

"I was always very open with whatever it was because I was always doing twenty-five things," says Gordy. "Multitasking, you know, problem over here, problem over there. . . . If I'm in the studio mixing or whatever it is, I just pick up the phone and do it. Michael listened to everything . . . he was *always* listening to everything."[27]

As he entered his teenage years, an increasingly confident Michael started to look for more artistic freedom. He told Gordy he wanted to sing songs his way; the Motown producers wanted him to be too "mechanical."[28] Gordy responded by allowing the young star to add more of his own creative input—and to debut solo material.

Jackson's first album, *Got to Be There*, came out in January of 1972. It featured covers of classic songs like "Ain't No Sunshine" and "Rockin' Robin." That same year, Jackson followed with *Ben*, a record whose title track was used in the movie of the same name (a 1972 horror flick whose titular character is a killer rat). Those first albums did reasonably well—they peaked at number 14 and number 5 on the US charts, respectively—but they were high school chemistry explosions compared to the sales supernova that would come just a decade later.

Jackson's international audience eventually became an essential element of his success. He now sells two albums abroad for every one sold stateside—a trend that began in the *Thriller* years, but whose roots were laid in 1972. That year, the Jacksons embarked upon their first world tour, a two-week whirlwind starting in the UK with a performance before the Queen of England.

Somewhere over the Atlantic en route to London, the Jacksons received the first concrete indication of their European fame: their pilot announced that there were already ten thousand fans waiting for them at Heathrow Airport. The boys made it through the pandemonium safely and arrived on time for their show, where they shared a bill with Liberace and Elton John. They shook the gloved hand of the Queen backstage before continuing on to France, Germany, Italy, Holland, and Spain.[29]

"England was our jumping-off point, and it was different from any place we'd been before," Jackson wrote, "but the farther we traveled, the more exotic the world looked. We saw the great museums of Paris and the beautiful mountains of Switzerland. Europe was an education in the roots of Western culture."[30]

———

By the fall of 1973, Michael Jackson was a teenager whom most of the world still believed to be twelve, indefinitely embedded in his age like a Jurassic mosquito in amber. This was all by the design of Motown, his father, and even Jackson himself. But his brothers were growing up rapidly. The year before, Tito married his high school sweetheart, Dee Dee; the year after, Jackie got hitched to his girlfriend, Enid. And in between the two, Jermaine officially fused the Gordy and Jackson clans by tying the knot with the Motown chief's daughter Hazel.

If Berry Gordy didn't spare any expense when recording "I Want

You Back," he certainly wasn't going to skimp on the wedding of his eldest daughter. The ceremony took place at the Beverly Hills Hotel on December 15, 1973—one day after Jermaine's nineteenth birthday—and included artificial snow, 175 white doves, and a musical performance by Smokey Robinson.[31]

The boys released two studio albums that year: *Skywriter* and *G.I.T.: Get It Together*. The former peaked at number 44 on the US charts and the latter topped out at number 100, not such an inspiring performance after 1972's *Lookin' Through the Windows* climbed to number 7. The boys' next two albums, *Dancing Machine* (1974) and *Moving Violation* (1975) did reasonably well, reaching the number 16 and number 36 spots on the charts.

Michael was growing up, too, and the transition from child prodigy to adolescent superstar wasn't always smooth. He had few meaningful interactions outside his family, which continued to be a major source of stress. His father and brothers teased him mercilessly about his looks—particularly his nose and the acne that was suddenly spreading across his face. Jackson later admitted he was so depressed that he'd often wash his face in the dark so that he wouldn't have to look at himself in the mirror. "I just hated it," he told Oprah Winfrey in 1993. "I cried every day."[32]

There was little time for brooding as the boys circled the globe in the early 1970s. They stopped in Japan and China, where, even as local economies were starting to boom, Michael Jackson marveled at how the locals "didn't value material things as much as they did animals and nature."[33]

They flew to Australia and New Zealand, where they received warm welcomes from English speakers and outback tribesmen alike. But it was their trip to Africa that influenced Jackson perhaps most of all. From the moment he and his brothers disembarked and saw a welcoming party of native performers dancing and drumming, Jackson was entranced. As he visited game lodges, crowded markets, and abandoned slave camps, he soaked up the rhythms and the sights of the continent. "The African people had given us gifts of courage and endurance we couldn't hope to repay," he later wrote.

The crowds seemed to follow the Jacksons wherever they went. When they traveled to Jamaica in 1975, they decided to play a basketball game against a local high school powerhouse, filling out their roster with students from Priory, a nearby school whose team didn't quite measure up. The squad typically drew crowds of twenty to fifty people to games at its outdoor home court, but when Michael and his brothers arrived, the setting was decidedly different.

"The place was packed, absolutely packed," recalls Neil Weinberg, who was a fourteen-year-old player for Priory at the time. "You could barely get to the basketball court."[34]

Michael skipped the game; his brothers and their new teammates were handily defeated. But in a gesture of gratitude, the Jacksons invited the Priory players to their hotel for a pool party afterward. The crowd never really receded (one girl even asked Weinberg, who couldn't possibly have been mistaken for a Jackson, for his autograph). By the time everyone arrived at the Sheraton, the edges of the hotel's pool were stacked five-deep with young women desperate to catch a glimpse of one of the Jacksons.

"It was really kind of creepy," Weinberg recalls. "It was like, 'I guess this is what it's like to be famous, but it's making me kind of nervous.'"

———

Michael Jackson had gotten used to many aspects of show business, including the crowds, but back in Los Angeles, he was beginning to feel musically stifled. After watching Stevie Wonder take creative control of his career from Gordy, he wanted the Jackson 5 to be able to do the same, instead of plugging along with the same bubblegum pop sound they'd been producing for years.

"Basically, we didn't like the way our music sounded at the time," Jackson wrote. "We had a strong competitive urge and we felt we were in danger of being eclipsed by other groups who were creating a more contemporary sound."[35]

Furthermore, the monetary value of songwriting was becoming clearer and clearer to Jackson. As he learned at a young age, the two main revenue streams for a song come from its master recording and its publishing rights. The former is the recording of a musical composition from which all future copies of the song are made. Record labels tend to own these "masters" and pay artists a royalty (typically 10 percent to 15 percent of the retail price) every time a copy is purchased as a CD, tape, vinyl record, or digital download.

Publishing rights, on the other hand, encompass songwriting and musical composition. The concept dates back to at least 1501, when Venetian printer Ottaviano Petrucci landed rights to publish "Harmonices Musices Odhecaton" for twenty-one years.[36] Publishing has since evolved far beyond sheet music; these days, a producer who uses synthesizers to come up with the backing track to a rap song would be entitled to a share of publishing royalties, as would the rapper who penned the words spoken on the track. Like recording artists, songwriters are entitled to a royalty every time someone buys a record, but only songwriters earn royalties from US radio play (though this is beginning to change); they also cash in when songs are covered or licensed for movies and television.

Like the early Jackson 5, many pop musicians don't write their own music—and lose out on the associated revenue. Of the ones who do, most sign away the rights to music publishing companies, which split the proceeds with songwriters. A select few musicians are able to gain complete ownership of their publishing rights—either by never giving them up in the first place or by buying them back—and simply pay a music publisher a small administrative fee (5 percent to 20 percent) to ensure that their creations continue to generate cash. Master recordings are similarly difficult to pry away from music companies.

Michael Jackson was one of the rare artists who eventually did both. He started by asking the right questions. "He was interested in what publishing was—what this was, what that was," says Gordy. "You know, he was just an inquisitive kind of person."[37]

As the 1970s wore on, many of Motown's top artists left the label in search of greater artistic freedom. Gladys Knight and the Pips departed in 1973, followed by the Temptations in 1977. Marvin Gaye convinced Gordy to let him write his own songs, as did the Commodores, who opened for the Jacksons on some of their tours. But Motown kept Michael and his brothers on a steady diet of compositions penned by the Corporation. That became a matter of increasing frustration for the young singer and his father. "I wanted my boys to be able to produce their own stuff, write their own songs," recalls Joe Jackson. "And that was kind of hard for Berry."[38]

Accounts differ as to how the duo addressed the issue with Gordy. Michael Jackson wrote that, without consulting his brothers or father, he arranged a one-on-one meeting with the Motown founder in the mid-1970s to discuss the situation—and he wasn't able to convince Gordy to allow the Jacksons to write their own music.[39] Gordy, however, remembers no such meeting.

"I didn't even know Michael could write as well as he did because he never expressed that to me," he says. "He was too busy listening. . . . He may have wanted to do that, but never mentioned it to me . . . as far as I was concerned, he was extremely happy."[40]

So it came as something of a surprise to Gordy when Jermaine approached him in 1976 with some unsettling news: Joe Jackson had landed a lucrative contract to move his sons to CBS's Epic Records. With the Jackson 5's Motown deal set to expire, the group was free to go to the highest bidder.

"Jermaine said that his father controlled everything and had made the deal," Gordy recalls. "I don't think the boys had even talked to the company."

Jermaine had to decide between going with his brothers or staying with his father-in-law and mentor. Both Berry and Hazel Gordy told the singer they'd support him no matter what he decided to do. In the end, he picked Motown, where he'd focus on making a solo career for himself.[41] But for the rest of his brothers—including Michael—the Motown days were coming to an abrupt end.

———

Berry Gordy has been talking for an hour and a quarter, he's nearly polished off his carrot juice, and he's about ready to get back to his work on *Motown: The Musical*. He's covered quite a bit of ground, from Michael Jackson's arrival at Motown as a cherubic prodigy to his untimely passing more than forty years later.

Gordy's eyes had twinkled at the beginning of our conversation while we discussed his first moments in the studio with his young charge, but as the topic turned to the end of Jackson's days, his sentences unfurled more slowly, his jovial manner replaced with a countenance of concern. With every syllable, it seemed he felt the pain of someone who'd watched a family member fade away, close enough to touch but impossible to reach.

"Let's close again with the fact that he was the greatest entertainer that ever lived," he says. "But . . . when you don't surround yourself with the best people, that's powerful."[42]

Chapter 3

EPIC CHANGES

"You were hungry," says Walter Yetnikoff, eyeing the empty plate in front of me, which had until recently been occupied by an omelet.[1]

The former chief of CBS Records had wanted to have lunch on Manhattan's Upper East Side at the Second Avenue Deli (which is actually on First Avenue), but it was closed for Passover. Upon arriving at its replacement, the unambitiously named 3 Star Diner, he had unsuccessfully attempted to squeeze his ample frame into a booth, prompting a waitress to usher us over to a roomier table. Decades ago, Yetnikoff was renowned for other appetites—women, booze, and cocaine, in particular—but he's been sober for years.

He's still loquacious as ever, and no topic is off-limits. For the past half hour, he's been sprinkling anecdotes about Michael Jackson between thoughts on my place of work ("*Forbes* has some clout—maybe it shouldn't, maybe it should, but it does"), my relationship status ("Are you thinking of getting married? Do you have a prenup?"), and his thoughts on matzoh toppings.

"I put schmaltz," he says. "You know what schmaltz is? Rendered chicken fat."

"Yeah," I reply, trying to steer us back to the topic at hand. "You said that you felt Michael had a good head for business."

"Always."

———

The first time Walter Yetnikoff saw the Jacksons perform, he wasn't sure if he wanted to sign them. The year was 1976, he'd just taken over as chief of CBS Records, and when he schlepped out to Long Island's Westbury Music Fair to see the boys in concert, he found Michael Jackson onstage singing "Ben," a song about a rat.

Two of his top lieutenants—Ron Alexenburg, head of CBS's Epic Records, and Steve Popovich, an A&R executive—were prepared to shell out $3.5 million to lure the Jacksons over from Motown. Perplexingly for Yetnikoff, nobody seemed to be able to confirm how many records the group had actually sold. Back then, there was no central authority keeping track of music sales as Nielsen SoundScan does today. Only individual labels knew their artists' numbers, and Berry Gordy wasn't about to offer up any clues.

"For $3.5 million, I don't know if we should do that," Yetnikoff told his colleagues. "We don't know that they're selling any records."

"You haven't been in this job long enough to turn down a deal like that," they replied.

He thought for a moment.

"You're probably right."

That same year, the Jacksons officially joined CBS's Epic Records. In addition to a lofty guarantee, Joe pushed for a high royalty rate and got 14 percent of retail (about 28 percent of wholesale)—much more than they were getting at Motown.[2]

One major downside of the deal: they'd have to ditch the Jackson 5 name, to which Motown retained rights, and instead call themselves the Jacksons. But they would finally gain the opportunity to write their own songs, a caveat that would unleash Michael's considerable capabilities as a composer.

"I don't think [Motown] had the idea that Michael would be as big as he was," says Joe Jackson. "I wanted to try other avenues and other better things."[3]

Berry Gordy, however, saw the move as less of a push for creative control and more as a power play by a patriarch eager to refresh his grip on his children's careers: "He was constantly trying to come in and dictate things. . . . I would imagine that Joe having absolutely no control at Motown, and having all the control at CBS [was the reason]."[4] Adds Smokey Robinson: "Joe never got used to Berry calling the shots on his boys. He figured because his sons came from his seed, he'd be their boss forever."[5]

Joe may not have been able to control Gordy, but he continued to hold sway over his boys, especially the younger ones. Michael and Marlon were still minors, limiting their say as to which label they worked for. Besides, Joe figured that after years of harsh punishment, all his children—even the ones who'd grown and started families of their own—had gotten used to obeying orders. But he underestimated twenty-one-year-old Jermaine, who refused to sign the CBS contract.

Jermaine couldn't believe his father was trying to force the group to jump from Berry Gordy's Motown, the label that had turned the Jackson 5 into America's answer to the Beatles, to a company run by what he saw as a bunch of suits "with no attachment to what we'd built." That included Walter Yetnikoff, who "made our father look like a pussycat," he later wrote.[6]

Joe was plenty tough, particularly when it came to dealing with Jermaine's defection. He cut off his son's weekly living allowance, and Jermaine no longer felt welcome with his family. He didn't talk to his brothers for the first months of 1976, and it wasn't until he had a heart-to-heart with Barry White that Jermaine started to see the end of the standoff. "Your brothers will come around," the older singer predicted. "There is family and there is business—don't confuse the two."[7]

By the end of the year Jermaine had been invited back to his family's inner circle, though he didn't officially rejoin the group. Michael would later recall feeling "totally naked onstage for the first time" without his brother performing next to him. But Joe was already busy making plans for the Jacksons, replacing Jermaine with fourteen-year-old Randy, and dreaming of future business ventures.[8]

One of those projects was a television show. The brothers had already been immortalized in a Saturday morning cartoon; this time, Joe had landed them a live-action variety show. For each episode, the Jacksons would don outrageous outfits, perform dance numbers, and spout witticisms accompanied by canned laughter while cameras rolled. Michael hated the idea. Now seventeen years old and becoming increasingly confident in his intuitions on marketing and promotion, he told his father and brothers that the production would overexpose them, hurting record sales.

"You lose your identity in the business," he later wrote. "The rocker image you had is gone. I'm not a comedian. I'm not a show host. I'm a musician. . . . Is it really entertaining for me to get up there and crack a few weak jokes and force people to laugh because I'm Michael Jackson, when I know in my heart I'm not funny?"

But they went ahead with the show. Sure enough, the group's next album, *The Jacksons*, never rose higher than number 36 on the US charts. Perhaps trying to make sense of the disappointing results, Michael quite literally took business matters into his own hands. Yetnikoff remembers visiting the family compound in Encino and seeing the young singer poring over contracts for performances and records, making notes in the margins of the pages.

"He'd read them like a lawyer would," Yetnikoff recalls. "Peering, peering, make a note on the side. . . . I'm sure he had a lawyer reading it also, but he wanted to read it and make notes on it [himself]. So it appeared that he knew what he was doing."[9]

Meanwhile, the Jacksons' music continued to produce lackluster results. Their 1977 release, *Goin' Places*, fared even worse than its predecessor. Though Michael learned a great deal from the album's primary songwriters Kenny Gamble and Leon Huff, the inventors of the Philadelphia soul sound, he felt their compositions didn't really fit with the Jacksons' ethos.

"We knew that the message to promote peace and let music take over was a good one," he wrote. "But again it was more like the old O'Jays' 'Love Train' and not really our style."[10]

Though the Jacksons had been lured to the label with the promise of a chance to write much of their own music, CBS wasn't contractually bound to give the brothers that opportunity, and they were able to land just two of their creations on each of their first two albums. So, along with his father, Michael decided to confront Epic's Ron Alexenburg in an effort to secure his creative freedom.

"We told Mr. Alexenburg that Epic had done its best, and it wasn't good enough," Jackson recalled. "We felt we could do better, that our reputation was worth putting on the line."

Alexenburg heeded Jackson's words, and the brothers—led by Michael—wrote all but one song on their next album. With greater creative control over their music, *Destiny* soared to number 3 on the US charts shortly after its 1978 release, eventually selling 4 million copies worldwide. The album featured "Shake Your Body (Down to the Ground)," a funky disco hit written by Michael and Randy; the song served as further validation of the Jacksons' musical talents beyond performing.

As Michael continued to record music and tour with his brothers, he found himself more and more interested in an expanded solo career. And he recognized a potential ally in Yetnikoff; the association would go on to help both men greatly.

"By the quirk of fate, I became associated with Michael Jackson, and it sort of made my career," says Yetnikoff. "I became sort of his good daddy. One of few people he could run to when things were not good at home."[11]

Two years after the Jacksons' arrival at CBS, Michael was ready to start thinking about the album that would eventually become *Off the Wall*. He had already released four solo albums for Motown, with all the songs penned by others. This time, he wanted to write and produce the bulk of the tracks himself, but wasn't sure if his new boss would like the end result.

So Jackson, just eighteen years old, arranged a meeting with the president of CBS Records to explain his plans. Yetnikoff liked what the young singer had to say, and encouraged him to stretch his creative muscles. If it didn't work out, he figured, CBS could always try to sell Jackson's contract back to Motown.

"He's this skinny kid in a T-shirt, he addressed me with great respect," Yetnikoff recalls. "And . . . it wasn't much of a dialogue. He said, 'You know, I think I ought to step out and perform on my own, I'm ready for it,' and such and such. And I said, 'I think you should try it.' It was sort of an easy call for me."

————

One of the many ideas about the music business that Michael Jackson learned from Berry Gordy—for better or worse—was the notion that budgets shouldn't constrain art. That was Gordy's stance when it came to filming *The Wiz*, an adaptation of the Tony-winning musical *The Wonderful Wizard of Oz* with Harlem replacing Kansas as a backdrop.

The production quickly became the most expensive musical film to date, with a budget estimated at $24 million.[12] Gordy brought in director Sidney Lumet, fresh off the success of the Oscar-winning film *Network*. To write the screenplay, he hired Joel Schumacher, who'd just penned the cult classic *Car Wash*. For the role of the Scarecrow, he reached out to his favorite protégé.

"It was Berry Gordy who said he hoped I'd audition for *The Wiz*," Jackson wrote. "I was very fortunate that way, because I was bitten by the acting bug during that experience. . . . The people, the performances, the story become a thing that can be shared by people all over the world for generations and generations."[13]

Gordy had also signed Stephanie Mills, a twenty-year-old singer and stage performer who'd played Dorothy in his film's Broadway precursor, and planned to have her reprise that role in *The Wiz*. But despite being thirty-three years old, Diana Ross wanted the role of Dorothy for herself, and eventually Gordy gave in. He wouldn't offer specifics when pressed in person, saying simply: "The question came up as to whether Diana should be the right person or not. But Diana wanted to do it."[14]

Ross joined Jackson, who'd impressed Lumet enough in his audition to win the part of the Scarecrow, along with a cast of legendary entertainers that included Lena Horne, Richard Pryor, and Nipsey Russell. When filming began in New York in mid-1977, the future King of Pop stood out on set both in terms of performance and professionalism.

"Michael was a great perfectionist, and it always showed," says Schumacher. "I mean, there never seemed to be a misstep. . . . Michael was very, very, very shy, and very, very, very soft-spoken, beautiful manners and obviously a great talent."[15]

His work ethic was particularly impressive for a teenager. Living in a high-rise apartment in Manhattan's ritzy Sutton Place with sister La Toya, he'd wake up at 4:00 a.m. most days to get to the set in Queens by 5:30 a.m. so that makeup artists could spend hours applying his elaborate costume: saggy neck folds, a Reese's Peanut Butter Cup–wrapper nose, and a massive wig that seemed to be made of big, floppy Brillo pads.[16]

Jackson's work regimen—and his father—had prevented him from having much of a social life outside the family since he was young. Despite his long hours on *The Wiz*, though, Jackson found time to explore New York on his own. In "Human Nature," he sings of his time there: "If this town is just an apple, then let me take a bite." Jackson took at least a nibble, mingling with glamorous residents like Jackie Kennedy Onassis (who would later acquire the rights to publish his autobiography at Doubleday).

At this point in his life, Jackson still considered himself a Jehovah's Witness like his mother. Though he sampled the nightlife at dance clubs like Studio 54, he didn't indulge in chemical or carnal diversions, as many patrons did. He nevertheless found himself intoxicated by the opportunity to be treated like a normal reveler.

"Everybody thought they were a star at Studio 54," says Susan Blond, the brothers' CBS/Epic publicist who'd go on to work with Michael during the *Thriller* years. "There were such interesting characters, and Michael wouldn't have been totally as much appreciated there as anywhere else because *everyone* was fabulous."

At the same time, Jackson had an air of childlike mischievousness, as evidenced by his habit of picking up Blond's purse and turning it upside down, spilling the contents. He was always serious, though, when it came to his followers. One day while Jackson was signing autographs, Blond suggested that he ought to simply write his initials rather than his whole name, a timesaving tactic often employed by Andy Warhol. "Oh, no," said Jackson. "These are my fans, they have made me, and I could never do something like that."

Dedicated as he was to his admirers, Jackson remained a bit of a mystery to his colleagues working on *The Wiz*. "I don't know how much life experience he had had by 1977 at the age of nineteen, I don't know how much outside of the family he'd lived," says Schumacher. "And he remained a very reclusive person, except when the spotlight hit him. . . . When the spotlight hit Michael, he gave you everything."[17]

Jackson was a natural performer, and he augmented his obvious talents with careful preparation. He'd study videotapes of gazelles and cheetahs, hoping to incorporate their grace into his dance routines in *The Wiz*. And on the set, he displayed an ability to learn a dance step simply by watching someone do it once. Recalls Schumacher: "Of the cast, Michael was really the true dancer."

His talents were so remarkable that they caused a bit of tension with his costars. One day on the set, Ross pulled him aside. "[She] told me that I was embarrassing her," Jackson remembered. "I just stared at her. Embarrassing Diana Ross? Me? She said she knew I wasn't aware of it, but I was learning the dances much too quickly."[18]

Jackson had a few embarrassing moments of his own. He read a quote from Socrates in an early run-through, mispronouncing the philosopher's name as "Soh-crates." Then he heard a whisper nearby: "Soc-ruh-tease." He recalls looking over to see a friendly face. "Quincy Jones," the man said, extending his hand. "I'm doing the score." Jackson had first met the producer in Los Angeles at age twelve, introduced by Sammy Davis Jr. as "the next biggest thing since sliced bread."

According to Jackson, he asked Jones on the set of *The Wiz* for advice on the best producers and sound engineers to hire for his upcoming solo album. "Why don't you let me do it?" replied Jones, much to the surprise of Jackson ("I just didn't think he would be that interested in my music," the singer would explain in his autobiography). "Oh, sure, great idea," Jackson stammered. "I never thought about that."

Jones remembers the interaction differently, tracing it back to a meeting at his home in Los Angeles. Jackson asked him for help finding a producer, which Jones interpreted as an invitation to work on the project—and said he'd think about it. Only after spending time with Jackson on the set of *The Wiz* and seeing his work ethic and talent on display did Jones come around. It was the Socrates incident that sealed the deal. When the producer corrected the youngster's pronunciation, Jackson simply said, "Really?"

"What a reaction!" Jones later wrote. "He was so sweet about it. Those big eyes opened wide, and right then and there I committed."[19]

Both men seem to agree that when Jackson approached the executives at CBS, there wasn't much support for the idea of bringing on Jones, a producer they thought was too jazzy. Jackson's response to his record label: "I don't care what you think, Quincy is doing my record."

Jackson and Jones assembled a bevy of talented musicians to help them in the studio, including Rod Temperton, the British master songwriter responsible for hits by Aretha Franklin and Donna Summer; bass guitarist Louis "Thunder-Thumbs" Johnson, of the Brothers Johnson; Greg Phillinganes, a keyboard prodigy who'd left school to start working for Jones five years earlier; and Tom Bähler, a vocal arranger known in part for his collaborations with Cher.

Another valuable addition was sound engineer Bruce Swedien. With his thick white mustache and burly physique, he was a pair of rosy cheeks short of winning a Santa Claus look-alike contest. An electrical engineering major at the University of Minnesota with a minor in music, he worked for the Minneapolis Symphony before leaping across genres to work with Count Basie and Duke Ellington. Even against that backdrop, Jackson seemed remarkable.

"Michael was a joy to be with in the studio, absolutely the best," says Swedien. "It doesn't get any better. For instance, there's two vocalists that I have worked with in my career—Michael Jackson is one, Siedah Garrett is the other—that I have never used pitch correction on. . . . He never wasted a take."[20]

Swedien would go on to work on every one of Jackson's solo studio albums (and Garrett would join forces with the singer on *Bad* for the duet "I Just Can't Stop Loving You"). Swedien and his wife, Bea, eventually became close friends with Jackson, and the singer would make frequent visits to the couple's ranch in California. ("Michael used to love our chickens," Swedien recalls.)

The first product of this extraordinary team was *Off the Wall*. Recording began in December 1978 at Hollywood's Allen Zentz Studios, where Jones and his crew (collectively known as the A-Team) began experimenting with some unfamiliar recording techniques. These ranged from relatively mundane (using a wide range of microphones plucked from Swedien's collection of more than a hundred) to bizarre (Jackson joined the engineer in the attic one day to record the sounds created by banging on assorted objects).

Jackson was a sound engineer's dream. When Swedien suggested recording in the dark, the singer happily obliged. Sometimes he'd stay up all night memorizing his lyrics so that he could deliver them with the lights off in the studio the next day; it allowed him to feel uninhibited, particularly on romantic songs. He grew to love Swedien's idea so much that he employed it on future albums as well.[21]

And though his Motown days were long behind him, Jackson never forgot the ethos that Berry Gordy had instilled in him at a young age. "He was a perfectionist," says his cousin Keith Jackson. "No matter what he did, if it was business or music, or just being in the studio or just writing . . . he always believed if you were going to do it, do it right."[22]

Off the Wall was no exception. From the album's opening track (the swirling, emphatic disco-funky "Don't Stop 'Til You Get Enough") to its other hits (the silky, mellow "Rock with You" and the tender, tremulous "She's Out of My Life"), the songs of Jackson's adult solo debut rocketed him to a musical place far beyond his Jackson 5 days.

"It was such a joy to work with Michael, so natural," says Swedien. "Music just came out of every pore of his body."[23]

———

The Wiz debuted in October of 1978, nearly a year before *Off the Wall*'s release. Roger Ebert was one of the critics who praised Jackson's performance. "It's good that the Scarecrow is the first traveling companion [Diana Ross's Dorothy] meets," he wrote. "Michael Jackson fills the role with humor and warmth."[24]

When it came to the rest of the film, they weren't so thrilled. "*The Wiz* had everything going for it—it could have been a musical *Star Wars*," lamented the *Globe and Mail*. "Now, it's suitable for children of all ages under twelve."[25] *TimeOut* would later name it one of the biggest flops in the history of cinema.[26]

The film bombed at the box office, too, grossing just $13 million—about $11 million less than its budget.[27] Even some of the people involved in making the film thought it was terrible; Jackson stood out as one of the lone bright spots.

"What's amazing is how he sparkles, and his dancing is just fabulous," says Schumacher. "It's a very saccharine film, because that's what we were expected to make . . . but those quick turns and some of the things he went on to embroider upon and make even more brilliant, you can see the seeds of some of the great Michael Jackson moves in *The Wiz*."[28] Adds Berry Gordy: "I frankly liked his performance in *The Wiz*. . . . Michael just kind of wanted to do everything."[29]

Jackson's talent and ambitions couldn't rescue *The Wiz*, but they powered the success of *Off the Wall*, which debuted the following summer. The album would sell 7 million copies in the US by 1982, and more than 30 million copies worldwide, making it the bestselling effort by any black artist at the time; *Rolling Stone* labeled it "a slick, sophisticated R&B-Pop showcase."[30] Adds Yetnikoff: "[*Off the Wall*] was really, I think, his breakout record as Michael."[31]

There was no doubt that Jackson had arrived as a legitimate solo act and was much more than just a member of the Jacksons—both the group and the family. Buoyed by a fresh sense of independence, Michael started to contemplate going his own way on a number of fronts, including business. Though his father had orchestrated the early success of the Jackson 5, he was a flawed manager in many respects. His aggressive approach came in handy during the chitlin circuit days when he bargained with small-time promoters to earn cash for modest gigs. But it wasn't so helpful as his sons' careers grew to superstar status.

"Joe wasn't a businessman," wrote Smokey Robinson. "In the end he was more of a hindrance than a help; business people didn't want to deal with him. Sadly, when they were old enough, his kids found managers of their own, with Michael leading the way."[32]

Jackson knew that taking the next step as a solo artist meant breaking off from his father. He turned twenty-one less than three weeks after *Off the Wall*'s debut and didn't waste any time asserting himself as an adult. He informed his father he wouldn't be retaining his services as manager.

"Trying to fire your dad isn't easy," he explained in his autobiography. "But I just didn't like the way certain things were being handled."[33]

Joe didn't take the move as seriously as he might have, perhaps because Michael retained Freddy DeMann and Ron Weisner—who also handled some of the Jackson 5's affairs—as his new managerial team. But Michael saw the move as a major step toward independence.

"All I wanted was control over my life," he wrote. "And I took it."

––––––––––

"We're running overtime," says Yetnikoff, after about an hour and a half at the diner. "I'll start billing you."[34]

"Okay, last one."

"You keep saying last."

Yetnikoff touches on one more topic before we wrap up: the multiple sides of Jackson's personality, sometimes at odds with each other, that he witnessed as the singer's career progressed.

"To me, it's very simple," says the former CBS chief. "They coexist. . . . He had the childlike, emotional kind of thing and he had the astute one . . . the astute businessman."

He continues.

"I don't see that as impossible, to have different sides to a personality. I may be the only one who says, 'Sounds all right to me.' Not sounds all right, but sounds almost normal."

Chapter 4

EMPIRE BUILDING

The walls of John Branca's Los Angeles office are covered with mementos from his clients—he has represented more than twenty-five members of the Rock and Roll Hall of Fame—but the artist best represented by the keepsakes is Michael Jackson. Among the highlights is a photo of the singer at his wedding to Lisa Marie Presley, with the inscription: "To John Branca, the greatest lawyer of our times," signed by Jackson.

The veteran attorney spent the 1980s helping build Jackson's business, negotiating a record-setting album deal with CBS among other landmark agreements. After an on-and-off working relationship in the following decades, he was asked to return to Jackson's camp shortly before the singer's death in 2009. Along with coexecutor John McClain, he has since guided the singer's estate to more than $700 million in earnings, so it shouldn't come as much of a surprise that, even on a Friday afternoon in August, his inbox is overflowing.

"Oh!" he exclaims. "We got the latest ticket report from Cirque du Soleil . . . we're up to 103,000 tickets sold in Mexico City. They sold out nine shows, so they just added four more at the basketball arena."

Another email rolls in—this time from Marty Bandier, the president of Sony/ATV music publishing, which the estate co-owns along with Sony. It's a list of songs played at the closing ceremonies of the London Olympics.

"This will give you an example of some of the songs [Sony/ATV owns or administers]," says Branca, speeding up as he rattles off names. "'Rolling in the Deep' . . . 'Rebel Rebel,' all this Bowie . . . 'Bohemian Rhapsody,' 'We Will Rock You' . . . Spice Girls, Amy Winehouse, Depeche Mode, Robbie Williams . . . 'Diamonds Are Forever' . . ."

He smiles.

"Not bad, huh?"

———

Branca first met Michael Jackson in January of 1980 as a baby-faced twenty-nine-year-old attorney whose only professional experience was doing legal work for the Beach Boys with accountant Michael Mesnick—the one who'd arranged the meeting with Jackson.

The singer had just turned twenty-one and was looking for a lawyer. Sunglasses seemingly glued to his face, Jackson settled into a conference room seat and quietly listened as Branca and David Braun, an older partner at the firm where Branca was working, made their case. Then, in the middle of the meeting, the singer lowered his shades and stared directly at Branca.

"Do I know you?" Jackson asked.[1]

"Well, I don't think we've met," the young lawyer replied. "But I'm looking forward to us getting to know each other."

"Are you sure we haven't met before?"

"Michael, I think I would have remembered."

"Oh," said Jackson, replacing his eyewear. "Okay."

The next day, Branca received a call from Mesnick. "Michael likes you," said the accountant. "He's hiring you."

Jackson hadn't interviewed any other attorneys, but going with his gut was a wise move in this case—he knew the firm was among the best for musicians, representing clients including Bob Dylan, Neil Diamond, and George Harrison. And Jackson's eyewear was more than a fashion statement.

"He would sit in the meetings with his sunglasses on," recalls

Karen Langford, who started working with Jackson in the early 1980s. "And you really couldn't tell how much attention he was pay-ing . . . but afterwards, he would say something and you would know he actually really was paying attention because he just likes to sit there and take it all in. And that's how he learns . . . the whole world was like his classroom and he just wanted to learn it all."[2]

Shortly after Jackson hired Branca, the lawyer received his first task: negotiating a new deal with performing rights company BMI. He recalls asking the singer how much he was looking for as an ad-vance against songwriting royalties. Though he was young, Jack-son knew his worth, and said he would settle for nothing less than $200,000.[3] So Branca went to BMI and made his case. It wasn't long before he knew he'd passed his first test.

"I got three times that amount," he remembers. "I'll never forget the day we sat down and I said, 'Well, Michael,' and when I told him what I got him, there was a big smile on his face. So I knew for then, we were good to go, for a long time to come."

Much as he'd done during his Motown days, Jackson continued to absorb lessons about the business of music. "While I think that he may have picked up a lot of that stuff from me," says Berry Gordy, "I think it was John Branca [who] talked to him about what he could do."[4]

The next move was to rework Jackson's deal with CBS's Epic Records. Renegotiation is a common reward for artists who release albums as successful as *Off the Wall*, but Branca was able to score a bonanza. He convinced Epic to draw up a new solo contract for the singer. Jackson had received 32 percent of wholesale on his previous record; Branca got that number bumped up to 37 percent escalating to 39 percent—about 20 percent of retail—the highest rate in the industry at the time. The deal called for Jackson to earn more than thirty times what he'd made at Motown (where each brother earned about 1 percent of wholesale) and guaranteed the label would retain the Jacksons even if Michael left the group.[5]

Branca added another handy stipulation to the deal: Jackson's five-album deal, which began with *Off the Wall*, would be governed by California law, the only such agreement in the New York–based CBS Records family. That may sound like a triviality, which is likely why the label didn't put up a fight. But it was actually quite a shrewd move—unlike New York, the Golden State's regulations stipulated that an employee had the right to terminate any contract after seven years—and it gave Jackson's team a great deal of leverage for future renegotiations.

Around the same time, Branca grew accustomed to receiving late-night phone calls from Jackson to discuss the status of his latest album or business deal. Some matters were of greater importance than others, as the lawyer learned on one particular night when he picked up the phone.

"John, we have something very serious to talk about," Jackson said.

"What is it, Michael?" Branca replied, grabbing a pen and paper from his bedside table.

"My pinball machine isn't working."

———

Branca's job would prove to encompass much more than law, business, and pinball machines (he outsourced the latter to an arcade technician). Jackson often leaned on him for help with family matters as well, and the two had quite a bit in common on that front.

Jackson grew up in the entertainment business and so did Branca, in a way: when he was four years old, his mother left him with his father in New York and moved to Hollywood to pursue an acting career. His uncle, Ralph Branca, was an all-star Major League pitcher and one of Jackie Robinson's first friends on the Brooklyn Dodgers. Like the team, John eventually moved west; as a teenager, he played keyboard in a band that sometimes opened for the Doors, planting his flag in smoky Los Angeles clubs around the same time his future client was doing likewise halfway across the country in Gary.

While working for Jackson, Branca was often sent on reconnaissance missions to learn more about the intentions of the singer's father. Though the elder Jackson had been relieved of his managerial duties, he still felt he could exert his influence over anybody in Michael's sphere.

"I met with Joe, who basically said I needed to do what he told me to do," he recalls. "Michael said, 'Branca, tell me everything my father said.' And I repeated it all back, and he said, 'You don't listen to a thing he says.' And the fact that I would have repeated [Joe's words] to Michael let him know that I was working for him and not his father."[6]

Dealing with Michael's family also meant unwinding a few sloppy deals that Joe and his associates had put together in the 1970s. One particular problem area: music publishing. Though Michael had realized the importance of songwriting as a revenue stream, he wasn't familiar with the intricacies of copyright law—and neither was his father.

Shortly after the Jacksons left Motown, Joe had helped his son form a company in which to place copyrights to his own compositions, like "Shake Your Body (Down to the Ground)," written with Randy. But he or one of his associates had signed away international publishing rights for next to nothing. Worse yet, this arrangement was scheduled to last for the life of the copyright.

As a result, Michael wouldn't get paid for the airplay of his songs abroad, and it seemed that fixing the situation was impossible. It might have been, had Branca not noticed a loophole: when making the unfavorable deals, nobody on the Jacksons' team had filled out the proper paperwork.

"I didn't see any corporate documents that showed chain of title going from Michael to the corporations," says Branca. "So I just blew off the corporations. I told the companies overseas these corporations don't own these songs."

Those songs formed the beginnings of a new publishing company called Mijac Music that would serve as home to Jackson's future compositions. Now administered by Sony/ATV and owned by the estate, the catalogue is likely worth somewhere in the neighborhood of $100 million (perhaps more, depending on what earnings multiple one uses to determine the value).

After Jackson's experience with *The Wiz*, he'd been emboldened to flex his cinematographic muscles as well. He came up with the idea for the music video to the Jacksons' 1980 hit "Can You Feel It," a psychedelic romp through a futuristic landscape whose diverse inhabitants are sprinkled with golden dust by the brothers, who are portrayed as giant, shiny-suited superheroes. Critics would later praise the nine-minute segment for being ahead of its time; in 2001, MTV named it one of the top hundred videos ever made.[7]

Full recognition would be delayed for Jackson's solo music as well. In February of 1980, Jackson won his first Grammy Award as a solo artist, taking home Best Male R&B Vocal Performance for "Don't Stop 'Til You Get Enough." But for the hyper-ambitious singer, who also earned a Best Disco Record nomination for the same song, the attention didn't feel sufficient.

"My pride in the rhythms, the technical advances, and the success of *Off the Wall* was offset by the jolt I got when the Grammy nominations were announced," he wrote in *Moonwalk*. "I remember where I was when I got the news. I felt ignored by my peers and it hurt."[8]

Jackson watched the ceremony at home, on television. In his mind, "Don't Stop 'Til You Get Enough" should have garnered consideration not just in the narrow category in which it prevailed, but also for Song of the Year (an award claimed instead by the Doobie Brothers for "What a Fool Believes")—and *Off the Wall* should have been in contention for overall awards like Album of the Year.

Jackson was keenly aware of how black musicians had been exploited or overlooked by the establishment over the years. ("Use the past as a teacher, as a reference as to what I should do," he'd later write in an unpublished note.)[9] When it came to the Grammys, the relative lack of recognition made him feel marginalized. He wasn't interested in making *black* music, anyway. Since his early days with the Jackson 5, he'd spoken of making albums that transcended skin color; his stated goal was "uniting people of all races through music."[10]

As disappointing as it was, Jackson's Grammy letdown may have ultimately been a useful lesson. "That experience lit a fire in my soul," Jackson wrote. "All I could think of was the next album and what I would do with it. I wanted it to be truly great. . . . I said to myself, 'Wait until next time'—they won't be able to ignore the next album."

———————

In the summer of 1982, Jackson summoned Quincy Jones and the rest of his A-Team to Westlake Recording Studios in Los Angeles to record his follow-up. The album that would become *Thriller* was known by a different name at first: *Starlight*.

Veteran songwriter Rod Temperton initially gave that name to the title track (with a chorus of "STAR-light! *Star*light sun . . ."). And it would have stuck, had Jones not challenged him one night to come up with something better. Temperton went home and brain-stormed hundreds of titles, including "Midnight Man." He still knew he could improve on that; Temperton woke up one morning and the title *Thriller* popped into his head.[11]

The next task was to concoct some more hits. Michael Jackson didn't only want to win awards and write perfect songs, he wanted to sell records—more than anyone else had ever sold. "Ever since I was a little boy, I had dreamed of creating the biggest-selling record of all time," he wrote. "I remember going swimming as a child and making [that] wish before I jumped into the pool."[12]

Jackson was so focused on his goal that when Jones and Tem-perton asked him if he'd be disappointed if *Thriller* didn't top *Off the Wall*, he became angry with them for even suggesting the possibility. Fortunately, he had a fresh face to help him in the studio: a young sound engineer from Syracuse named Matt Forger. The son of a pilot, Forger grew up repairing mangled airplanes, learned to play guitar in high school, and studied mechanical engineering in college. In his spare time, he applied his multifarious talents by mixing live shows first for his friends; frustrated by the poor quality of the sound equipment at the venues where he worked, Forger started building his own.

"That challenge taught me a lot, but I wanted to get into a serious environment to be able to make recordings," he says. "I understood very early in my life [that] I could be listening to the radio and three or four songs would play, and then one song would come on and it would be like, 'Wow, this song is great—there's something about it—there's some quality that *this* song has that these other songs, while they're good, they don't seem to have this magic quality.'"[13]

He found a home at Westlake, working as a technology guru for Quincy Jones shortly before the production of *Thriller* began in earnest. When Forger met Jackson on the first tracking day for "The Girl Is Mine," a duet with Paul McCartney that would become the album's first single, the engineer immediately recognized Jackson as an avid accumulator of knowledge. A voracious reader, Jackson often spoke of studying the best to become better—in all sorts of fields.

"He didn't study the greats just in music," Forger remembers. "He studied people like Michelangelo, he studied the Beatles, he studied Thomas Edison, Henry Ford. . . . His quest was to figure out what it was, what these qualities are, how these people became successful."

One of those qualities was attention to detail. Jackson and the A-Team listened to rough cuts of more than six hundred tracks, including thirty-three submitted by Temperton.[14] Jackson himself wrote four of the album's nine total songs, including "Billie Jean" and "Beat It." To broaden the record's appeal, he secured musical contributions from other big-time artists: a guitar solo from Eddie

Van Halen, vocals by McCartney on "The Girl Is Mine," and songwriting by Steve Porcaro (of the pop-rock band Toto) on "Human Nature."

Quincy Jones proved to be a big help in convincing some of those guests to record. He lured Van Halen to the studio with two six-packs of beer and the promise of a killer guitar solo on "Beat It." The song turned out to be so hot that, in the midst of an early playback, it caused a speaker to actually burst into flames.

Sound equipment wasn't the only casualty of *Thriller's* aural pyrotechnics. One day on his way home from a recording session, Jackson found himself lost in the melody of "Billie Jean," which he was composing in his head at the time. He was so wrapped up in the music that he didn't notice the smoke spewing from the bottom of his Rolls-Royce until a man on a motorcycle pulled up to his window and shouted, "Your car's on fire!"[15]

In the 1980s, computers and samplers weren't commonplace, and digital music was in its infancy. But the A-Team had mastered the technology of the day, namely the twenty-four-track tape. In particular, Bruce Swedien had gotten into the habit of using dual multitrack tapes and linking them together with a synchronizer. So instead of having twenty-four audio tracks, there would be nearly twice that number (forty-six, to be exact, as two tracks had to be devoted to time codes). On *Thriller*, he and Forger took that strategy to extremes, often using a dozen different twenty-four-track tapes per song. A less advanced recording might use one track for the entire string section, but the A-Team could dedicate an entire track to a single violin.

"One of the things that created the richness and the character and the sound of *Thriller* was this ability to use this vast number of multitrack tapes," says Forger. "There was an entire organizational strategy of how to make this work. . . . We sat in the studio every single day and utilized this technique. And with Quincy's vast knowledge of how to draw on sound characters and textures, Rod's arrangement ability, Bruce's knowledge of the sonic quality of how to create these signature sounds . . . everything was driven by the creative sense of how to create and make the best recording possible."

While Epic prepared to release "The Girl Is Mine" as the album's first single in October 1982, Jackson and the A-Team worked feverishly—often stringing together multiple sixteen-hour days—to place the finishing touches on the rest of *Thriller*. The day before Epic's drop-dead date to turn in the album, a group including Jackson, Branca, the A-Team, and Yetnikoff gathered in the studio to hear the final mix for the first time. As they listened, it quickly became clear that something was wrong.

"It doesn't make me want to dance," Jackson said.[16] He put it more bluntly in his autobiography: "*Thriller* sounded so crappy to me that tears came to my eyes."[17]

The problem was not the songs themselves, but the sound quality. In an effort to fit the long intros that Jackson favored—he dubbed them "smelly jelly"—they'd packed twenty-eight minutes of sound on each side of the record. On a digital album, that wouldn't have been an issue. But on vinyl, where each track must be physically cut into the actual record, it's a different story. In order to cram half an hour of audio on one side, each groove must be a little narrower than usual. For *Thriller*, the initial result was a thin, tinny sound that wiped out the A-Team's tireless work on sound quality. And Jackson wouldn't let it be released in such a state.[18]

The *Thriller* team took a weekend to cool off before embarking on a grueling schedule of revisions, editing, and remixing the entire album in a week. They all made compromises. Jackson agreed to wipe away some of his treasured "jelly," while Temperton chopped a verse off of "The Lady in My Life." They managed to shave a handful of precious minutes from other places as well, leaving the final product with about nineteen minutes on either side. At last, they were able to cut a record that had what Jones described as the "big fat grooves to make a big fat sound."[19]

Swedien still remembers Jackson's reaction when he first heard the retooled record: "His eyes lit up and he said, 'Oh, it makes me want to dance!'"[20]

Still, Jackson had his doubters. In advance of the album's release, Yetnikoff and Branca lobbied *Rolling Stone* chief Jann Wenner to run a story on the nascent King of Pop. Though he had put Michael on the cover during the Jackson 5's heyday, Wenner wasn't interested in the singer as a solo artist. His reasoning at the time: "Michael Jackson's not cover material."[21]

———

Shortly after *Thriller* finally made its debut, Quincy Jones found himself in a panic. He'd discovered that Jackson had decided not to renew the recently expired contract with his managers DeMann and Weisner (both declined to comment for this book;[22] "I'm tired of talking about Michael Jackson," added the latter[23]). With no agent and no manager, it seemed the young singer had sabotaged what he'd envisioned as his greatest triumph.

The only person left on Jackson's business team was Branca, the baby-faced lawyer who'd been with the singer for just two years. Jones picked up the phone and punched in the attorney's number.

"Branca, what's going on here?" the producer asked urgently. "It's like a 747 with no pilot!"[24]

"There is a pilot, Quincy."

"Who?"

"Michael."

Chapter 5

KISSING THE MONSTER

"Michael's not going to kiss the monster," growled the voice on the other end of the line.

"What are you talking about?" asked Branca, who'd just been rushed from a meeting to take the call.

"Tell 'em he's not kissing the monster!"[1] [2]

The voice in question belonged to Yetnikoff. The monster in question was E.T., the lovable alien with a penchant for racking up terrifying intergalactic phone bills. He was also the titular character in a film that had captured the imagination of millions—including that of Michael Jackson, who'd agreed to record a song and narrate the movie's companion audiobook at the personal request of director Steven Spielberg. Jackson was set to appear on the LP's cover embracing E.T.; MCA Records would release the package. But the label hadn't obtained the proper clearances from CBS, and Yetnikoff was irate.

Success had made the blustery executive even more confident— and cantankerous—than usual. Under his watch, other top CBS artists including Bruce Springsteen, Marvin Gaye, and Billy Joel had seen their latest releases rocket into uncharted commercial strata. And he certainly wasn't planning to let Michael Jackson appear on a rival company's product so close to the release of *Thriller*.

"The monster, he's not kissing the monster!" Yetnikoff repeated. "You can tell those fucking guys at MCA to go fuck themselves, they're not using my artist."

Yetnikoff ended up threatening to sue MCA unless the label pulled the E.T. album from stores or provided proper compensation. "I was very litigious," the former CBS chief recalls with a hint of glee. "We'd always duel. . . . I was always suing MCA."

After getting off the phone with Yetnikoff, Branca panicked. He thought Jackson might blame him for the situation, perhaps even fire him. But the singer recognized his lawyer wasn't at fault. Eventually, MCA settled with CBS, agreeing to pay $500,000 to put the matter to rest.[3]

It was Jackson, however, who'd eventually reap the biggest reward from the fiasco.

In 1983, there were 9.1 million cars sold in the United States.[4] That same year, Michael Jackson's *Thriller* moved more than 10 million copies.

For what would become the bestselling album ever, though, commercial success accelerated more like a Pinto than a Porsche. The full *Thriller* LP was preceded by its first single, "The Girl Is Mine," which eventually reached number 2 on the *Billboard* charts. Critics blasted it as a step back from the diverse rhythms of *Off the Wall*. One reviewer from *Rolling Stone* called it "wimpoid" and lashed out at the song's featured guest, Paul McCartney, for being too "tame."[5] (Given that the chorus ends with the line "the doggone girl is mine," he may have had a point.)

The complete album would earn a much warmer reception from other critics and consumers. *Thriller* hit stores on November 30, 1982, making its debut at number 11 on *Billboard*'s Top LPs & Tapes chart (the precursor to today's Billboard 200), behind such classics as *Built for Speed* by Stray Cats and . . . *Famous Last Words* . . . by Supertramp. Still, it was a strong opening—back then, albums rarely debuted at number 1, and the most common path to the peak was a slow climb.

Reviewers seemed to like *Thriller* much better than its first single. *Billboard* praised its "irresistible pulse and energy,"[6] while the *New York Times* called it "a wonderful pop record, the latest statement by one of the great singers in popular music today."[7] Perhaps more important, Yetnikoff loved the album. After hearing the final cut—and seeing its early sales—the CBS chief offered Jackson his thoughts with the same obscene fervor he'd employed with Branca just a few weeks earlier.

"You delivered like a motherfucker."[8]

"Please don't use that word, Walter."

"You delivered like an angel. Archangel Michael."

"That's better. Now will you promote it?"

"Like a motherfucker."

Even as *Thriller* sailed off record store racks, Jackson wasn't satisfied. He still hadn't hired a manager, assigning most business-related tasks to Branca and picking up the rest himself. He'd call Yetnikoff at all hours to discuss the latest sales numbers on his album. And he was right to think more was possible.

By the early 1980s, promotion meant much more than just convincing radio DJs to spin a hit single: to truly break *Thriller* as a mainstream pop album, Yetnikoff needed to get videos played on MTV. The network had only been on the air since August of 1981, but in barely a year, its reach had grown from 300 cable outlets and 2.5 million homes to 2,000 affiliates and more than 17 million households. Partly due to the new burst of exposure, the music industry went from negative growth in the late 1970s to a 5 percent uptick in 1983.

"Since the beginning of time—1956—rock and roll and TV have never really hit it off," the Rolling Stones' Keith Richards told *Time*. "But suddenly, it's like they've gotten married and can't leave each other alone."[9]

Jackson had planned to take advantage of that trend with an initial vision for *Thriller* that called for three videos. Brimming with ideas in the wake of his involvement with *The Wiz* and "Can You Feel It," he was determined to personally elevate the music video genre, which he saw as "primitive and weak" in the early 1980s. He believed videos shouldn't be treated as promotional throwaways, but as works of art in their own right.

Jackson convinced CBS to shell out $250,000 to fund production for "Billie Jean." Helmed by Steve Barron (who would go on to direct *Teenage Mutant Ninja Turtles* in 1990 and *Coneheads* in 1993), the video featured Jackson twirling through a desolate film noir landscape (the singer had to convince Barron that there should be dancing in the video at all). Throughout Jackson's quixotic romp, he is tailed by a nefarious paparazzo. In the climactic scene, Jackson sneaks into a hotel room and slips into bed with a figure obscured by sheets—presumably Billie Jean herself. Just as the snoop arrives at the window to take a photo, Jackson vanishes in a golden glow that explodes like a miniature atom bomb beneath the covers.

"I wanted something that would *glue* you to the set," Jackson later wrote. "I wanted to be a pioneer in this relatively new medium and make the best short music movies we could make."[10]

Though Jackson had certainly lived up to his end of the bargain, Yetnikoff encountered fierce resistance when he tried to get the video played on MTV. The network's brass insisted that Jackson's music wasn't rock; they played only rock videos because that's what their listeners wanted. The subtext: they essentially only played music by white musicians.

"[MTV] just had this real apartheid mentality toward black music," recalls Fab 5 Freddy, who went on to host the show *Yo! MTV Raps* after the network eventually expanded beyond rock. "They were trying to mirror the segregated format of mainstream radio at that time."[11]

Jackson wasn't happy about that reality. Neither was Yetnikoff, particularly now that the policy was affecting his biggest artist—and CBS's bottom line. He placed a call to MTV's offices. Within moments, he had chief executive Bob Pittman on the line. As usual, he didn't start with pleasantries.

"Are you the chief schmuck?" Yetnikoff remembers asking.[12]

"Yeah . . . ?"

"I want you to play ['Billie Jean']."

"It's not up to you."

"Well, let me tell you what's going to happen," Yetnikoff continued. "I'm going to pull every [CBS Records video]."

"What are your artists going to do?"

"They're not going to have to worry about MTV. If I pull everything, Quincy Jones, who is very close to Steve Ross, who owns the other half of MTV, is surely going to pull out. And then you're going to have Warner Bros. and CBS pulling their stuff."

Not all of CBS's acts were actually making videos at that point, but in theory, Yetnikoff's ultimatum meant that MTV would never get to run anything by major acts like Billy Joel and Bruce Springsteen. To add pressure, Yetnikoff told Pittman that he'd publicly brand MTV as a bunch of racists if the network continued to refuse to play Jackson's videos. ("I don't think it was racism in the sense of 'We don't like black people,'" Yetnikoff explains. "I think it was racism in the sense of, 'We're a white rock and roll outlet and we want to play white rock and roll.'")

MTV caved, and as "Billie Jean" entered heavy video rotation, *Thriller* shot up the *Billboard* rankings. There were actually separate charts for black artists at the time (titled "Black LPs" and "Black Singles"). By the end of February, *Thriller* occupied the number 1 position on the general pop, black album, and singles charts,[13] making Jackson the first artist to accomplish such a feat.[14]

A few weeks later, rumblings of Yetnikoff's threats made it all the way to the pages of trade publications. But they were rumors then, not music business lore, and MTV shot them down. "The only pressure [CBS has] ever given us is Billy Joel's," said a spokesperson for MTV's parent company, speaking of a popular song by the Piano Man.[15]

Although Yetnikoff had pledged to push *Thriller* "like a motherfucker," Jackson's album didn't need much help. "It almost took off on its own," the former CBS chief recalls. "I don't think we had to do anything, we just did normal promotion. There was no specific thing. We didn't have to. I think at that point, the intelligent thing was to get out of the way."[16]

Jackson pressed on with his videos, or short films, as he liked to call them. Next up was "Beat It," directed by Bob Giraldi, who'd go on to direct the cult classic film *Dinner Rush* (he also had experience filming commercials and would later direct Jackson and his brothers in a fateful Pepsi ad). For the "Beat It" video, Jackson wanted a literal interpretation of his song: two rival gangs preparing for a potentially lethal throwdown as they wander through an urban dystopia. In an effort to make the video feel as authentic as possible, Jackson had his team go around Los Angeles and round up actual gang members for the shoot.

In the video, Jackson eventually defuses the dispute between the warring groups by—what else—dancing (a narrative that would re-play itself on the title track of his next album). Strangely enough, it also resonated in real life. Jackson found that the gang members, many of them from warring factions on the street, were quite pleas-ant when united for his video. They complimented him on his danc-ing, asked nicely for autographs, and even cleared their own trays at lunchtime.

"I came to realize that the whole thing about being bad and tough is that it's done for recognition," Jackson later wrote. "All along these guys had wanted to be seen and respected, and now we were going to put them on TV . . . they were so wonderful to me—polite, quiet, supportive."[17]

But "Beat It," like "Billie Jean" before it, had ramifications far be-yond the career of Jackson and those who worked on the video. "It really spawned what turned out to be a wave of Top 40 stations play-ing artists that had a harder, rougher edge and an R&B sound," says Berklee College of Music professor John Kellogg, speaking of songs like Aerosmith's "Walk This Way" collaboration with Run-D.M.C. "All of that started with 'Beat It' and Michael Jackson."[18]

———————

It was a different sort of video, however, that really sent *Thriller* into uncharted commercial territory. In 1983, Suzanne de Passe decided to put together a television special called *Motown 25: Yesterday, Today, Forever.* She initially had to convince Gordy to authorize the project. He didn't want to go up onstage and "be phony and smile at all the people" who'd left his company, he says.

"Come back for one night to celebrate Motown and me?" he asked de Passe. "For what, why should I be there?"[19]

"Everybody is coming," she countered. "You have to be there because it is a legacy that you started twenty-five years ago."

There was another consideration on Gordy's mind: he was having financial troubles at the time and thought he might have to sell Motown (he would, five years later, for $61 million). Meanwhile, de Passe enlisted Smokey Robinson to help convince Gordy. "It doesn't matter who owns the company," the legendary songwriter said. "We got a legacy of love . . . and you need to help Suzanne."

As soon as Gordy agreed, de Passe told him he needed to start working on Michael Jackson, who was ambivalent about coming and didn't want to be part of a television special. The Motown chief's own reluctance quickly turned to outrage at his former charge: "How dare he not want to come?"

So Gordy headed over to Epic's recording studio and asked to see Jackson. He got right to the point.

"What do you mean you don't want to come celebrate *Motown 25*?"

"I'm doing too much TV now," Jackson replied.

"This is not TV—this is *Motown 25* . . . and they're honoring me. Are you saying you don't want to come?"

"Well, they didn't tell me that specifically. Do you want me there?"

"Yeah, I want you there."

Jackson agreed to perform a medley of hits with his brothers, followed by "Billie Jean," and went back into the studio.

Later, worried that the show would overexpose him, he briefly reneged, claiming it was because Branca didn't want him to do "Billie Jean" on television. Gordy called his bluff.

"I know you, I taught you that," the Motown boss said. "'If you don't want to do something, I'll be the bad guy.' . . . Now it doesn't work. So you want to do it or not?"

"I'll do it."

Jackson choreographed the set and spent days practicing with his siblings at their Hayvenhurst home, videotaping each rehearsal so that they could go back and analyze what was working and what wasn't. During his rare moments of downtime, Jackson mulled the options for his solo performance. "I had no idea what I was going to do at first," he wrote in an unpublished note. "I just had one major thought in mind and heart: It had to be the best, incredible, the unexpected. I had determination of fire to be incredible on this show."[20]

The night before the performance, Jackson decided he wanted to use his solo time to showcase his version of a move that was particularly popular with inner-city break dancers at the time. ("All I did was enhance the dance," he told Oprah Winfrey in 1993.[21]) He gave it a name: the Moonwalk.

On March 25, 1983, after he and his brothers finished their routine in front of an enthusiastic live studio audience at the Pasadena Civic Auditorium, Jackson took the microphone to make an announcement. "Those were the good old days; I love those songs," he said. "Those were magic moments with all my brothers. . . . But, especially, I like the new songs."[22]

With that, Jackson whisked a fedora to the top of his head and started gyrating to the tune of "Billie Jean." The crowd squealed with delight as he swirled around the stage, but it was a five-second sequence in the song's bridge that would unleash the flashbulbs of history on Jackson's performance. After pointing at the crowd and letting out one of his trademark whoops, Jackson planted his feet and glided backward across the stage—his feet appearing to move forward and backward at the same time like mystical pistons— before easing into a spin and landing on his toes. Though the audience erupted in applause, the perfectionist Jackson's first reaction was frustration.

"The audience loved it, I got an incredible response, more than I imagined, standing ovation, screaming, dancing," he wrote. "But still I was disappointed that after the big spin, I didn't stay on my toes long enough."[23]

Walter Yetnikoff has an explanation for Jackson's feelings: "He was a star at six. And he had his father hovering over him, smacking him in the head when he didn't do it well . . . this will tend to give you a perfectionist kind of thing."[24]

Any lingering doubt as to the merits of his performance dissipated when he received a call from Fred Astaire. "You're a hell of a mover," the dance legend said. "Man, you really put them on their asses last night."[25]

Some fifty million people had tuned in to watch the *Motown 25* special on NBC, and quite a few shared Astaire's attitude. Many of them went out and bought *Thriller*. The album had sold 2 million copies in the United States by March of 1983. After *Motown 25* and the videos for "Beat It" and "Billie Jean," *Thriller* would sell an additional 10 million before the end of the year.[26]

The album spent eighty weeks in the top ten on the US charts, including thirty-seven at number 1. *Thriller* fared almost as well overseas: in Japan, it spent sixty-five weeks on the charts; in the Soviet Union, it became a valuable trading chip on the black market; in South Africa, it became the segregated country's top seller. In 1984, the *Guinness Book of World Records* named *Thriller* the top-selling album of all time, a title it still holds.[27]

"He did what other people couldn't," says former Def Jam president Kevin Liles. "It's the spirit in which he did things—'I'm going to moonwalk, and you ain't gonna know what the hell I just did.' . . . He definitely was an inspiration to a lot of us."[28] Adds rapper Ludacris: "He was the definition of what a superstar was to me . . . there's an intangible energy whenever you listen to his music that you can't even explain."[29]

And like the hip-hop moguls he inspired, Jackson was determined to monetize his success to the greatest extent possible. He often spoke of the many great artists of the 1950s and '60s—particularly black musicians—who had signed away vast swaths of their future musical interests because they were so eager to land record deals.

"He studied people who had attained success in their field . . . but he also studied people who, although they were successful in the popular sense, they may not have been successful in a business sense," recalls Forger. "And he studied those people and the mistakes that they made so that he would not make those same mistakes."[30]

One afternoon at the height of the *Thriller* frenzy, Jackson and Branca were sitting in the living room at Hayvenhurst when the singer decided to give his lawyer a motivational speech.

Jackson often did this with his closest lieutenants in those days, a habit he picked up from Berry Gordy. This time, he had something very specific on his mind: renegotiating his record deal. Given *Thriller*'s record-shattering success, Jackson knew he could squeeze just about anything out of CBS.

"You sure you can get me a great deal with Walter Yetnikoff?"[31]

"Yes, Michael."

"Well, you know, Frank Sinatra uses Mickey Rudin."

Rudin, who would pass away in 1999, was one of the biggest names in Hollywood during the second half of the twentieth century. As Sinatra's right-hand man, he guarded his client's interest with the vigor of a mother bear. Four years after hurling a $2 million lawsuit at author Kitty Kelley over her 1987 unauthorized biography *His Way*, Rudin sued her for including his name in the acknowledgments of her next book, a dishy tome on Nancy Reagan that suggested that the First Lady had a long-term affair with Sinatra.[32]

Jackson expected the same level of excellence—and ferocity—from his attorney.

"Are you as good as Mickey Rudin?" he asked.[33]

"Yes, Michael," Branca replied. "And, you know, Mickey Rudin's a little older now. I probably have more energy than he does."

"Oh, okay, I like to hear that. You know, when people speak to me about Sinatra and Rudin . . . [I want them to] speak about us that way, Branca. We need to be the model for the world. We need to be the people that people point to and say, 'I want to do it like those guys do it.'"

Evidently, Jackson knew how to motivate those who worked for him. Branca would go on to renegotiate his deal three different times during *Thriller*'s historic run. After that afternoon at Hayvenhurst, Jackson homed in on something even more important than percentage points: ownership of his master recordings. And Branca knew that to accomplish such a momentous feat, he'd need to wait for just the right moment.

————

Thriller continued to get scooped from store shelves at a record pace as 1983 wore on. But by the summer, it was no longer number 1 on the charts, and Jackson was peeved. Rather than sit back and watch the royalties roll in, he decided to make another late-night call to Yetnikoff.

"The record, it's slipping from number one," he said. "What are we going to do?"

"Michael, what we're going to do is we're going to go to sleep, and we're going to pick this up tomorrow."[34]

But Frank Dileo, Epic's chief of promotions, had some ideas. A squat, cigar-chomping fireplug of a man who looked so much like a mobster that he was later cast as Tuddy Cicero in Martin Scorsese's film *Goodfellas*, he suggested making a third video as Jackson had initially planned. *Thriller*'s title track seemed a good target ("It's simple," Dileo said. "All you've got to do is dance, sing, and make it scary").[35]

It wasn't quite so easy, though, once Jackson developed a vision for the video. He wanted to hire John Landis, director of *An American Werewolf in London* and many other movies, to lead an ensemble of dancing zombies in a short film three times the length of a typical video—and an order of magnitude more expensive. Yetnikoff wasn't buying it: "What are you, fucking crazy, making a video about monsters?"[36]

In fairness to Yetnikoff, "Billie Jean" and "Beat It" had already gobbled up a big chunk of CBS's cash, and the record company generally didn't bankroll more than two videos per album anyway.[37] That was mostly because, at the time, it was rare to have more than two singles from one album. To top it off, Jackson's plan for "Thriller" called for a budget of at least $900,000—in era when budgets rarely exceeded $50,000 per video—and the film had to be flawless.[38]

"He became more of a perfectionist than I was," recalls Berry Gordy. "I would spend whatever money it took, and he knew that. . . . I said the money is less important than the quality of the work. So when he started doing his [own projects], he took that to major extremes."[39]

Jackson's message to Branca about the budget: "I don't care, figure it out." The lawyer's solution was to find partners willing to finance an entertainment special on the making of the "Thriller" video, thereby covering the budget of the video itself at the same time. He was able to convince Showtime and MTV to cough up about $300,000 apiece—marking the first time the latter had ever paid for programming—and got another $400,000 from home video outfit Vestron (CBS agreed to pick up an additional $100,000 to $200,000 as the video's budget ballooned to $1.2 million).[40]

By mid-1983, Landis and Jackson had written the screenplay and completed filming. The result seemed poised to live up to even the singer's lofty expectations. There was something for everyone: the spooky voiceovers of Vincent Price, the good looks of *Playboy* centerfold Ola Ray, an opening scene in which the world's top entertainer turns into a werewolf (and then, famously, a zombie). Just days before the film was to be delivered to MTV, however, Branca received a phone call spookier than anything that happened in the video.

"Get the tapes for 'Thriller,'" said Jackson in a whisper. "We have to destroy them."

"Michael, think about it tonight. Call me tomorrow."

The next day, Jackson called back.

"Did you get the canisters?"

"No, Mike, but they're coming."

After having a handful of similar calls with Jackson over the next few days, Branca realized that—for some reason—his client was serious about destroying the film. So he phoned John Landis, who had the precious cargo in his possession.

"John, you gotta bring me the [canisters]."

"Why?"

"John, just give them to me," said Branca urgently. "Do you want ["Thriller"] put out or not?"

"Yeah."

"All right, then, get me them!"

As soon as Landis turned over the film canisters to Branca, Jackson called again.

"Did you get them?"

"Yeah, I got them here, Mike."

"Destroy them."

When Branca pressed Jackson as to why he wanted the tapes obliterated, the singer finally admitted that the Jehovah's Witnesses—

whose beliefs he still shared—had heard about the video. Outraged by its supernatural suggestions, they essentially told him he'd lose his spot in heaven if he ever allowed it to see the light of day.

Branca scrambled for a way to soothe his client.

"Mike, you remember Bela Lugosi?"

"Yeah."

"He played Dracula," said Branca, stalling for time. "Well, you know he's a very religious man."

"What do you mean?"

"He's a very religious man and yet he's playing Dracula . . . did you ever see the disclaimers in his movies that it didn't reflect his personal convictions?"

Jackson said he hadn't.

"Michael, why don't we put a disclaimer at the beginning of the video?"

After a long pause, Jackson agreed. What he didn't know was that Branca hadn't a clue as to Lugosi's piety—and that the actor had never made a habit of including sly disclaimers at the beginning of his films. But that bit of shrewd maneuvering ended up saving the "Thriller" video, not to mention the making-of special that would pay its bills. More important, it prevented Jackson from making a then-rare disastrous business decision—the sort that the sycophants who later came to surround him would never have had the gumption to help him avoid.

Branca next called Landis to notify him of the impending addendum. The director initially resisted, but when the attorney fully conveyed the gravity of the situation, Landis gave his approval. The video went live in December of 1983 with the following note in the introduction:

> Due to my strong personal convictions, I wish to stress that this film in no way endorses a belief in the occult.
>
> Michael Jackson[41]

The fourteen-minute flick would later be named the best music video of all time by MTV,[42] and was certainly the most important chapter in Michael Jackson's revision—and reinvention—of the medium. The video on the making of "Thriller" eventually sold 9 million copies, making it the bestselling home video of any kind at that point.

"Michael pioneered videos as an art form," says Branca. "I really think when you talk about his business contribution and business acumen, it was especially in the area of marketing and music."[43]

In the meantime, Jackson's ghoulish gallivantings sent sales of the album itself skyward once again. "After the 'Thriller' video, I remember [the records] were running out the door," says Yetnikoff. "He was selling a million records a week."[44]

By age twenty-five, Jackson had become one of the richest entertainers on the planet, earning $43 million in 1983 and $91 million in 1984. His financial success was matched by *Thriller*'s accolades. In addition to a slew of positive reviews, the album received twelve Grammy nominations.[45] And Jackson wanted to be sure he got the credit—sometimes at the expense of his collaborators. The night before the ceremony in Los Angeles, he called Yetnikoff.

"I'm winning a bunch of Grammys and Quincy is winning a bunch," said Jackson. "He shouldn't get a Grammy for producing the record, I produced it."

"Michael, you're crazy."

"No, go to the Grammys, tell them to take Quincy's nomination off, I want to be the only one getting the Grammy for producing the record."

"Michael, I can't do that. I can't do that. One, it's too late. Two, this is a TV show, they don't care what you and I do at this point; it's Quincy's town more than it's my town. And they're not going to do it; they're not going to take my word over his. And three, I saw him produce the fucking record! I saw him rolling the dials or whatever. This is ridiculous, I can't do it."[46]

In Yetnikoff's autobiography, the former CBS chief writes that he ended the conversation by saying, "Go to the goddamn Grammys, Michael, and act like you're happy."[47] It seemed Jackson heeded that advice when he arrived at the ceremony the next day. He was all smiles as he and Jones celebrated victories including Record of the Year for "Beat It" and Album of the Year for *Thriller*.

Jackson took home eight awards in all, and to this day, no other artist has collected more Grammys in a single night. It's even more impressive given that the number of categories expanded from 67 at the 26th Annual Grammy Awards to a peak of 110 a quarter-century later.[48] In the year that followed, the acknowledgments continued to pour in—and not just from Grammy voters. In May, Jackson agreed to waive the fee for the use of "Beat It" in an anti-drunk-driving campaign in exchange for a visit to the White House. There, on a sunny spring day, Ronald Reagan introduced the singer as cameras rolled.

"Well, isn't this a thriller?" the president began as he formally welcomed Jackson to the White House, discharging a salvo of additional puns before turning serious.[49]

"Michael Jackson is proof of what a person can accomplish through a lifetime free of alcohol or drug abuse," Reagan continued, turning to present the singer a plaque the size of a small coffee table. "Thank you, Michael, for the example that you've given to the millions of young Americans who look up to you . . . your success is an American dream come true."

———

"John, I think I fucked up."

It was Yetnikoff on the phone, calling Branca with the closest thing to an apology that he could muster.

"Why, Walter?" the lawyer replied.

But he already knew: Yetnikoff was feeling remorseful for berating Branca—and not taking Jackson's opinion into consideration—

during the E.T. fiasco. Since then, *Thriller* had broken just about every sales record there was to break. Even the E.T. album in question managed to crack the top 100 on the UK charts and earned Jackson a Grammy for Best Recording for Children. Yetnikoff's stature had received an incredible boost as a result of *Thriller's* success, and he wanted to keep his star happy.

"Well, Michael told me how big [*Thriller*] was going to be," Yetnikoff continued. "But I didn't realize how big it was going to be. I didn't realize that. I think I fucked up. Is he mad at me?"[50]

"I don't know, Walter. Would you be mad if you were him?"

"I gotta make it up to him," said Yetnikoff. "How do you think I can do that?"

Branca's moment had arrived.

"Give him ownership of his masters," the lawyer said.

There was a long pause on the other end of the line.

"Okay."[51]

Chapter 6

THE BUSINESS OF VICTORY

Charles Sullivan describes many things as "grand and glorious." On our first phone call, he used the phrase to characterize institutions of higher learning (Harvard, his alma mater), publications (*Forbes*), and the way he was feeling that day.

When we met for lunch at the Yale Club in New York a few days later, his outlook hadn't darkened a bit. Decked in a blue blazer, a blue-and-white striped dress shirt, and neatly knotted yellow tie, the seventy-year-old came from a family accustomed to grandness and glory. His father founded the NFL's New England Patriots and owned the team for three decades. Sure enough, when the waiter asked how he was doing, Sullivan's reply was swift: "Grand and glorious."[1]

Those two words also happen to be the best way to describe the vision of Michael Jackson and his brothers for the Victory Tour—the Jacksons' post-*Thriller* reunion romp of 1984—bankrolled by none other than Sullivan. The tour would go on to gross $70 million, of which Sullivan would end up guaranteeing $55 million to the brothers. He wouldn't see a dime from the tour. Then again, neither would Michael Jackson.

They both planned it that way, more or less. For Sullivan, the goal was expanding the scope of his business from sporting events to include live music. For Jackson, it was giving back (on the eve of the tour, he announced that he'd be donating his $6 million cut to charity) and doing right by his family (the excursion was his last with his brothers) so that he could move into the next phase of his solo career with a clear conscience.

"I had a much better story to tell: that this was the reunion of the Jackson 5, the group that really defined Motown and American music," says Sullivan. "And that was a message that I was able to sell."

Though Jackson didn't end up keeping any money from ticket sales, the Victory Tour helped turn his already sparkling star into a supernova. He'd find other ways to add millions to his bulging coffers along the way.

As Jackson racked up record sales and Grammy Awards, his family watched his explosive success with great interest—and more than a bit of envy. Jermaine was in the process of leaving Motown after his solo career at the label had fizzled. The brothers hadn't recorded an album since 1980's *Triumph*, which had earned platinum certification for sales of more than 1 million, about what *Thriller* sold on a very good week.

Between Michael's supernatural success and the overwhelmingly positive reaction to the brothers' reunion on the *Motown 25* special, it seemed the time was right for new material. An album and a tour with Michael was just what Jackie, Marlon, Randy, Tito, and Jermaine needed to give their careers—and bank accounts—a boost.

Concocting a new album proved to be easy enough. The brothers started recording *Victory* in November 1983, bridging gaps in both musical taste and schedule by structuring the album mostly as a collection of solos. Jermaine made his return to the group with opening track "Torture" (written by Jackie Jackson), while Michael contributed a handful of songs including "State of Shock," a duet with fellow Branca client Mick Jagger ("He sings flat," Jackson teased his lawyer after recording the song. "I can't believe you recommended him"[2]).

When it came to touring, however, Michael would prove to be a tough sell. He had already spent over a decade toiling alongside his brothers, and even his father acknowledged that the singer was tiring of the grind. "He was getting fed up doing all these tours," recalls Joe Jackson. "He wanted to write and produce music."[3]

Moving on made sense from a financial standpoint, too: though Michael had long been the Jacksons' undisputed frontman, they still divided the spoils evenly. That didn't seem to bother him as much as the fact that everything about the concerts was a group decision, from the set list to the dance steps. As always, though, he found it very hard to say no, especially when his mother got involved. She urged him to think about hitting the road with his brothers one last time, and eventually he relented.

"I felt the wisest thing for me to do would be *not* to do the tour," Jackson later explained. "But my brothers wanted to do it, and I did it for them."[4]

Even with Michael on board, the tour's beginnings didn't match its grand and glorious moniker. The search for a concert promoter began with an offer from music executive Cecil Holmes, who'd later sign New Kids on the Block to their first record deal. Holmes showed up to meet Joe Jackson and his sons with a check for $250,000 as an advance for the entire tour—about enough to cover one of the giant mechanical spiders that Michael wanted to be part of the show.

"Are you kidding me?" shrieked Joe, ripping up the check and dropping the remnants at Holmes's feet. "We're not going to be undersold like this!"[5]

Shortly thereafter, a new candidate emerged: Don King, the flamboyant promoter of boxing matches. He gave each brother a check for $500,000 to seal the deal. Per the Jacksons' initial agreement with King, the promoter would take 7.5 percent of tour proceeds and the Jackson parents 7.5 percent; the brothers would split the remaining 85 percent evenly.[6]

There would be plenty to go around—the tour was expected to top $50 million in ticket sales. In preparation, Michael hired Frank Dileo to be his manager. The rotund former Epic executive (who passed away in 2011 due to complications from heart surgery) had a wit as sharp as his promotions expertise. "We stand next to each other," he once said of Jackson, "and we look like the number ten."[7] He quickly came to appreciate his new boss's intellect.

"A lot of artists don't want to know anything about business affairs, but Michael is involved in every facet of his career," he said shortly after signing on. "He's not one of those people who stops thinking when he walks out of the recording studio or off the stage."[8]

Dileo and Branca combined to form the two-headed business monster that oversaw a burgeoning Michael Jackson, Inc., but the singer had final say on all major decisions. "The business was me, and the imaging and marketing was Frank, and Michael oversaw both," says Branca. "So Michael was the chairman and we reported to him."[9]

As such, the two men accompanied Jackson to all the planning meetings for the Victory Tour, while Jermaine hired his own counsel and the other four brothers brought a representative of their own. Don King had an unusual plan to get these players on his side, as Branca learned one day at Hayvenhurst, where Jackson was still living. One of the promoter's associates sidled up and informed him that King wanted to "give" the lawyer a boxer.

"He was trying to buy me off," Branca remembers. "So I kept my mouth shut. I said, 'What do you mean?'"

"Don wants to give you a boxer to own," the man replied.

Branca politely declined.

"It was this war," he says, recalling the days that followed. "Michael would lock himself in his room, and Joe Jackson and Don King would come banging, 'Open up the door!' 'I don't want to.' 'Open!'"

It was King's performance at the press conference to announce the tour—along with Michael's discovery that King had spent four years in jail after a 1966 manslaughter conviction[10]—that pushed the young singer over the edge. Rather than trumpeting Michael's success at the event held at New York's posh Tavern on the Green, King seemed more interested in promoting his own triumphs, bloviating about legendary boxing matches he'd arranged, such as the Thrilla in Manila.

"The wrong *Thriller*!" explains Sullivan, who emerged as a candidate to replace King soon after the fiasco. "So Michael said to his father, 'I don't want to have anything more to do with this guy.' He said, 'I want a tour that will promote me, not promote him.' And so he said, 'We need to get rid of him.' And Branca then sent King a [termination letter]."[11]

Sullivan entered the picture after calling Dileo in hopes of bringing the Victory Tour to his family's 60,000-seat football stadium (his father bought the Boston Patriots for $25,000 back in 1959, moving the franchise to Foxborough in 1970 to play in what would become Sullivan Stadium as the NFL's New England Patriots). Dileo asked if Sullivan might be interested in promoting the whole tour, and days later, the latter was on a plane to Los Angeles to meet the Jacksons.

The mild-mannered Sullivan, with his Brooks Brothers style and Harvard pedigree, couldn't have been more different from the outrageous Don King. That certainly bolstered his case with Michael Jackson. It didn't hurt that Sullivan was the managing partner of the New York office of law firm O'Melveny & Myers, where one of his clients was CBS Records. His first meeting with the Jacksons may not have been grand or glorious, but it did the trick.

"When I met them, you know, I got on well with them," Sullivan recalls. "Met Michael, met the others. And they asked me to take the whole tour."

Even at the outset, the proposed deal didn't seem like an easy run to the end zone for Sullivan. He'd get 25 percent of ticket sale revenues and 22.5 percent of merchandise sales, with the rest going to the Jacksons—but he'd have to pay them a $55 million guarantee regardless (with 7 percent going to Joe and Katherine, 3 percent to Don King as part of his exit agreement, and the remainder split between the six brothers, who kept their original checks). Sullivan also gave each brother a check for $500,000 up front; in order to afford that, along with setup costs, he had to take out a $12.5 million bank loan. If sales fell short, he'd be on the hook for the difference.[12]

Originally, Sullivan was to have a partner in the endeavor: San Francisco 49ers owner Eddie DeBartolo Jr. But the elder DeBartolo vetoed the deal. Sullivan's own family expressed similar reservations—Chuck himself admits that he only expected to net half a million dollars on the tour, not much for an NFL football owner, especially considering the eight-figure risk he'd be shouldering.

For Sullivan, though, immediate financial gain wasn't the main goal. In those days, no national concert promoters were around to front cash for an entire tour. Artists had to negotiate with scores of smaller regional players, the sort that entrepreneur Robert F. X. Sillerman would later buy up and roll into what would become Live Nation. Sullivan's previous experience hosting sold-out shows for Madonna and David Bowie in the early 1980s gave him confidence that he could create a live music behemoth of his own—and the Victory Tour was a perfect way to prove it.

"I thought it would provide a basis for future tour deals," says Sullivan. "I also thought it would give me a leg up in getting major tours into Foxborough. That was the rationale."

Sullivan agreed to the deal. He was happy, the Jacksons were happy, and even Don King had grudgingly accepted the terms of his buyout. Al Sharpton was brought in as a "consultant" in case King changed his mind and tried to convince the regional and local promoters to boycott the tour. When King was running the show, they had assumed that he was going to follow the old model and farm out the task of planning concerts to them. The promoters would collect their fees, book the venues, and hire caterers, limo companies, and security teams, thereby preserving a profitable status quo.

With Sullivan on the scene, it seemed they'd been cut out—he was planning to do all the legwork himself, bypassing the middleman in an effort to create a more efficient business model for the future. The regional and local bosses, of course, didn't take kindly to this. Many of them had booked the Jacksons several times in previous years, and felt they'd played a crucial role in establishing the brothers' careers.

"They were planning major protests and boycotts, but they didn't have them because the regional promoters were paid [off], and the regional promoters paid off the local promoters," recalls attorney Cynthia Minor, who was brought in as an advisor to the regional promoters. "Everybody got their little cut. And a lot of folks got paid off with tickets, depending on how far up the chain you were. Because the tickets were impossible to get."[13]

To expedite shipment, tickets would only be sold directly by mail, rather than through a third-party ticketing company. Sullivan added that they could be purchased only in blocks of four, for $30 apiece (about $65, adjusting for inflation). When fans protested, Michael asked Sullivan to change the policy, which he did.

Pepsi sponsored the tour, calling for the Jacksons to film two commercials. There was a problem, though: Michael wouldn't touch the can. He insisted on writing clauses into his contract stipulating that he wouldn't have to hold the soda on camera, and that he wouldn't be in the ad for more than three seconds, lest he cheapen his image or overexpose himself.[14]

The first commercial, helmed by "Beat It" director Bob Giraldi, was filmed at a Hollywood lot made to look like a New York street. The second took place across town at the Shrine Auditorium, where a Jacksons concert was staged—complete with throngs of fans waving Pepsi cups in the air. But something went awry.

Michael was to appear at the top of a stairway, at which point he'd be illuminated in silhouette by a shower of sparks from magnesium flash bombs. Getting the timing right was tricky. After five takes, the director suggested that Michael wait a bit longer atop the steps before walking down and joining his brothers onstage. On the sixth take, he lingered just a moment too long, and the sparks ignited his spray-drenched hair.[15]

"I was dancing down this ramp and turning around, spinning, not knowing I was on fire," Jackson wrote. "Suddenly I felt my hands reflexively going to my head in an attempt to smother the flames. Jermaine turned around and saw me on the ground, just after the explosions had gone off, and he thought I had been shot by someone in the crowd."[16]

Michael was rushed into an ambulance and taken to the nearby Brotman Medical Center, where he was treated for third-degree burns to his scalp, nearly down to the skull. Once the relief that the singer was still alive had subsided, the executives at Pepsi immediately began worrying he'd sue them. Instead, he scored a new deal worth $5.2 million,[17] the highest endorsement fee ever paid to a musician at that point—and $1.5 million to establish the now-defunct Michael Jackson Burn Unit at the hospital.[18]

Ten days later, Jackson was back in action, appearing at a gala held at New York's Museum of Natural History in honor of *Thriller* selling 35 million copies. Epic's Susan Blond devised an unusual invitation: a single white glove with the date, time, and occasion printed on the palm. Roughly one thousand guests arrived to find the building's towering dinosaur skeletons illuminated by thousands of flickering candles, casting eerie shadows across a crowd that included most of the Jacksons, Andy Warhol, Calvin Klein, and Brooke Shields. Outside in the frigid February night, an even bigger crowd had gathered in hopes of catching a glimpse of Jackson.

"Even though Michael had just been on fire, he realized that these were his fans," says Blond. "It was quite chilly, too, and he went out and gave a big wave and made sure everyone saw him. They went bananas, totally screaming."[19]

He ducked back into the party for a good while, but kept popping outside to wave to his fans. His motivation was simple, says Blond: "He wanted to go and to give them what they had come to see."

Yet the Pepsi incident would take its toll. The surgery Jackson had to undergo in order to stretch his scalp to cover the burned area left him in terrible pain. His only respite would come in the form of prescription painkillers such as Demerol—and he wouldn't soon forget the relief they provided.[20]

———

As soon as Michael was back in shape to perform, rehearsals began in Birmingham, Alabama. And with the goal of making the Victory Tour the grandest and most glorious in history, the staging of the show became just as important as the performance.

There was a levitation sequence with Marlon, a skit where Jermaine threatened to leave the group again unless they played one of his solo songs, and a grand entrance where Michael emerged from a hole in the ground to sing "Beat It." Sullivan was able to book dozens of concerts across the country—though, ironically, the Jacksons wouldn't make it to Sullivan's home stadium at Foxborough (the town council voted down a proposed three-night stand due to noise concerns). To spread the word about other concerts, he enlisted Michael's help.

"I would talk to him about the marketing plan for each venue," says Sullivan. "He had toured since he was five years old, so he had a sense of the nuances of the markets we were visiting . . . he knew what radio stations got the most play, who were the dominant entertainment figures in each market. He was a very tuned-in person."[21]

As the summer approached, the Jacksons had plenty of new material to offer those stations. "State of Shock"—Jackson's collaboration with Mick Jagger—dropped on June 5, followed by the rest of the *Victory* album on July 2. Bruce Swedien remembers telling Jagger that one Los Angeles disc jockey played the song for twenty-seven consecutive hours (the rocker's response: "How boring").[22]

There was less enthusiasm, at least on Michael's part, for "Tell Me I'm Not Dreamin' (Too Good to Be True)," a duet with Jermaine intended for the latter's 1984 self-titled album.[23] Shortly after the brothers had finished recording, Michael called Yetnikoff.

"I don't want it released as a single."[24]

"Are you crazy? This is your brother."

"I know, but I did it. I shouldn't have, but I agreed to it. I don't want it released. So you call Clive [Davis] and tell him he can't do it."

"Are you out of your fucking mind? This is your brother."

"That's what I want."

Yetnikoff then called Davis, the head of Arista Records, the label that was slated to release the duet, and explained the situation. It appeared that Jackson didn't want the collaboration competing with his solo singles on the charts. Davis eventually compromised and released the song as a promotional single, which meant it could still garner ample radio play (which it did) but couldn't be considered for *Billboard*'s prestigious singles chart. And as time went on, Jackson would only grow more tired of watching his brothers ride his coattails.

When the Victory Tour opened on July 6 at Kansas City's Arrowhead Stadium, however, the outside world had little clue as to the discord that was already rankling the Jacksons. The first show had drawn reporters from Asia, South America, the Middle East, Europe, and all over North America; there were more total requests for press credentials than for the preceding Super Bowl.[25]

As the brothers prepared to take the stage, a sold-out crowd of 45,000 started chanting "Jacksons" in the dark. All the fans could see at first was a giant boulder with a sword sticking out of it. Randy, dressed as a knight, dashed out and pulled the sword from the stone, then ran back behind the stage to join his brothers on a platform below the stage. Decked in aviators and military-inspired garb, they waited as the platform began to rise toward the crowd. Floodlights illuminated the stadium, the brothers whipped off their sunglasses, and with the flash of a sequined hand, Michael Jackson took the stage at his first concert since completing *Thriller*.

"I don't even know how to explain the level of crazy that it was," Minor recalls. "Screaming, yelling, crying, fainting, pushing, shoving. Those were the things I remember the most. Just continued screaming. I mean, how could you even hear them, you're screaming! And that was the case everyplace."[26]

The fans' reactions seemed to be even more extreme than they were in the group's early days. Not only would the sight of Michael Jackson leave many in a state of hysteria—or unconsciousness—but some truly believed him to be superhuman. "When they see you, they feel it's a miracle or something," he wrote. "I've had fans ask me if I use the bathroom. I mean, it gets embarrassing."[27]

One night in a Dallas hotel, a young woman decided to open a twentieth-floor window and attempt to lower herself into Michael's room on a string of sheets tied together. When members of the Jacksons' entourage spotted her dangling on the other side of the glass, they called the police, who removed her without further incident.[28]

There were other issues on the tour, particularly on Sullivan's end. His costs were so high that some insiders began to believe he'd have to shut down the tour early. That group included Michael Cohl, a future chief of Live Nation, whose company at the time was handling the tour's merchandizing.

"I just knew if the tour went down, which is what everybody said was going to happen three or four weeks in, it'd be a warm day in the Arctic before I'd see my money," says Cohl. "And our merchandise company would go down the toilet."[29]

In August, Cohl convinced Sullivan to bring the tour to Toronto during a free weekend in October. He ramped up revenues by selling more VIP tickets and travel packages that included hotel stays; the shows were so profitable that Sullivan decided to bring him on to help run the tour going forward. Cohl immediately started cutting costs, beginning with redundant staff members and unnecessary furniture that had been lugged from city to city. Though the changes weren't enough to make the tour profitable for Sullivan, they ensured it would generate sufficient cash to keep going.

Despite the drama, the Jacksons still made time for self-indulgent hijinks. Jermaine had decided to bring his pet tiger, Bakana, on the road with him; Michael especially enjoyed taking the animal on jaunts through hotel kitchens. They also amused themselves by going out on their balconies and dumping buckets of water on unsuspecting passersby. Sometimes they'd throw $100 bills instead. Food fights often occurred after shows.[30]

"I got a sense that they had a very brotherly type of relationship, that kind of jokey-friendly-but-I'll-sock-you-in-the-stomach kind of fun," says Minor. "They did travel kind of separately because they had their families with them; some of them had their wives and kids with them from time to time."[31]

Yet a cloud hung over Michael. He felt restricted—perhaps in part because of the two Jehovah's Witnesses who traveled with the brothers and "monitored" Michael, a result of the church's concerns over its most famous member, no doubt spurred by *Thriller*. He was also confined mostly to his hotel suite for his own protection, as fans circled and stalked outside. Some people close to him, including Yetnikoff, felt that he never forgave his family for pressuring him into doing the tour.

"Everybody's family is dysfunctional, that I've ever known," says the former CBS chief. "I'm sure Eisenhower maybe had [a normal family]; there aren't too many people. I'm in AA, so I don't know anybody that's not dysfunctional. But his family was more dysfunctional than most."[32]

In addition to the pressures of family and religion on the tour, Michael felt the decision-making process limited his artistic freedom, particularly when it came to showcasing his new solo work. "It was a nice feeling, playing with my brothers again," he stated in his autobiography. "But I was disappointed with the tour from the beginning. I had wanted to move the world like it had never been moved. . . . I was disappointed in the staging of 'Billie Jean.' I wanted it to be so much more than it was. I didn't like the lighting, and I never got my steps quite the way I wanted them. It killed me to have to accept these things and settle for doing it the way I did."[33]

Some who observed Jackson on the tour also noticed that he occasionally drifted into a state somewhere between restlessness and loneliness. Around four o'clock in the morning after one show in Dallas, Minor happened to peer out the window of her hotel room. Below, a thin figure ambled through the courtyard, trailed by a bodyguard. It was Michael. With the adrenaline from that night's performance still rocketing though his veins, the singer couldn't fall asleep. But he couldn't leave the hotel, either—not without creating a major scene, anyway.

"The heaven he lived in was not a paradise," says Minor. "It's got to be a very sad thing when you can't go anywhere, can't do anything. You're just kind of in a cage . . . these people would tear you to pieces."[34]

The Victory Tour wrapped up on December 9, 1984, at Dodger Stadium in Los Angeles, the last of seven consecutive sold-out shows there. As the crowd danced and cheered in the warm California rain, Michael stopped for a moment between songs to make a surprise announcement. "This is our last and final show," he said. "It's been a long twenty years, and we love you all."[35]

The brothers weren't thrilled—they'd been hoping to continue the Victory Tour abroad—but Michael had spoken. He had left his family in an excellent financial position (though that wouldn't prevent them from trying to get money from him in the future): the Jacksons had sold 2.25 million tickets. With merchandise revenues, the final tally was a tad north of $70 million, far surpassing the tour's projected $55 million total.[36] Could Jackson have sold that amount by himself on his first tour after *Thriller*? "Yeah," says Cohl. "Of course."[37]

Yet Jackson's brothers would take home about $6 million apiece. The picture wasn't quite so rosy for Chuck Sullivan. Long before the Victory Tour's last note, he knew he wouldn't be getting his money back. Even with Cohl's changes, the setup expenses for three sold-out shows at Meadowlands Stadium in New Jersey had ballooned to $1 million, plus another $1 million for exit costs. With all the tour's accoutrements, from swords in stones to rising platforms to magic tricks, the story was the same all around the country.

In the end, the tour's costs totaled $78 million—$8 million more than the total ticket sales—and Sullivan was on the hook for the difference.[38]

———

Michael Jackson donated his share of the Victory Tour's proceeds to a handful of charities, including the T. J. Martell Foundation and the United Negro College Fund—about $6 million in total—as promised. Still, he wasn't about to spend half a year of his life on the road and come away empty-handed.[39]

While traveling the country during the summer of 1984, Jackson noticed that many of the fashion statements he made in his videos had been picked up by some of the millions who'd flocked to see him perform with his brothers. But someone else was profiting from all those imitation "Thriller" jackets. So Jackson and his advisors huddled to formulate a plan. Rather than let the market be overrun with third-party knockoffs, why not offer the genuine article? For funding, they didn't have to look further than Chuck Sullivan, who offered them $28 million, including $18 million up front. The licensing deal also included a fragrance—Jackson tested more than fifty different combinations before deciding on one.[40]

"He had quite an awesome command of rights and rights values," says Sullivan. "This really was generated by him."

And so, in 1984, Michael Jackson became the first music star to have his own clothing line. Sullivan brought in Warren Hirsh, the fashion maven who'd launched a line of Gloria Vanderbilt–branded jeans in the late 1970s, to help oversee the effort. They planned to debut the Jackson clothing line in the fall of 1986, around the time Jackson's new record was set to hit stores. Expectations were high: $70 million in retail sales for the first fifteen months of 1986 (about $150 million, adjusting for inflation).[41]

Unfortunately for Sullivan, *Bad*'s release would end up being de-layed for a year, but the clothing came out as scheduled. Without the boost of an album's buzz—and more important, free advertising in Jackson's music videos—the products were met with lukewarm sales, leaving Sullivan with far less than the $28 million he'd paid for the rights. Still, Michael Jackson walked away with double-digit millions—and paved the way for the hip-hop fashion boom of the 1990s and 2000s.

As for Sullivan, his family sold the Patriots to Victor Kiam, owner of Remington shavers, in 1986 for $87 million.[42] He says the deal had nothing to do with financial troubles related to the Victory Tour or Jackson's clothing line and everything to do with estate planning for his father, who'd been diagnosed with prostate cancer.[43]

Two years later, the Sullivans sold the Patriots' stadium as well. The buyer? Robert Kraft, who paid $25 million for the building. He'd go on to buy the Patriots for $172 million in 1994, amassing a multibillion-dollar personal fortune while guiding the team to three Super Bowl victories in four years.[44] For contributing to the set of circumstances that circuitously led to that run, Patriots fans can thank Michael Jackson.

———

Back at the Yale Club, Sullivan hasn't displayed a hint of bitterness toward Michael Jackson, his family, or his handlers. Remarkably, he doesn't even seem to regret signing up to promote the Victory Tour. Though he lost millions on the project, he's still reaping dividends as an indirect result.

For example, he explains, the Rolling Stones were playing a show at Madison Square Garden in 2003 that was being filmed as an HBO special. By then, Sullivan's brother Pat was running a mobile television broadcasting company called Game Creek, and he wanted the contract to provide production services for the show. So Chuck called Cohl, who was working the Stones' tour, and asked for the business.

Game Creek's previous experience was only with sporting events, but Cohl vouched for the company, and the Stones agreed to let the company handle production at the Garden. HBO was so happy with the results that they hired Game Creek again. The company subsequently worked to provide production for the likes of Oprah Winfrey, Justin Timberlake, David Letterman, Céline Dion, and both inaugurations of Barack Obama.

"So the bottom line is that, not directly from the Jacksons but as a result of doing the Victory Tour, we have made up the losses," says Sullivan. Or, in other words, "The Victory Tour did have a grand and glorious silver lining for the Sullivan family."[45]

Chapter 7

BUYING THE BEATLES

When Sony/ATV chief Marty Bandier was a long-haired twenty-three-year-old, he got his first job in music simply because he looked the part. A senior partner at his law firm took one glance at him and assigned him to work on a music publishing deal.

"'We're going to make an acquisition . . . and we think you have some knowledge of music,'" Bandier recalls the partner saying. "Only looking at my hair."[1]

In the wake of its 2012 acquisition of EMI Music Publishing, Sony/ATV controls more than two million songs by artists ranging from Eminem to the Beatles, making it the world's largest music publishing company—and Bandier still looks the part. High above the corner of Madison Avenue and Fifty-sixth Street in Sony's New York headquarters, the septuagenarian executive sits behind a caramel desk as big as a barn door, sporting a monogrammed dress shirt with the top two buttons undone. His flowing locks are mostly intact, though perhaps a bit shorter, bright white and combed back neatly against his scalp.

Bandier's office brims with mementos related to his company's most treasured artists: next to his computer there are figurines of John Lennon, Paul McCartney, George Harrison, and Ringo Starr; Elvis Presley curls a sausage-sized lip from a black-and-white poster that occupies the entire west wall.

On a ledge by the window, though, there's a less showy artifact from an artist to whom Bandier is even more inextricably tied—

Michael Jackson. The musician was responsible for creating the $2 billion company Bandier now runs, and he's represented in this particular room by a blood-red volume the width of two telephone books, titled *THE OFFICIAL MICHAEL JACKSON OPUS*.

"Once I got here, the first signing was Lady Gaga," recalls Bandier. "[We have], you know, Taylor Swift. Those are all things that Michael owns half of."

Though Jackson didn't play an active role in bringing those two on board, he was the one who shelled out the cash to buy the catalogue's core. Says Bandier: "Michael had a great sense of the value of music . . . the guy picked out songs that have lasted forever."

———

One night in 1981 at Paul McCartney's estate just outside of London, the former Beatle handed Michael Jackson a binder. Inside was a list of all the songs whose publishing rights were owned by McCartney. After letting much of his own songwriting catalogue slip away as a youngster, he'd been buying up copyrights for years.

"This is what I do. I bought the Buddy Holly catalogue, a Broadway catalogue," McCartney told the young singer. "Here's the computer printout of all the songs I own."[2] Jackson was fascinated. He wanted to start doing the same, and his entrepreneurial instincts quickly clicked into gear. "Paul and I had both learned the hard way about business and the importance of publishing and royalties and the dignity of songwriting," Jackson wrote in his autobiography.[3]

When he got back to California, he found himself with an enviable problem. He'd earned $9 million in 1980 and was sitting on a pile of money that needed to be invested. Inflation was rampant in the early 1980s, meaning that fallow cash would start to lose value quickly. In short, he needed to find some worthwhile places to park the reserves of Michael Jackson, Inc.

His accountants brought him a number of real estate deals, but he wasn't excited enough to buy anything. Branca even discovered that the Century City building that was home to CBS Records' Los Angeles headquarters was on the block, and tried to persuade the singer to consider purchasing it. "You'd be Walter Yetnikoff's landlord!" the lawyer enthused. Though Jackson got a chuckle out of the idea, he declined. He wanted to buy songs.

So Branca started combing around, talking to people in the publishing business to find out what was for sale. He talked to songwriter Ernie Maresca, who had two big rock songs available: "Runaround Sue" and "The Wanderer." When Branca told Jackson, the singer didn't recognize them. The lawyer gave his client a tape and told him to have a listen. A few days later, Jackson called back. "You gotta get those songs!" he said. "I danced to them all weekend."[4]

Thus began a buying binge for Branca and Jackson. They picked up a small catalogue that included "1-2-3," a 1960s soft-rock love song by Len Barry; "Expressway to Your Heart," a Gamble and Huff composition released by the Soul Survivors in 1967; and "Cowboys to Girls," a 1968 hit by the Intruders composed by the same duo. If Jackson didn't know a song, Branca would send him a recording; if the singer fell in love with it, he'd give the go-ahead to acquire it.

Longtime associate Karen Langford remembers sitting around with Jackson during this period and discussing which of the greatest songs of all time would be best to own (he often mentioned ones by the Beatles, Elvis, and Ray Charles, among others). Sometimes he'd quiz Langford, singing a snippet of a song and asking if she could give the title and performer. Even then, he had his eye on ownership at a scale few could have fathomed at his age.

"He wanted to be the number one publisher in the world," she says. "And . . . it would come up in lots of different ways, but [his goal] was always number one, getting to that number one spot. Being the biggest, being the best."[5]

One day, Branca was talking to radio station owner Kenny Roberts, who owned half of the Sly and the Family Stone catalogue. He'd been advancing Sly cash against his publishing royalties and wanted out. Jackson didn't need to hear those songs played over the phone—they were right in his wheelhouse—and he bought Roberts's half for $250,000. The rest was owned by Warner Music's publishing arm, which administered Jackson's own songs at the time. Branca sensed another opportunity and arranged a meeting with the company's chairman, Les Bider.[6]

"We want to buy the other half of the songs," said Branca.[7]

"Why would we sell them?"

"Well, if you want to renew [Jackson's] deal . . ."

Bider agreed to sell the catalogue to Jackson for about $250,000 on the condition that he kept administration of his Mijac Music with Warner. So Jackson ended up paying half a million dollars for the entire Sly and the Family Stone catalogue—and made it all back shortly thereafter when a cover by Status Quo went to the top of the UK charts.

Yet Jackson was selective. When offered a catalogue that included hits like "Help Me Make It Through the Night" by Kris Kristofferson, Jackson chose not to buy it—the songs just weren't that meaningful to him. Ultimately, he decided to buy just three of the ten to fifteen catalogues presented to him from 1981 to 1984.

What the singer really wanted was Gordy's Jobete catalogue, home to most of Motown's greatest hits, including those of the Jackson 5. Gordy says Jackson offered him a "competitive" price for it at one point, but the Motown chief wasn't ready to sell—and didn't, until EMI paid him $132 million for half of the catalogue in 1997.[8] But watching Gordy manage his publishing interests had set something ablaze inside Jackson.

"He got the bug," says Gordy. "And that gave him the [urge] to want to do something even greater."[9]

———

"Michael," began Branca, coyly, at a meeting in September 1984, "I think I heard of a catalogue for sale."

"What's that?"

"It's ATV."

"Yeah, so what's that?"

"I don't know, they own a few copyrights, I'm trying to remember," said Branca, pausing for effect. Then he offered a few names: "Yesterday," "Come Together," "Penny Lane," and "Hey Jude."

"The Beatles?!" Jackson exclaimed.[10]

The only problem: the catalogue belonged to billionaire Robert Holmes à Court, an Australian corporate raider known for a steely patience, a penchant for backing out of deals at the last minute, and a stubbornness that rivaled that of any rock star. He also had plenty of other suitors for ATV, including billionaire real estate developer Samuel LeFrak, Virgin Records founder Richard Branson, and the duo of Marty Bandier and fellow publishing executive Charles Koppelman.

For Holmes à Court, there were few pleasures greater than a grueling business negotiation. He took particular glee in toying with overzealous Americans ("They are just looking for me to play according to their rules and make it a big game," he once said of his stateside counterparts. "The Viet Cong didn't play by the rules, and look what happened."[11])

None of that mattered to Jackson. His instructions to Branca: "You gotta get me that catalogue."

The lawyer remembers the frenzied days that followed. His first task: to check in with Paul McCartney and Yoko Ono, both friends of Jackson. As John Lennon's widow, Ono was in charge of his estate and was rumored to have had some interest in making a joint offer for ATV with McCartney. Jackson was hoping to avoid a showdown.

"I got Yoko on the phone," recalls Branca. "And then I said, 'Michael asked me to call you and find out if you're bidding [on] ATV Music that owns all the Beatles songs.'"

"No, we're not bidding on it."

"No?"

"No, no, if we had bought it, then we'd have to deal with Paul," replied Ono. "It'd have been a whole thing. Why?"

"Because Michael's interested."

"Oh, that would be wonderful in the hands of Michael rather than some big corporation." (When I asked Ono about the conversation some thirty years later—in the midst of a brief interview prior to an anti-fracking rally at New York's ABC Carpet & Home, of all places—she said she didn't have "a complex dialogue" with anyone on Jackson's team, but wouldn't elaborate.)[12]

Branca says his next move was to check in with John Eastman, Paul McCartney's lawyer and brother-in-law (he represented the singer along with his father, Lee Eastman, who started working with McCartney before the Beatles broke up). According to Branca, Eastman said McCartney wasn't interested because the catalogue was "much too pricey."[13]

This was one of many reasons that neither Branca nor Bandier believed McCartney would lay out such a large amount of cash. Though the Beatles' songs made up roughly two-thirds of ATV's value, the remaining third consisted of assets McCartney didn't want: copyrights to thousands of other compositions, a sound effects library, even some real estate.

"Paul's demeanor was very, very much more financially structured," says Bandier.[14] Adds Joe Jackson: "The only reason Michael bought that catalogue was because it was for sale! [McCartney and Ono] could have bought the catalogue themselves. But they didn't."[15]

There's also an artistic explanation for McCartney's unwillingness. "I never thought Paul McCartney would buy it because it's very difficult for a creator of something [to buy] it," says Bandier. "It would be like Picasso, who spent a day doing a painting, to buy it for $5 million like twenty years later. It wouldn't be a thing that Paul would do."[16]

Branca opened with an offer of $30 million. But Holmes à Court wanted more, especially since Bandier, Koppelman, and a few other suitors were still interested in buying ATV. By November, Jackson had authorized Branca to raise his offer beyond $40 million. With the exception of John Johnson, Jackson's advisors—even music executives like David Geffen and Walter Yetnikoff—thought the singer had lost his mind.

The latter told Jackson he was making a mistake and that he should stick to being an artist. "That was my advice," says the former CBS chief. "And he disregarded it, luckily."[17]

Jackson didn't have a business school education, and multiples of cash flow meant little to him. But he had a tremendous sense of value—and in Branca, a lieutenant able to help him make the most of that.

"John was the financial concierge in executing Michael's instincts," says billionaire Tom Barrack, who'd go on to work with Jackson later in the singer's life. "So Michael said, 'Wow, I think there's incredible value [in the Beatles' songs] over time. Quite honestly, Michael didn't know if they were worth $12 million or $18 million or $25 million. He just knew and anticipated correctly that over time the intellectual property was going to be worth a lot of money."[18]

Jackson's constant refrain: "You can't put a price on a Picasso . . . you can't put a price on these songs, there's no value on them. They're the best songs that have ever been written."

During a finance committee meeting, he wrote Branca the aforementioned note that still sits in the lawyer's home: "John please let's not bargain," it says. "I don't want to lose the deal . . . IT'S MY CATALOGUE."[19]

———

A bid of $45 million was good enough to earn Jackson and Branca a meeting in London that winter, but Holmes à Court refused to go himself. Since the deal was far from being completed, Branca did the same, sending his colleague Gary Stiffelman in his stead.[20]

The two sides agreed on a nonbinding statement of mutual interest, and Jackson's team embarked upon a four-month due diligence review of the 4,000-song catalogue. To verify ATV's copyrights, a team of twenty spent some 900 hours examining close to one million pages of contracts. Branca met Holmes à Court in New York that April and agreed to a handshake deal. Within weeks, however, the mogul had backed out. So, with Jackson's blessing, Branca sent another letter: accept the last offer of $47.5 million, or there would be no deal.

Around the same time, Branca learned that Holmes à Court had tentatively agreed to sell the catalogue to Koppelman and Bandier for $50 million. But he knew his rivals—and some of the places they were getting their money. As it happened, their company had picked up a hefty publishing advance from MCA Records, headed at the time by Irving Azoff, who'd served as a consultant for the Victory Tour.

"I went to Irving and I said, 'How can you fund Charles and Marty? They're bidding against Michael and you're the consultant,'" Branca recalls. "[Azoff] pulled the deal, and [their ATV agreement] fell through."

Shortly thereafter, Branca received a call from one of Holmes à Court's colleagues. Could he come to London and close the deal?

"If Holmes à Court wants to say something to me, he can say it to me personally," Branca replied. "I'm not discussing it with you."

"Well, I'll talk to him, this is highly unusual."

"I'm not coming to London [if he's not]. Don't call me again."

When Holmes à Court finally called, Branca played it tough, telling him they'd decided to buy another catalogue instead.

"We're happy not to buy your company, so go ahead and sell it to Charles or Marty or whoever the hell else you want to sell it to," he said, knowing the duo had lost their funding. "We're not buyers."

"Would you please think this over?"

"Give me a call in a couple of days."

"I promise you I'll pay your ticket over."

"I don't need you to pay my ticket."

"I promise you, you come over here and within twenty-four hours, we'll have a deal done."

"Yeah, at what price?"

They agreed on $47.5 million. Jackson granted Branca power of attorney, and the lawyer flew to New York. While waiting in the Concorde lounge at John F. Kennedy airport before his flight to London, he heard his name echo across the loudspeaker and raced to the phone. It was Richard Branson, who'd been keeping his eye on the ATV negotiations himself. To further complicate matters, Branca had been doing some consulting work for the billionaire's music company, Virgin Records.

"Should I bid on the Beatles catalogue?" Branson asked.

Branca, whose firm had spent about $1 million on due diligence for ATV, was caught in an awkward situation. But he wasn't going to let Jackson's prize slip away.

"You know, Richard, if you do, you're going to have to deal with Yoko, and there's all these things, and all this stuff . . ."

Branson backed off. Content to have thrown another potential rival off the scent, Branca boarded his Concorde flight. Once inside the supersonic jet, however, he noticed two familiar faces also on their way to London: Bandier and Koppelman.

"What are you doing over there?" Bandier asked.

"Oh," said Branca, "just some business."[21]

Bandier was ready to do some business of his own. Even after Branca had convinced Azoff to pull his funding, he and Koppelman thought they could scrounge up enough capital to make a $50 million bid for ATV—and that all they needed was to buy themselves a little time. Recalls Bandier: "We actually went to London to sort of finalize a more formal contract."

He and Koppelman figured that Holmes à Court had no interest in music publishing and was simply looking to unload ATV as quickly as possible. They weren't counting on his patience, or the glee he may have derived from a bit of corporate sport. They certainly weren't expecting what Holmes à Court was about to tell them when they arrived: that he was set to unload ATV to another party for $2.5 million less than they had offered.

Face to face with Holmes à Court and on the verge of losing the deal, Bandier immediately upped his offer by another $500,000. The Australian wasn't impressed.

"There's one aspect of the deal that you guys can't do," he replied. "And that is do a concert in Perth for my favorite charity."

"We can do a charity concert," Bandier pressed, figuring he could easily leverage his connections, and perhaps his cash, to lure just about any big act.

"No, no, you don't understand," continued Holmes à Court. "I'm selling this to Michael Jackson."[22]

———

Fittingly, Jackson had sealed his biggest deal by throwing in a personal appearance as a sweetener. It wasn't an easy favor, either—he would have to fly fifteen hours from Los Angeles to Sydney, change planes, and then fly another five hours to Perth. But not even a pack of dingoes could have stopped him from getting his catalogue.

Bandier later learned that Jackson had offered another perk. Holmes à Court's daughter was named Penny, and they were willing to exclude the song "Penny Lane" from the deal so that the billionaire could give it to her as a present (Jackson's company continued to administer the song for her). It was far from a minor concession. "Any song that you own of the Beatles earns money," says Bandier. "There's only like two hundred fifty of them, and everybody has a favorite of the two hundred fifty. Believe me, 'Penny Lane' is a popular song."

But the kicker was the appearance in Perth.

"We knew that we couldn't do the moonwalk, so there was no question," Bandier remembers. "It wasn't going to happen."

When Branca boarded his Concorde flight to return home from London, he found one more surprise: sitting in the row behind him were Koppelman and Bandier. "Okay, you outmaneuvered us," said Bandier. "If we're ever in a position to buy a major company, we want to hire you."[23][24]

Other bidders for ATV didn't react quite so kindly. "I think it's dodgy to do things like that," said McCartney. "To be someone's friend and then buy the rug they're standing on."[25] In some subsequent interviews, however, the former Beatle has admitted Jackson told him in advance of his intention to buy ATV—and that he thought the future King of Pop was joking.[26]

Though Jackson and Ono continued to have a cordial relationship, the McCartneys never invited him to be their houseguest again. Richard Branson was also displeased. The normally mild-mannered Brit made that clear when he called Branca shortly after hearing the news of Jackson's ATV acquisition. "So what's the word for you?" Branson asked. "Prick?"[27]

"I felt terrible," Branca recalls. "Nowadays I would have said to him, 'Richard, please, I'm about to sign.' I might have handled it differently . . . but I was a young lawyer at the time. I couldn't lose this deal."

Sure enough, Branca was well rewarded for his efforts. He earned a small fortune in legal fees, a 5 percent cut of the catalogue's future earnings, and a gift from Jackson: a brand-new Rolls-Royce Corniche convertible.

Six months later, he received a call from Bandier asking if he could come to New York the next day to close a big deal. He hung up the phone, thinking it was a prank. Moments later, Bandier's associates called and asked him the question again. He declined. Then Yetnikoff rang.

"John, listen to me, these guys are for real," he said. "I'm going to sell CBS Songs. . . . I'm going to sell it to them, and they want you to represent them. You need to get on a plane and come."

Branca went to New York, and they closed the deal for $125 million. Three years later, Koppelman and Bandier sold their company to EMI for $297 million; Koppelman went on to become the chairman of EMI Records, while Bandier ended up at the helm of EMI's music publishing division.

And, to close the loop, Bandier was hired to run Sony/ATV in 2007.[28]

————

Michael Jackson, of course, was thrilled to finally acquire ATV in 1985. His organization had outmaneuvered some of the smartest in the business, somehow managing to convince a reclusive Australian billionaire to sell one of the most valuable assets in music for millions less than the next-highest bidder. And that was just the beginning.

The catalogue contained a background music library called Bruton Music, an outfit that licensed mundane sound effects (a door closing, for example) to commercials and low-budget movies. Branca flipped it to Clive Calder's Zomba Music for $6 million, lowering Jackson's net cost to $41.5 million; Jackson took out a business loan of $30 million to finance part of the acquisition and paid for the rest in cash.[29]

Then Branca hired a team of international tax experts to help sort out the transaction—and save Jackson a raft of money. At the accountants' suggestion, they moved ATV's corporations to the Bahamas, eventually liquidating them and distributing the assets to Jackson. His accountants also realized that tax laws allowed them to write off about $5 million of the catalogue's purchase price annually as a business expense over eight years. As a result of this and the Bruton Music sale, Jackson's net cost for the purchase would end up being only $20 million or so.

The ATV catalogue had been generating roughly $6 million per year from physical sales and radio spins of its four thousand copyrights, propelled by low six-figure payouts for individual hits like

"Yesterday." But there was an opportunity to make much more. Shortly after acquiring ATV, Jackson and his team decided to lay off the bulk of the company's forty employees and move administration of the catalogue to CBS Songs in exchange for 3 percent to 5 percent of publishing revenues. That slashed ATV's overhead by $5 million to $10 million per year.

To prevent his copyrights from getting lost in the shuffle at such a large company, Jackson hired veteran song plugger Dale Kawashima, who'd previously worked to get licensing deals for the likes of Prince and Bruce Springsteen, to serve as ATV's president. Kawashima would spend his time pursuing new ways to make money on both ATV and Jackson's Mijac catalogue while looking for new songwriters to sign, reporting directly to Branca and Jackson. The singer carved out a list of dozens of titles that were considered untouchable, at least when it came to advertisements.

"The most important copyrights of Lennon-McCartney, like 'Yesterday' or 'Let It Be' or something, would never be used in any commercial," says Kawashima. "It was other songs that were not deemed to be in the approximate top fifty or sixty that could be licensed in the right situation."[30]

———

"We're the largest, most profitable, and best music publishing company that there is, and Michael has a significant interest in it," says Bandier, who's winding down our interview (he's got Berry Gordy coming in next). "So his investment is a pretty good investment. Like buying Apple [computer] stock when it first came out."[31]

That's not necessarily hyperbole. A $47.5 million investment in Apple stock shortly after its 1980 initial public offering would be worth about $6.5 billion today, considerably more than Sony/ATV. But it's all a matter of timing. Had Jackson spent $47.5 million on Apple shares at their 1987 peak, their value would now stand at $1.6

billion; factor in his catalogue's fat dividends, and the two purchases would be roughly equivalent.

Jackson's single-minded focus on buying the catalogue despite vociferous objections from the record industry's brightest minds might strike some as impetuous. But in hindsight, it's clear that he was correct to follow his instincts, even to those who doubted him at first—and that his sense of the value of copyrights was impeccable.

"I think if you were his advisor at that time you would have told him, 'Don't do it,'" says Yetnikoff. "Turns out that it was a very lucrative investment. . . . So I would have to say that his business acumen is better than mine."[32]

Jackson certainly never forgot that he'd been right. In 2007, on a conference call with Bandier, the executive recounted the story of ATV's 1985 sale. Jackson was delighted to relive the experience.

"See," he said. "I told you I knew the music publishing business."[33]

Chapter 8

DANCING WITH THE STARS

It's a gray February day at Disneyland and business at Tomorrow-land is sluggish, even for a Thursday afternoon. The Astro Orbitor is half empty. There are no aspiring Jedis queued up in front of Star Tours. And the wait for Space Mountain is a mere ten minutes. One bright spot: a crowd is gathered to see Michael Jackson in *Captain EO*, the futuristic featurette he headlined in 1986.[1]

Two decades before 3-D films came to the mainstream, *Captain EO* became the first so-called 4-D flick—meaning viewers not only donned glasses that made onscreen asteroids seem as close as the seat in front of them, but also felt the whoosh of air from a spaceship lifting off and found their seats shaking in tandem with interstellar turbulence.

As a result, *Captain EO* was the most expensive film per minute in history when released. The budget for its seventeen minutes was about $30 million[2] ($1,764,705.88 for every sixty seconds), including a $3 million salary for Jackson.[3] He played the lead role opposite evil space queen Anjelica Huston, while Francis Ford Coppola served as director and George Lucas as executive producer. The film aired in Disney's parks around the world for varying chunks of time from 1986 to 1998, returning the year after Jackson's death.

Standing next to me in line today is Rusty Lemorande, perhaps the only person who doesn't seem thrilled at the prospect of seeing *Captain EO*. He's got a good excuse: he wrote and produced the film.

"I don't want you to feel bad," he says. "But the prospect of seeing it was not . . ."[4]

". . . the most exciting?" I offer.

"Maybe if I hadn't seen it in years, but I saw it last time I was here," he continues. "If I come here with friends, then it's like, 'Oh, we've got to go see *Captain EO*.'"

"I could imagine it would get to be tiresome to see the same thing you produced, over and over again."

"Well, when you know every shot . . ."

"Is there still some element of butterflies in your stomach?"

"If people react to it around us, which may happen, that's great. They may not. It was cutting edge at its time."

He pauses.

"*The Wizard of Oz* still endures even though it's incredibly period. So I'm hoping that, you know, fifty years from now, people will still be watching *Captain EO*."

———

Lemorande was in Spain in 1985 when the call about *Captain EO* came in from Disney. After finishing the films *Yentl* with Barbra Streisand and *Electric Dreams* with Richard Branson, he had traveled to Europe to research a stage musical about Goya.

"We want you to come in right away," explained the voice on the other end of the line. "We'll fly you in to meet with Jeff Katzenberg."

Katzenberg, who would go on to found DreamWorks with David Geffen and Steven Spielberg, was already a Hollywood force in his new role as head of Disney's movie studio. But Lemorande wasn't particularly eager to cut his trip short.

"I'm in Spain," he said. "I'm busy."

"We'll send you back, just come in for this meeting."

"Well, tell me what it's about."

"No, I can't tell you."

When Lemorande insisted, the executive offered one nugget of information about the project: it involved George Lucas and Michael Jackson. A few hours later, Lemorande settled into a business-class seat on a jetliner bound for Los Angeles.

The Disney executives' urgent desire to meet with him was part of a larger corporate sea change brought on by Michael Eisner, who had just taken control of the company. As part of a massive modernization program, he wanted to knock down the organizational walls between his theme parks division and film studio, which he'd just hired Katzenberg to run. Conveniently, two of Disney's biggest fans were Jackson and Lucas, and the sides began discussing a collaboration that would combine a ride with a movie.

"They said they didn't care what I did, as long as it was something creative," Jackson later wrote. "I had this big meeting with them. . . . I wanted to do something with them that Mr. Disney himself would have approved."[5]

Disney's famed Imagineers then dreamed up the broad outline of an interstellar adventure in which a ragtag band of loveable misfits, headed by a charismatic leader, liberates a planet of enslaved creatures from an evil tyrant by using the magic of song and dance. The role made sense for Jackson, who was looking to build himself a Hollywood career following his performance in *The Wiz* and the record-shattering success of the *Thriller* video. As always, he wanted to be in the vanguard of whatever field he was working in; *EO* seemed like a suitably novel endeavor.

"There were no 3-D movies, really, at the time," says Branca. "So it was an opportunity to do [something] ahead of its time."[6]

Katzenberg met with Lemorande—who'd become something of an expert on the industry's latest technology after working on a 3-D flick about a boy in space (which never made it to theaters)—to discuss the possibility of writing and producing the movie. Then Katzenberg sent him to San Francisco to meet with Lucas for final approval.

"You really know 3-D," said the *Star Wars* creator. "You really understand it, that's great . . . would you like the job?"[7] Lemorande accepted.

His next stop was a conference room in Disney's Burbank headquarters, where he quickly noticed two things: the dimly lit ambiance and the entrance of Michael Jackson. "I sensed from working with other superstars that Michael would determine the potential depth of our working relationship with the first eye contact," says Lemorande. "I do remember the importance of 'Do not turn away.' I sensed that was a really important bonding moment. I recall saying something that made him laugh."

With that, the ice was broken, and a productive partnership began. Lemorande treated Jackson with a mix of familiarity and deference; the singer responded by offering the writer-producer unlimited access and feedback. Jackson told Lemorande he loved his first draft of the script—the dialogue, the characterization, the storyboards. With the music and the choreography, Jackson did more micro-managing, as one might expect. But Lemorande didn't mind.

"Michael was funny and playful and curious and animated and full of energy," he recalls. "And had a high aesthetic, one of the best, and made you want to please him. Because if you pleased him, you knew you did something well; it wasn't faint praise. It was the mark of a top person in his field."

Very early on in the production of *Captain EO*, Lemorande came to understand why Jackson was so interested in the role—and the film business in general.

"Making movies for Michael was a number one priority in his life, and understandably so," he says. "He had conquered videos; he'd kind of created them. He'd conquered pop music, and he'd staked his claim in the field of dance and choreography. So what was left?"

————

The first time designer Michael Bush met Michael Jackson, he had just walked into a dark trailer—and found himself being pelted with cherries. Lemorande had hired him to handle Jackson's wardrobe for *Captain EO*.

"I'm standing there, nervous," Bush recalls. "And here's Michael Jackson someplace over there in the dark. Another cherry came at me. The third cherry came at me. I picked it up and threw it back."[8]

Then Jackson emerged from the shadows, laughing, with a whole bowl of cherries. The pair started talking, and eventually the conversation turned to music. Bush mentioned that his favorite singer was Patsy Cline. Though Jackson didn't know much about her at first, he returned to the *Captain EO* set the next day singing one of her songs, suddenly knowing how she died and how old she was when it happened.

"I'm going, 'How the hell did this man have the time?'" says Bush. "He didn't go on Google, there was no Google then, this man educated himself about me, to talk to me. . . . With everything going on with this man's life, even getting ready to step [before] a camera and perform, he knew how to make me feel comfortable around him."

Along with partner Dennis Tompkins, Bush would go on to generate some of Jackson's most iconic outfits over the years, perhaps most notably his costumes for the Bad Tour in the late 1980s. Jackson had another long-term ally on the set: Matt Forger, the tech-savvy engineer who'd worked with him on *Thriller* and would reprise his efforts for many of the singer's subsequent albums.

Forger's expertise was required to support some of *Captain EO*'s technological advances. The film was the first production with regular showings that featured discrete digital 5.1 channel surround sound, which would go on to become an industry standard. Much of the equipment that would be required didn't yet exist, so Disney's Imagineers designed a proprietary system from scratch.[9]

Having not yet chosen a director, Lucas and Katzenberg left Jackson and Lemorande plenty of room to inject their own ideas into the movie. Lemorande asked himself what Walt Disney would do—and came up with a plan to add the in-theater effects that would make *EO* a 4-D trailblazer. He brought in John Napier, a costume and set designer from London's theater scene, and together they worked with the Imagineers to figure out how to incorporate real smoke, laser beams, and fiber-optic stars that descended from the ceiling. Accomplishing all of this, however, would require extensive modifications to Disney's custom-built theater.

"We had to raise the ceiling by like five feet," Lemorande says, recalling that the construction cost about $500,000. "You have to understand, if you raise it five inches, you're still raising metal beams, and so that created a huge expenditure. George said, 'Let's do it.' So he called Michael Eisner and talked him into it."[10]

Still, *Captain EO* had no director. Jackson wrote in his autobiography that Steven Spielberg had been offered the gig, but it seemed he just couldn't fit the film into his crowded schedule.[11] That didn't dampen Jackson's dedication to the project.

"Michael was my constant ally," Lemorande remembers. "He would, at the drop of a hat, do anything, be anywhere, answer any question, look at anything—and want to—because this was so desperately important to him. He thought this would show Hollywood that he could be as big a film star as Elvis Presley."

———

"What do you think about Francis Coppola?" George Lucas asked Lemorande. It seemed he had finally narrowed down his search for a director.[12]

"Wow, are you kidding?" replied Lemorande. "I'd be thrilled if he did it. What made you think of him?"

"He'll get a great performance out of Michael, he's got experience with musicals, we can help him with the special effects. And most importantly, he's a genuine artist, and genuine artists can do anything."

Coppola joined the production and began filming. Though the flick had a record-setting budget, it wasn't unlimited: two weeks were allotted for filming. Immediately after that, Coppola was due to begin directing *Peggy Sue Got Married*—on the same lot in Culver City where he was working on *EO*.

Jackson soaked up every aspect of the filming process. According to Bush, he even learned how to take apart a film camera and put it back together again.[13] Beyond its technical aspects, the storyline of *Captain EO*—something like an interstellar version of "Beat It"—fit him like a rhinestone glove.

"He brings his message of love and light and music and transforms the planet," explains Matt Forger. "This is a theme that reoccurs to Michael many times in his life and on many songs that he does . . . how to improve the world, how to make it a better place."[14]

At the conclusion of principal photography, the *Captain EO* team went to work on a preliminary edit. Lemorande remembers trekking to Lucas's Skywalker Ranch to watch the rough cut. In those days, when a sequence hadn't yet been filmed all that showed up on the screen was a white cardboard placeholder with a drawing of the anticipated shot. And that was the case with about every third shot in *Captain EO*. Lucas assured his small audience that the film would look fantastic once the missing special effects sequences were added—a laser battle between starships zooming just above the surface of a Death Star–like planet, for example.[15]

As Jackson watched, new ideas swirled through his mind. He believed from the beginning that *Captain EO* could be the next step in the evolution of the music video—from promotional throwaway to short film—a process that began with "Billie Jean" and "Thriller." As such, he wanted *EO* to have a similar feel, which meant adding more shots to capture the speed and sizzle of his dance moves.

Lemorande had anticipated the possibility of additional filming. So rather than discarding everything at the conclusion of principal photography, per usual, he had used a technique called pack storing, where major elements were cut apart and saved. If necessary, the crew could reassemble enough of the set to make a backdrop suitable for filming. This step was one more expense for an already costly movie, but it proved invaluable. With critical parts of the set revived, the desired shots were added.

Afterward, as he did following every edit of the film, Lemorande took a copy of *Captain EO* to Jackson. The singer liked what he saw. "A compliment from Michael was very, very rewarding because he wasn't going to give them freely," Lemorande recalls. "And it made him happier and happier that this had the chance to be a real hit."

———

Captain EO debuted at Disneyland in the fall of 1986; the film's premier featured speeches, a ribbon-cutting ceremony, and appearances by George Lucas, Anjelica Huston, and Francis Ford Coppola. Even Janet Jackson, suddenly a superstar in her own right after her 1986 breakthrough album *Control*, made an appearance. But her most famous brother was nowhere to be found.

"Rumor has it Michael Jackson is here, but it's as a robot or a zombie or an old lady," said Michael Eisner in a speech to the crowd that had gathered at Tomorrowland. "So look to your left and your right, and that might be Michael Jackson standing next to you."

Why had Jackson suddenly abandoned the project into which he'd thrown so much time and energy—and staked his Hollywood dreams on—at the last minute? There are multiple theories. Yetnikoff recalls Jackson suddenly expressing reservations about being seen gallivanting around Disneyland at the premier, an about-face as he prepared to transition to the harder-edged look he would soon bring to his upcoming album, *Bad*.

"I want a more grown-up image," Jackson told Yetnikoff. "I'm not a child anymore, I don't want to be publicized holding hands with Pluto."[16]

There were also rumors that Jackson had skipped the premier

due to dissatisfaction with Disney's final edit, and that he believed the studio was preventing him from attaining perfection, at least as he saw it. Not being allowed to execute his creative vision in its entirety—and not getting exactly what he wanted—was simply unacceptable to him, hence his absence.

Still, *Captain EO* debuted as planned, and the reports were generally positive. The *Los Angeles Times* praised the film's special effects and costumes, noting that viewers at the premier called it "brilliant," "outstanding," and "genius." The *New York Times* called it a "smashing, 3-D extravaganza,"[17] and *EO* remained a popular attraction in the US until it was replaced by *Honey I Shrunk the Audience* shortly after Jackson was first accused of child molestation in 1993. When *EO* returned to Disney following the singer's death in 2009, *Wired* posited that "the twenty-four-year-old space opera still holds up. Mostly."[18]

————

Lemorande sits through his umpteenth screening of *Captain EO* with me, and we watch as the crowd oohs and ahhs at all the appropriate points. After toying with the notion of a quick run to Space Mountain, we decide instead to hightail it back to Los Angeles before the traffic gets too bad.

It's dusk as we approach Hollywood, and Lemorande is telling me a story. Years ago, a screenwriter he knew was working on a script commissioned by a producer in London—and had a sneaking suspicion this fellow would stiff him in the end. "So I go, 'Do what Michael Jackson would do,'" he recalls.[19]

Before many of his concerts, Jackson insisted on personally accepting his share of the box office revenues in his dressing room before taking the stage. Lemorande suggested the screenwriter equivalent: contact the employer, personally deliver the script to London, and accept the payment there. But the screenwriter allowed himself to be talked into accepting his fee by wire—and never received it.

"He should have done what Michael Jackson said," says Lemorande. "Any stage performer from that era probably knows that lesson. But [Jackson] really advocated it. . . . I don't think he was against stonewalling at the last minute to get what he wanted."

That strategy would work for Jackson at many points throughout his career, but not always—and *Captain EO* was one such occurrence.

"He should have been there to enjoy it and appreciate it, and Disney should have had the benefit," says Lemorande. "That was kind of a very sad closure."

Chapter 9

GOOD AND BAD

In early 1986, a young publicist named Michael Levine received a phone call from a talent manager who, to many observers, seemed more like a mobster than a Hollywood operative. And he was about to make Levine an offer he couldn't refuse.

"Mr. Levine, my name's Frank Dileo," the manager said. "I see you're doing very well, you represent a lot of big people. How would you like to represent Michael Jackson?"[1]

"Okay," said Levine. "Let's just say you got my attention."

"Come to my house."

The manager lived in a generically affluent neighborhood on the west side of Los Angeles, and he greeted Levine at the door alone, no entourage.

"Look, we decided to try you out," Dileo began.

"I didn't know I'm auditioning."

"We'll give you a project. You do this well, you'll represent Michael Jackson."

"What's the project?"

Recalling the meeting a quarter of a century later, Levine describes feeling like he was about to enter a parallel universe that night at Dileo's abode. What the manager proposed was exciting, crazy, and somewhat dangerous—and not very financially rewarding, at least in the short-term.

"You're not getting paid," said Dileo. "You do this, and if it's great, you'll have Michael [as a client]."

———

That same year, Michael Jackson gave copies of the P. T. Barnum biography *Humbug* to Branca and Dileo, along with some advice: "Study the greats and become greater."[2]

Jackson was already widely acknowledged as one of the top music stars of all time, and he had earning power to match. In 1986, he landed a $10 million endorsement deal with Pepsi, shattering his own previous record. His ATV catalogue was generating profits of nearly $10 million annually. And *Thriller* was still paying dividends as well: In the four years following the album's release, he'd earned a total of $191 million.

By the end of 1984, *Thriller* had sold more than 20 million units in the US alone, but other artists were beginning to catch up. Madonna released *Like a Virgin* that same year, selling 6 million US copies in just twelve months; Prince starred in the film *Purple Rain* and released a soundtrack of the same name that quickly sold 8 million.[3] They were encroaching on Jackson's turf both commercially and culturally, bringing raw sexuality to the pop sphere with songs like Madonna's title track and Prince's "Darling Nikki," which prompted Tipper Gore to push for the inclusion of "Parental Advisory" stickers on potentially offensive music.[4]

Jackson would adopt an edgier image for *Bad*, but first, to help build anticipation, he decided to remove himself temporarily from public view (says biographer and historian Joe Vogel: "He hated the idea of overexposure after *Thriller*"). So after he co-wrote the charity single "We Are the World" in 1985 with Lionel Richie (and recorded it with a cast that included Bruce Springsteen, Ray Charles, Diana Ross, and Billy Joel), Jackson more or less disappeared, avoiding awards shows, interviews, and public appearances that year.

In the meantime, he and Dileo plotted his grand return, with Levine's covert assistance. Jackson delineated this philosophy in a series of unpublished notes (a few of which I was allowed to view while writing this book), including one titled "Thoughts on Work and Secrecy":

> When working on any project, work with the best people in the business, the best people in the world—expertise in every field of endeavors, the best chemistry, the best unity— and work in secrecy. And when it's least expected, hit everybody between the eyes with the phenomenal, the most powerful, unexpected project. Then it becomes historical because you have a perfect gem. But strive for excellence and perfection in everything. Study the greats and become greater—in secrecy.[5]

Jackson planned to reemerge in September 1986, launching a Barnum-inspired publicity blitz that would take him all the way up to the release of his next album. *Humbug* describes Barnum as someone with whom Jackson might have identified at the time: "intelligent and energetic, a devoted family man, an abstainer from liquor," someone who exhibited a "mastery of showmanship."[6]

Of course, Barnum wasn't the greatest role model in all areas. The book points out that he made his fortune on the backs of indentured "freaks," advertising grandiose (and, often, completely false) stories about their respective histories. He sometimes sabotaged the parts of his business that were grounded in fact, spreading rumors that an old woman in his troupe was an automaton and that his "bearded lady" was actually a man. As the author puts it: "Deception, humbugging, cheating, these were some of the words that Americans commonly associated with Barnum, during his life and ever since."[7]

Barnum's primary interest was to create a spectacle. For Jackson, that's where Levine came in. Dileo gave him some photographs of the singer lying down in a hyperbaric oxygen chamber—a medical contraption that looks like a clear coffin with dials on the side— with the goal of making the world believe Jackson was sleeping there every night so that he could live to age 150. Levine's task was to plant the story with members of the tabloid press by any means necessary.

"The truth is stranger than fiction," says Levine, recalling his conversation with Dileo. "There was nothing in my first meeting that Rod Serling couldn't have written."[8]

Predictably, the *National Enquirer* took Levine's bait: "Michael Sleeps in Hyperbaric Chamber," a headline declared. Somewhat more surprisingly, the mainstream press picked up on the story as well. These writers may have known it was all a ruse, but they couldn't stop themselves from covering the singer's purported antics. The Associated Press ran a piece on September 16 revealing Jackson's alleged ambitions of eternal youth while noting that doctors considered such strategies dangerous.[9]

Levine's work continued to cause ripples. A few days after the Associated Press story, Jackson's personal physician went on the record with words that seemed to lend credence to the rumors about his patient: "I would not recommend that he undergo treatment," Dr. Steven Hoefflin was quoted as saying. "Michael has many bizarre ideas and sometimes these ideas are ahead of his time."[10]

The media mentions continued to pile up, but the whole scenario was already seeming a little too bizarre for Levine. "At this point, who's crazy? Me?" he asks, recalling the episode. "Possible, right? Definitely. Or Michael?"

A month after the hyperbaric story became international news, Levine called Dileo.

"Frank, you didn't pay me for this," he said. "Am I going to represent Michael Jackson?"

"I'll get back to you."

Levine didn't hear back after a few days, so he called again.

"It's gonna happen," said Dileo. "You gotta trust me. . . . Michael and I [are] going to hire you, you'll see what we've got planned for you. We're just getting warmed up."[11]

Levine wasn't involved in the next stunt, and it was a doozy.

Exhilarated by the press generated by the hyperbaric chamber articles, Jackson and Dileo decided to leak a story that the singer wanted to pay $500,000 to acquire the skeleton of Joseph Merrick—a nineteenth-century sideshow act whose physical deformities earned him the nickname Elephant Man—from the London Hospital Medical College.[12]

When stories began to circulate, representatives from the institution insisted they hadn't received such a bid, and that even if they had, the bones weren't for sale. Suddenly incensed by the rejection of his nonexistent offer, Jackson reportedly resolved to buy the bones. He made an offer of $1 million, which was, of course, rebuffed (the negative publicity also contributed to a growing rift between Jackson and the Jehovah's Witnesses, and he withdrew from the church).

Perhaps he was simply following Barnum's example too closely. The author of *Humbug*, the book Jackson so enthusiastically gave to Branca and Dileo that same year, explains that Barnum believed controversy wasn't a bad thing, and that "the only requirement was to keep the issue alive and in print. Any statement was better than silence."[13]

There's a fine line between feeding the media stories about a star's eccentricities, real or constructed, and becoming a tabloid punch line. By trying to buy human remains—or at least wanting to be seen as trying to buy human remains—it seemed Jackson had slipped past a crucial midpoint.

————

By 1987, Jackson's business dealings were also generating plenty of controversy. The Beatles' own recordings had never been licensed for use in a commercial. That changed when Nike paid $500,000 to put "Revolution" in a television spot.

Jackson's team obtained permission from Yoko Ono before signing off on the deal. ("John's songs should not be part of a cult of glorified martyrdom," she reportedly said. "They should be enjoyed by kids today.")[14] At any rate, neither Jackson nor his company was named in the lawsuit. Though he owned the composition of "Revolution," EMI Records held the rights to the song's master recording—with the Beatles' actual voices—and could have blocked its use. Under that scenario, Jackson could still have licensed a cover of the song to Nike; die-hard fans might not have been pleased with that either, but it would likely have caused much less of a stir. "The thing that disturbed the [living] Beatles was that [the commercial] used their master recording," says Bandier.[15]

Paul McCartney was furious. He felt the Beatles' recordings shouldn't be in commercials, period. So he joined the surviving Beatles in a lawsuit targeting Nike, its ad agency, and Capitol-EMI. Jackson's reaction: "Why is he fussin'? Paul owns Buddy Holly['s catalogue], doesn't stop him from licensing songs."[16] (McCartney later told David Letterman that, when he expressed his dissatisfaction with the way the singer was handling his songs, Jackson told him, "It's just business, Paul."[17])

Even though Jackson had turned down dozens of offers to license the songs, including one for a Beastie Boys recording of "I'm Down" slotted for the group's *Licensed to Ill*[18]—the "Revolution" controversy became part of a broader backlash over Jackson's purchase of the ATV catalogue. The *Houston Chronicle* slammed him for "exploiting" a counterculture anthem in the name of a $75 pair of running shoes, while the *Los Angeles Times* called the commercial "revolting" and "sacrilegious."[19]

John Lennon biographer Jon Wiener blasted Jackson in the *New Republic* as a Pepsi-flogging sellout, compared to other musicians like John Mellencamp, Bob Seger, and Joan Jett, who "have had the integrity to refuse to license their music."[20] (In 2007, Mellencamp would catch some flak of his own for allowing one of his songs to appear in a Chevy commercial.[21])

Even Tom Petty weighed in. "I hate to see these Beatles songs selling sneakers and stuff," he said. "Because the music always meant more to me. I don't wanna think of 'Good Vibrations' as a Sunkist soft drink commercial. I think it cheapens that value of the song."

Says Jackson biographer Joe Vogel: "If you look through news archives around this time, he was shredded by the media. People really didn't like the idea of him owning the Beatles catalogue (and using it for commercial ends). The catalogue was a great financial investment, but it also made him a big target in the years to come."[22]

––––––––

It was against this backdrop that Jackson recorded his follow-up to *Thriller*. Branca initially suggested that the singer release an album of covers before embarking on his next original project.

"I was trying to get him to record Sly and the Family Stone, and some of the other songs that I bought for him, because I figured that'd be another way to make a profitable deal," Branca recalls. "I said, 'That'll take the pressure off of having to top *Thriller* and compete with yourself.' . . . He looked at me like I was from Mars."[23]

Jackson couldn't fathom not competing with himself—both commercially and artistically. Before he started recording songs for the album that would eventually become *Bad*, he taped a note to his bathroom mirror with the number of copies he was determined to sell: 100 million.

Many of those close to Jackson felt that his lofty sales goals stemmed from the way Joe Jackson had taught his sons to measure their success. "If you sold a lot of records, if when you did a concert you sold out, then you were doing the right thing," says Forger, who spent a great amount of time with Jackson while working as an engineer on *Bad*. "[And] his family was very poor. And he wanted to not have to return to never having money."[24]

To top *Thriller*, Jackson knew *Bad* would have to be flawless. Before joining Quincy Jones at Westlake Recording Studios, Jackson spent months with a skeleton crew that included Forger, tinkering with tracks at the studio he'd built at Hayvenhurst (he called it "the laboratory"). They worked on about sixty songs, nine of which eventually made the eleven-track album.

Jackson also hired a musician named John Barnes—both to play piano and synthesizers on *Bad*, and to help fill the album with sounds not usually found on mainstream pop albums. They'd wander around Southern California and record everything from machinery clanking to birds chirping to cars whizzing past, hoping to capture something that could be woven into the fabric of a hit song.

By the time Jackson got to Westlake and began recording with Quincy Jones and the reunited A-Team, he had plenty of novel tracks to choose from. In order to simplify the process, he and Jones covered a big bulletin board in the studio with index cards, writing the name of a song on each. Those that didn't quite measure up were quickly removed; the best remained on the board.[25]

Jackson's abilities were clear to everyone around him, even those who weren't music aficionados. "One time, I asked Michael, 'Where do you come up with these incredible lyrics and melodies?'" remembers Bea Swedien, Bruce's wife. "He said, 'I just wake up and they're in my head.'"[26]

During rehearsals for the *This Is It* concerts two decades later, Jackson joked that if he didn't write down these ideas and turn them into music, God would give them to Prince. Jackson had initially envisioned the title track of *Bad* as a duel with his rival, but when they met to discuss a potential collaboration before the recording process began, Prince startled Jackson by bringing him a voodoo amulet. "I never want to talk to that guy again," said Jackson afterward.[27]

Bad launched a record five consecutive singles to the number 1 spot on the charts, three more than *Thriller* (though all seven of that album's singles reached the top ten, only "Beat It" and "Billie Jean" actually claimed the top spot).[28] It took a quarter of a century for another album (Katy Perry's *Teenage Dream*) to match *Bad*'s feat. Jackson penned nine of the eleven songs on the album—all but

"Just Good Friends" and "Man in the Mirror"—and some, including "Dirty Diana," "Leave Me Alone," and "Smooth Criminal," remain among his most iconic efforts.

Yet when *Bad* was released on August 31, 1987, many reviewers—white critics, in particular—seemed to focus more on Jackson's changing physical appearance than his music. Vitiligo treatments had left his skin noticeably lighter, and he'd had multiple plastic surgeries as well. Says hip-hop pioneer Fab 5 Freddy: "It was such a stark physical transition . . . it became the only thing you could think about, in a sense, when you are in a space where how we look and 'look at me' is so much a part of it all."[29]

The *New York Times'* album review noted his new chin cleft before discussing his music,[30] while the *Los Angeles Times'* response began by referring to Jackson as "the world's favorite frail manchild."[31] *Rolling Stone* said the album was better than *Thriller,* but buried the observation toward the bottom of a review that opened by calling Jackson a "*faux*-porcelain elephant man."[32]

A readers' poll conducted by the same magazine named Jackson the year's Worst Male Singer. He did earn Grammy nominations in a handful of categories including Album of the Year, but *Bad* won only for Best Engineered Recording—Non-Classical (and, in 1990, for the "Leave Me Alone" video). The negative press didn't stop *Bad* from debuting at number 1 in the US and many other countries; to date, the album has sold 35 million copies worldwide[33]—placing it among the most successful of all time, but nowhere near the 100 million figure that Jackson had initially envisioned.

Still, *Bad*'s commercial success during the fall of 1987 was one of the many factors that helped put CBS Records on pace to top the previous year's record profits of $162.1 million (on $1.5 billion in revenue) by more than 20 percent. Because of this virtuoso financial performance—and the musical acts that drove it—Sony agreed to buy CBS Records for $2 billion[34] that November.

"Look at the roster: Billy Joel, Bruce Springsteen, you know, they had a lot of artists," says Yetnikoff. "The whole classical thing was very interesting, too. [But] Michael was a big star . . . it contributed."[35]

―――――

If Sony's executives needed any additional persuasion to close the deal, they may have received it in September of 1987 when Jackson played a string of shows in Tokyo to kick off the *Bad* tour.

Godzilla himself would have been hard-pressed to re-create the level of hysteria that accompanied Jackson's arrival in Japan. He landed in a Boeing 747 packed with twenty-two truckloads of equipment, including 700 lights and 100 speakers.[36] The authorities shut down half of Tokyo's Narita airport to accommodate the hordes of local and foreign press who'd arrived to greet him. Bruce Swedien remembers the scene when he and his wife disembarked with Jackson, Dileo, Quincy Jones, Bubbles the chimpanzee, and a host of others.[37]

Sensing danger, Dileo ordered Jackson's entourage to make a protective circle around the singer in order to get him through the airport. Jones and the others closed into formation and ushered Jackson into his limousine without incident. (Swedien thinks they could have saved time by simply unleashing Bubbles: "He would have straightened out those reporters!")

Jackson opened his tour with three sold-out shows at Tokyo's 45,000-seat Korakuen Stadium—and that was just the beginning. His sixteen-month tour grossed $125 million (a quarter of a billion dollars, adjusting for inflation) on 123 shows, drawing 4.4 million fans— the most of any tour to that point. Former Live Nation chief Michael Cohl figures Jackson might have gotten $300 per ticket if the excursion had happened today. "It could be an astounding number," he says.[38] Indeed, by that math, the tour would have grossed more than $1 billion, making it the biggest of all time by a wide margin.

After the cumbersome democracy of decision making during the Victory Tour, Jackson took advantage of the control he had over his first solo excursion. To bring visual ideas to life, he personally collaborated with his costume designers—including Michael Bush, who remembers Jackson leafing through magazines, tearing out images that inspired him, and Scotch-taping them floor-to-ceiling. The two would then sit down with one piece of paper, one eraser, and two pencils: "He would draw, I would erase," says Bush. "I would draw, he would erase."[39]

In addition to costumes, Bush helped design a special shoe for the "Smooth Criminal" performance—one that allowed Jackson to execute his magical, gravity-defying forty-five-degree lean.

"You're sure it works?" said Jackson when he eventually saw Bush's creation.

"Well, Michael, I wouldn't bring it to you if it didn't work."

They laughed, and Jackson took another look.

"This is not going to work."

"Michael, it works; I did it, Dennis did it, we're here now to show you."

Jackson placed his feet in the shoes.

"Now lean toward me," instructed Bush. Sure enough, Jackson floated toward the ground, his body diagonal from the floor, as though he were doing a push-up with no hands. When he returned to his upright posture, he was crying.

"Oh my God, I can't believe you made this work!"

"That's the job you gave me."

"We have to patent this."

Four years later Bush discovered Jackson had gotten the patent, sharing the credit with Bush and Tompkins.

———

Even after he arrived in Japan, Jackson was deeply involved with the underpinnings of every show. He had a practical thirst to understand what everyone around him did and know how everything worked, from the costumes down to the staging. "I got my lighting designer for the tour," he'd say. "I need to understand what that board does. Because if I tell the guy I want this light up here to do this, and he says, 'I can't,' I need to understand why he can't, but I also need to understand why maybe we can."

All the while, Jackson kept up with music industry goings-on between concerts, scouring the charts for up-and-coming songwriters to sign to ATV. One such musician was Bryan Loren, who at the time was producing for the likes of Sting and Barry White. Jackson exhorted ATV president Dale Kawashima to get the new prospect on board.

"He wanted to be involved not just with buying older songs, classic songs like the Beatles," says Kawashima, noting that Loren was later added to the roster and would go on to work on Jackson's next album. "He was interested in signing new writers to ATV. . . . It was not John Branca who'd call up and say, 'Oh, there's this great writer Bryan Loren, we have to sign him.' That was Michael Jackson."[40]

Jackson's primary concern, however, was being in top shape for his performances. That was quite clear to those in his inner sanctum, and to those who briefly passed through—including, by a strange twist of fate, Jon Bon Jovi. "I don't have a lot of Michael Jackson anecdotes," the Jersey-born rocker said over the phone. "But I can tell you one, and you can make of it what you will."[41]

In September of 1987, Bon Jovi and his eponymous band were still riding the buzz of *Slippery When Wet*, which had catapulted the group to international superstardom a year earlier. They were playing a handful of shows in Tokyo's 20,000-seat Budokan arena while Jackson drew 135,000 fans over a sold-out three-night stand at nearby Korakuen Stadium. As it happened, they were all staying at the same hotel.

One night, Dileo called and asked if Bon Jovi would like to meet

Jackson, an invitation the rocker gladly accepted. The hotel was shaped like a hand, with the palm containing an elevator bank. The fingers radiated outward, each its own wing with multiple rooms; on the top floor, one wing was blocked off for Jackson and his inner circle. Dileo led Bon Jovi and his bandmates down a long corridor to the singer's suite, pausing to slick back his hair and extinguish his cigar before opening the door.

"The room had been ripped to shreds and redecorated," says Bon Jovi. "They put up mirrors against the wall so [Jackson] could practice his dancing, and a wooden dance floor in there. And they took over a wing of this hotel. Needless to say, spending money was not really an issue."

Jackson, however, was nowhere to be found. So Bon Jovi and his pals waited on the couch. When the singer finally arrived, he made quite the entrance, decked out in one of his trademark outfits from the Bad Tour: all black leather and buckles, a spandex shirt, belts draped over his shoulder. "When he entered the room, your eyes sort of had to focus again," Bon Jovi remembers.

The Jersey rockers, fresh from a string of tour dates in Australia—and new to the trappings of superstardom—immediately began regaling Jackson with tales from their trip. They were so big Down Under, they told him, that they had to buy wigs and fake mustaches to avoid paparazzi; the only way out of their hotel was in the laundry van. Jackson smiled and nodded, never giving away the fact that he'd been doing the same since his Jackson 5 days.

"So we made small talk and he couldn't have been nicer," Bon Jovi says. "We kept saying, 'Michael, you're sitting up here by yourself, man, we're down two floors below you . . . we're all here, on nights off we're hanging out, come on down.'"

Again, Jackson smiled and nodded. Eventually Bon Jovi and his band bid their new friend adieu and headed back downstairs, hoping they might get to party later on with one of the only acts in the world bigger than them. But with each passing minute, they grew more certain that Jackson wouldn't be coming. Imagine their surprise when Jackson sent down Bubbles to entertain them.

"We proceeded to get very drunk, have a bunch of water fights, knock on doors, typical classic rock star things to do in the eighties," Bon Jovi recalls. "And [we] blamed it all on Bubbles."

Jackson never came downstairs. And despite the fact that Bon Jovi showed up at Jackson's show, the singer didn't return the favor. It wasn't out of any personal animosity, but rather an unstoppable focus on his work.

"We were having a blast two floors below with Bubbles, and he was up there practicing his dancing," says Bon Jovi. "While we were being goofballs and enjoying our success, he was practicing even after the shows because he was just so ultra-über-focused on being Michael Jackson. The blessing was the curse."

As the tour wore on, another future music legend witnessed Jackson's perfectionism—and the toll it took on him—up close. Sheryl Crow, then twenty-five years old, served as a backup singer and often performed duets with Jackson on "I Just Can't Stop Loving You."

"I got to witness on a nightly basis what made him so completely different from everybody else," she recalls. "And that is that quality in somebody that is true stardom, for lack of a better word. I think he had such an understanding of the divinity that existed in him, and was also cursed by a fragility of the human spirit that existed from all the wounding that went along with making him who he was."[42]

Crow felt he had internalized the pressure of becoming the focal point of the Jackson 5, and thereby his family's meal ticket, at such an early age. Initially, she was amazed at how the Bad Tour was in many ways like a Broadway show, with everything consistent from one night to the next, down to the banter between songs.

In the midst of the tour, even as stadiums swooned before Jackson across the globe, Crow noticed how hard he was on himself—and at times "sort of the crumbling of his confidence in who he was," she says. "But when he would sing on songs like 'Human Nature' and 'Billie Jean,' you could look out at the audience and see people's faces just be transfixed."

————

By the end of 1987, Jackson had won eleven Grammys and earned a quarter of a billion dollars, all before the age of thirty. He had paved the way for black artists to dance and sing their way into living rooms all around the country—and for acts of all races to not only profit immensely from previously unheard-of brand extensions but to own the entities behind them as well.

Yet the noise around Jackson—some of it generated by him, some by others—was beginning to drown out some of his accomplishments. "When the conversation was more about the bizarre than the music for a prolonged period of time, you know, you can do that when the music is so extraordinary," says Levine. "[But] it all started to become a little too far out."[43]

As outlandish as the stories of hyperbaric chambers and Elephant Man bones were, some observers believed there were more insidious forces behind the backlash over his success. "The Michael Jackson cacophony is fascinating in that it is not about Jackson at all," writer James Baldwin opined. "All that noise is about America, as the dishonest custodian of black life and wealth. . . . I hope he has the good sense to know it and the good fortune to snatch his life out of the jaws of a carnivorous success. He will not swiftly be forgiven for having turned so many tables."[44]

Chapter 10

OFF TO NEVERLAND

The only way to truly appreciate the scope of the Neverland Valley Ranch is to climb the Giving Tree—the majestically gnarled oak up in which Michael Jackson composed many of his songs—and slowly turn clockwise.

To the east, a driveway stretches out from the main house, crossing a stone bridge on its path to a public road roughly a mile away. To the south, a meadow bigger than a football field sits behind an equally prodigious pond. To the west, a redbrick train station sits atop a knoll; embedded in the hillside is a twenty-foot-wide clock made of living flowers, the word "NEVERLAND" spelled in bushy yellow plants at the top.[1]

To the north of the tree (one of the property's 67,000 sycamores and oaks[2]) is Neverland's 2,700-acre backyard, about four times the size of Monaco. There's a swimming pool, a video game arcade, and a full-size movie theater; beyond, a sepia savannah gently slopes up to the tip of a 3,000-foot peak that Jackson dubbed Mt. Katherine, after his mother.

Neverland's more extravagant features are now gone. Its amusement park rides and train cars were hauled out long ago, and the ranch's nonhuman inhabitants—which once included alligators, elephants, giraffes, lions, tigers and, of course, Bubbles the chimp—are nowhere to be found. A dusty inflatable pool is all that remains inside the building that was once home to Jackson's vaunted video game collection. And the main house, a sprawling mock Tudor with seven bedrooms and thirteen bathrooms, sits pristinely empty in the center of it all.[3]

But traces of the property's longtime owner remain, most notably in the dance studio adjacent to the movie theater. In the center of the mirrored room, velvet ropes hang from four brass poles, marking off about ten square feet of the floor. Lift back the piece of plexiglass below and you'll find a well-worn spot, a series of swooping scratches carved into the caramel wood. Illuminated by a single spotlight, it was once Michael Jackson's favored location for practicing spin moves.

The indentations from Jackson's Florsheims started to accumulate shortly after he returned from the Bad Tour and bought what was then called the Sycamore Valley Ranch. Up to that point, Jackson had lived at his family's home in Encino—it was only at age twenty-nine, after selling tens of millions of albums and embarking upon what was then the highest-grossing tour of all time, that he finally stopped living with his parents.

Neverland's initial asking price: $60 million. Branca jumped in and helped Jackson negotiate, eventually closing at $17.5 million. The final sale included a fully stocked wine cellar, and the sprawling main house came fully furnished. A grateful Jackson gave his lawyer a fittingly grand token of thanks: another Rolls-Royce.[4]

———

"Frank Sinatra was the Chairman of the Board, Elvis was the King," sighed Michael Jackson one day to Branca and Dileo. "What am I, the Gloved One?"

The year was 1988, and though Jackson was already the lord of the *Billboard* charts and had a veritable kingdom of his own at Neverland, he conspicuously lacked something very important: a royal nickname. The best of his extant monikers was the Gloved One; one of the worst, in his opinion, was Wacko Jacko.

Jackson was fairly certain that the regrettable state of his informal nomenclature had something to do with the racial bias of his detractors. He used to tell Branca he thought the press didn't want him to be bigger than Elvis because Jackson was black, and that they insisted on labeling him Wacko Jacko in part to tear him down.

Fortunately for Jackson, a dear friend had a better name in mind. He first met Elizabeth Taylor in the early 1980s after he reportedly saw her walking out early from one of his performances. Insulted, he called her in tears. She explained that she'd left because she couldn't see the stage or hear the music; the explanation was good enough for Jackson, and the two soon became friends, bonding over their early life experiences in show business.[5]

"Our childhoods are very similar, and we have that from the very beginning in common," Taylor told Oprah Winfrey in 1993. "I was a child star at nine, had an abusive father, and that kind of brought us close together."[6]

"I love Elizabeth Taylor," Jackson wrote in his autobiography, echoing his friend's sentiments. "I'm inspired by her bravery . . . I identify with her very strongly because of our experiences as child stars. When we first started talking on the phone, she told me she felt as if she had known me for years. I felt the same way [about her]."[7]

After *Thriller* established Jackson's supremacy on the charts, Taylor suggested a new title for him, one that she'd already taken to using in public: the King of Pop, Rock and Soul. He was delighted. The only question was whether people would start using it. Conveniently, Jackson had been invited to appear at the fifth annual MTV Music Video Awards to receive what was then called the Video Vanguard Award, honoring lifetime achievement in the medium (it was later renamed in Jackson's honor).

He decided to make the appearance on one condition: that from then onward, the network's executives would make sure that their taste-making video DJs would refer to him only as the King of Pop.

"They agreed, and then the name stuck," Branca recalls. "Everybody called him the King of Pop. . . . It was part of Michael's genius to recognize [good branding] when it was suggested to him."[8]

Jackson's success continued on the publishing side as well. One day Branca got a call from Les Bider, the head of Warner/Chappell Music, which was then administering his Mijac catalogue. A Warner employee had forgotten to file the paperwork needed to retain the US copyright to one of the songs Jackson owned.

"We fucked up," Bider began.

"Yeah, you did, Les."

"We'll write him a check."

"He doesn't need money."

"Well, what am I going to do?"

"Les, the only way out of this—I won't tell him—is to sell him [other] copyrights at a good price."

Branca then convinced Bider to send over a computer printout of all the songs in Warner's catalogue, and picked out a group of the best, reiterating that Jackson might be pacified if he were given the copyrights at a discounted price. Bider agreed, leaving Branca to clear the decision with his client.

"Michael," Branca began, "I've got some bad news for you."

He then explained that Warner/Chappell had lost the US copyright to one of Jackson's songs.

"Branca, how could they do that!"

"But Michael, okay, listen, they want to offer you money."

"I don't want [that]!"

"Michael, hold on, hold on, I came up with this idea," said Branca. "I think I might be able to get them to sell you [some songs] at a really good price, not market value."

"Like what?"

Branca listed the songs.

"Close that deal."

Between that move and additional purchases Branca made around the same time, Jackson added hits including "When a Man

Loves a Woman" by Percy Sledge, "Great Balls of Fire" by Jerry Lee Lewis, "Love Train" by the O'Jays, and "What'd I Say" by Ray Charles to his collection. He usually had a very specific motivation for wanting to buy certain copyrights, and these all fit the bill: "He wanted to cover those songs," recalls Bider. "That's smart business."[9]

In 1988, Michael Jackson earned $125 million, a sum that would stand as the highest annual total of his life (and one that's even more impressive when viewed as an inflation-adjusted $247 million). His bottom line was bolstered by a rapidly broadening business portfolio. In addition to recorded music, touring, motion pictures, clothing, real estate, and music publishing, he launched a trio of products that bore the name of his most famous dance move.

There was the film *Moonwalker*, which costarred Joe Pesci and tied together a string of Jackson's music videos from *Bad*. The budget of $22 million was more or less covered by an advance from production company Lorimar,[10] and the flick went on to sell more than 800,000 units in the US.[11]

Then there was the Sega Genesis video game of the same name, also starring Jackson, this time in animated form. Through connections in Japan, he was able to get an introduction to the executives at Sega;[12] the company cooked up a popular side-scroller where the Jackson character runs around rescuing children, vanquishing enemies with a toss of his hat (or by dancing them to death).

Finally, there was the memoir *Moonwalk*—edited by Jackie Kennedy Onassis and Shaye Areheart. The latter, who ended up writing parts of the book, eventually flew to Australia to take a draft to Jackson for approval during the Bad Tour. For two weeks, she'd sit at the edge of his bed every night and read him the manuscript because he wanted to hear it after marking up several drafts; he'd dictate changes. Just as he did with the "Thriller" video, however, he got cold feet at the last minute.[13]

"He didn't have a problem with the book per se," says Areheart. "It wasn't that he thought it could have been better, that wasn't why. He just got worried about having it out." Adds Branca: "He didn't want it out because he didn't want to be overexposed."[14]

Ironically, the book's publisher had initially worried that it didn't reveal *enough*. But a call from the publisher, along with a bit of massaging from Areheart and Branca, ultimately convinced Jackson to change his mind and allow the book to be released without any reworking.

When *Moonwalk* eventually hit stores in February 1988, it zoomed to the top of the *New York Times* bestseller list. And indeed, the main criticism was that it didn't reveal enough—as the *Times* itself opined, the book "could be dismissed as an assiduously unrevealing, frequently tedious document. Ultimately, however, these are precisely the qualities that make it fascinating."[15]

Thanks to close associates who were willing to challenge him, Jackson had narrowly avoided dashing a worthwhile project. He couldn't have been happier with the result.

"He thought the book was great," says Areheart. "Michael loved it."[16]

Hollywood couldn't have designed two men more suited to be rivals than David Geffen, chief of his eponymous record label, and Walter Yetnikoff, who ran Sony Music.

For much of the 1980s, Yetnikoff was the unreformed Tony Stark (an arrogant, skirt-chasing boozehound who happened to be incredibly intelligent) to Geffen's Obadiah Stane (a brilliant operator who played business like chess and always seemed to know where to find an opponent's weaknesses). Yetnikoff also enjoyed tweaking his foe.

"[Geffen] used to say, 'You should have your eyes done,'" Yetnikoff recalls. "I'd say, 'David, I'm not a fucking fairy like you are.' We were very friendly at one time."[17]

For Geffen, the idea of luring the King of Pop to his label while spiting his rival seems to have been enormously appealing. Jackson liked having one of Hollywood's richest men on his investment committee for the free advice, but also for the help he could lend to Jackson's movie career. The mogul's Geffen Company had produced a string of hits in the 1980s including *Risky Business*, *Little Shop of Horrors*, and *Beetlejuice*.

Geffen declined multiple requests for an interview for this book, both through an assistant[18] and directly ("I don't want to talk about MJ," he wrote in an email. "All too sad").[19] His influence on Jackson's career, however, is undeniable. Starting in the mid-1980s, he served as one of the singer's advisors and even signed him to a movie development deal.[20]

So when the billionaire called to ask for a song to use on the soundtrack of the Tom Cruise auto-racing flick *Days of Thunder*, it seemed fitting that Jackson agreed to record the Beatles' "Come Together," to which he already owned the publishing rights (supporting Les Bider's point that Jackson often acquired songs with the intention of recording them himself).

But Jackson became concerned that contributing to the soundtrack might amount to overexposure and decided he wanted out. He called Yetnikoff and asked what he should do.

"Tell Geffen he can't use it," the CBS chief suggested.[21]

"Well, I already told him he could."

"Well, call him and tell him he can't."

"No, you tell him."

Yetnikoff wasn't terribly enthused about the plan. But this time, he figured, the task was at least possible. That wasn't the case a few years earlier when Jackson had called Yetnikoff the night before the Grammys and demanded he find a way to get Quincy Jones's name removed from nominations for the production of *Thriller*. The two incidents were indicative of a larger pattern where Jackson would agree to something, change his mind, and then rely on Branca or Yetnikoff to get him out of the deal.

The next time Geffen called, Yetnikoff delivered the news: "You can't use that song."

"What, are you crazy?" Geffen fumed. "Michael told us we could."

"He doesn't have the authority to do that."

"I wouldn't do that to *you.*"

"I have to protect his career as an artist . . . you can't use it."

Geffen appealed to Branca, but received the same response. The *Days of Thunder* soundtrack made its debut in June 1990 with nothing from Jackson on its track list; despite contributions from Guns n' Roses, Cher, and Elton John, it never climbed higher than number 27 on the *Billboard* album chart.[22] That was a decent performance for a soundtrack, but one that could well have been improved by a contribution from Jackson.

————

As intrigue engulfed the executive ranks of Michael Jackson, Inc., the singer found comfort at his Neverland hideaway. Frequent guests included family members (his brothers and their families), friends (Elizabeth Taylor), and disadvantaged children (busloads of inner-city youths from Los Angeles in need of a bucolic afternoon retreat[23]).

Jackson particularly enjoyed acting as a mentor. One day, his brother Jackie showed up at Neverland with an eight-year-old boy named Donny B. Lord, whom he'd been mentoring in hopes of managing him through a music career of his own (he even called the youngster "Little Michael" on account of his precocious dancing skills and vocal abilities). Now in his mid-thirties, Lord remembers waiting in the library with Jackie to meet Michael.

"He opened up the door and swung his arms out like a king," says Lord. "And . . . I just thought, 'Wow, he knew who the hell he was'— 'I'm Michael Jackson, I'm the King of Pop, I'm the greatest entertainer in the world, and you know what, I have the right to open up my own library door and just do it, arms open, like I have *arrived*.'"[24]

Most of all, Lord remembers the advice Jackson gave him as an aspiring—albeit eight-year-old—entertainer. Instead of lecturing Lord about how to write a song or how to capture an audience, he began with business.

"The value comes from when you own [your work]," Jackson explained, detailing a philosophy that he applied increasingly to physical goods as well as intellectual property. "It's yours. It's yours forever. And you can give it to your children, you can give it to your family. That's how you build your wealth."

With Michael's words of wisdom and Jackie's continued guidance, Lord went on to become a musician with his own small entertainment company. But Jackson family visits to Neverland didn't always have happy endings. Less than five years after completing the Victory Tour, Jackson's father pestered him for months to join his brothers for four shows in South Korea after being offered millions by operatives of the late Sun Myung Moon, a popular reverend (or cult leader, depending on your perspective). When the shows did not materialize, Moon's organization sued the family for millions (Jackson's parents filed for bankruptcy protection in 1999[25]).

There were plenty of other schemes afoot; Joe Jackson even tried to convince his son to open a vineyard at Neverland. "I wanted to turn it into some type of an orchard where they raise grapes and things of that sort," says the elder Jackson. "Because that area is real good for that."[26]

Michael never acted on that advice, though he didn't need grapes to financially justify Neverland's purchase. The property was appraised at $50 million in 2002, while recent estimates have placed its value much higher. Southern California realtor Josh Altman, who's sold numerous stars' homes, believes Neverland could fetch $75 million to $85 million on the open market—perhaps more if a foreign billionaire decided to acquire it as a trophy. Says Altman: "There are only so many mega-properties."[27]

Chapter 11

NEW SHOES

50 Cent isn't known for being giddy.

Born Curtis Jackson (no relation to Michael), the Queens native put himself on the hip-hop map with the 1999 hit "How to Rob," in which he outlines his plans to relieve stars from Jay Z to Will Smith of their cash. He rose to international superstardom after releasing *Get Rich or Die Tryin'* in 2003; on the album's cover, his face is contorted into a fierce scowl, perhaps a consequence of getting shot nine times at close range a few years earlier.

These days, he's more concerned with entrepreneurial ventures (though he still keeps a framed photo of a pistol in his office, behind a gold placard that reads "CJ Enterprises"). He took home $100 million on a single deal in 2008—payment for a stake he'd taken in vitaminwater parent Glacéau in lieu of a one-off endorsement fee—when Coca-Cola bought the beverage company for $4.1 billion. He's launched his own video games, record label, sneakers, clothes, headphones, and energy shots.

Yet it still comes as something of a surprise when, a few minutes into an interview in his Manhattan penthouse office, he jumps up from his plush leather chair and begins bouncing around the room, gesturing with cartoonishly muscled forearms and smiling uncontrollably. The topic responsible for his good humor? Michael Jackson, the man whose early shoe and clothing lines helped open the door for the brand extensions of the next generation of entertainers, 50 Cent included.

"When he did 'Billie Jean,' I had that poster on my wall," says the rapper. "Like, he could have sold me penny loafers . . . the show-manship that was involved in his presentation was so much more ad-vanced than the things that we'd seen in the past."[1]

Long before 50 Cent created his G-Unit sneaker for Reebok or Jay Z launched his S. Carter line, Nike had MJ.

To be clear, those initials don't refer to the King of Pop, but Mi-chael Jordan. In 1987, the Chicago Bulls legend became the first en-tertainer to be paid on a scale commensurate with today's stars when he inked a seven-year, $18 million contract with Nike to launch his Air Jordan brand. The agreement marked the apotheosis of the rap-idly growing athlete shoe deal, which was virtually nonexistent just ten years earlier.[2]

In the 1970s, Nike's first signing was University of Oregon track star Steve Prefontaine. He agreed to wear the fledgling company's shoes for a then-whopping $5,000. The scales quickly shifted when Adidas signed Kareem Abdul-Jabbar to a $100,000 deal in 1982; shortly thereafter, New Balance spent $1.2 million to lock up fel-low basketball star James Worthy before Nike upped the stakes by another order of magnitude with Jordan; the company's revenues soared from $10 million to just shy of $1 billion over that span.

Athletes were finally getting paid to wear shoes, but musicians didn't begin to break into the market until pioneering hip-hop act Run-D.M.C. released the song "My Adidas," an initially uncompen-sated ode to shell-toes. In 1986—after a handful of Adidas executives showed up to a Madison Square Garden show and witnessed some twenty thousand onlookers raise their own sneakers toward the raf-ters at the behest of the rappers—Run-D.M.C. signed a deal worth more than $1 million.[3]

By 1990, upstart sneaker purveyor LA Gear was desperately looking to grab a bigger piece of a multibillion-dollar market. So the company's chief, Robert Greenberg, turned to cofounder Sandy Saemann and said, "Let's get Michael Jackson."[4]

Saemann, a loquacious Californian who later resigned from the company after amassing millions in stock holdings—and now runs a high-end hot dog stand in Manhattan Beach—thought this was a bad idea. Even without a big-name endorser, he believed LA Gear had a shot at eating into its rivals' domestic market share.

The way he saw it, Michael Jackson's image was still smarting from recent tabloid fiascoes and wouldn't necessarily help sell sneakers in the United States. Greenberg saw things differently. Even if the singer couldn't help with their domestic efforts, he was still huge overseas, as the Bad Tour had shown. If Jackson could sell over 4 million concert tickets—with more than half his tour dates occurring abroad—why couldn't he move a million sneakers worldwide?

Thus began the relationship between Jackson and LA Gear. When Greenberg and Saemann finally reached out to his camp, they found the singer was amenable to doing a deal as long as his financial conditions were met: $20 million. That surpassed even the seven-year, $18 million Nike deal signed by Michael Jordan in 1987 (though the basketball legend would earn far more after receiving a royalty on every Air Jordan shoe sold). But Jackson knew his worth, even when it came to sneakers.[5]

"He wanted it to be the biggest deal known to man," recalls Saemann. "He was very conscious of where the scale was. . . . That's the side of him that nobody understands. He knew where he was. He wanted to be number one and he wanted to stay number one, he wanted to be the largest entertainer with the most deals."

During early conversations over the venture, Saemann and Greenberg told Jackson and Branca, who was negotiating the deal, that they wanted to launch the shoe abroad only. That way, they figured, it wouldn't be such a gamble. But Jackson refused. If he was going to launch his own sneaker, it had to be the biggest and the best—bigger even than Jordan's—and there was no way he'd settle for an overseas-only deal.

LA Gear agreed, and Jackson accepted the offer of $20 million, about one-fifth of the company's annual advertising budget, to help launch a line of co-branded sneakers that would be sold both in the US and around the world; he'd get half of that sum up front.[6] The press release announcing the shoe would refer to him as the King of Pop, and his agreement with LA Gear would be described as "the largest entertainment endorsement ever made."[7]

In return, says Saemann, Jackson promised he'd shoot television commercials for LA Gear and wear the sneakers in the promotional materials for his upcoming album, *Dangerous*, which was supposedly almost finished. When Jackson showed up at a press conference in Los Angeles on August 6 to announce the agreement, it seemed a perfect match.

"The theme of our ad campaign is 'unstoppable,'" said Saemann, introducing the singer. "This word epitomized what LA Gear and Michael Jackson represent. . . . I want to tell the competition, we'll up you a Jackson."[8]

"Thank you very much," said Jackson, looking spiffy as ever in sunglasses, a sleek dark suit, and a purple dress shirt. "I'm very happy to be a part of the LA Gear magic."

———

As the 1980s drew to a close, Michael Jackson seemed to be asking his closest advisors more questions than usual. Sometimes he'd ask Branca for his thoughts about Dileo's managerial work. Others, he'd ask Dileo if he thought Branca was spending too much time with the Rolling Stones, whom he was also representing.[9]

Branca knew that method of operating from the outset of his relationship with Jackson, when the singer would ask him if he was as good as Frank Sinatra's lawyer. It was Jackson's way of motivating his lieutenants. But Dileo's means of motivation sometimes rankled

Jackson: at one show in Pittsburgh, the singer showed up a half hour late—and the manager yelled at Jackson in front of his whole family.

Dileo imagined himself as something like an updated version of Colonel Tom Parker, Elvis Presley's boisterous manager (though, to be fair, Jackson was too shrewd to allow Dileo the 50 percent cut of earnings that Elvis gave Parker). He was also loyal, to a fault. He didn't take on extra acts to manage, thinking Jackson wouldn't permit it. Then rival advisors would whisper in Jackson's ear that Dileo didn't know anything about the music business. Coupled with his occasionally overbearing attitude, this made Dileo an easy scapegoat for Jackson's disappointment in the sales figures for *Bad*, which hadn't approached those of *Thriller*. In 1989, Jackson fired his manager.

The purge was just beginning, and not only at Michael Jackson, Inc. In 1990, Sony's chief dismissed Yetnikoff, citing his "behavior." Ironically, Yetnikoff had given up many of his notorious vices well before his dismissal, but that didn't necessarily help his cause. ("In my first year of sobriety, I may have been crazier," he says.) He also saw too late that his former protégé and eventual replacement, the lounge-singer-turned-song-plugger-turned-manager Tommy Mottola, had been planning a coup. (Geffen's gleeful response to his rival's demise: "Ding dong, the witch is dead!")[10]

Shortly before Yetnikoff's departure from the label, Mottola called Branca and offered to put him on a lucrative retainer; the attorney declined (he and Mottola were never close, and per his longstanding policy, Branca felt it would be a conflict of interest to represent both an artist and his record label).[11]

And despite the *Days of Thunder* incident, Jackson and Geffen seemed close as ever. "Michael wanted him to manage him," recalls Yetnikoff. "Geffen didn't want to manage him. He said, 'Do you wash windows?' And Michael said, 'No.' He says, 'Well, I don't manage.'"[12]

But Geffen had Jackson's ear. He also had a handful of attorneys he preferred, and it started to look like Branca might be the odd man out. Sure enough, later in 1990, Branca received a letter by messenger: Michael Jackson no longer required his services. His colleagues Ken Ziffren and Gary Stiffelman met with the singer one last time to try to change Jackson's mind. They told him they'd be willing to represent him themselves if his issue was with Branca, at which point Jackson became tearful and passed a note to Stiffelman: "Tell John and Karen I'm sorry and I love them. . . . I truly appreciate all the firm has done."[13]

––––––––

The executive ranks of Michael Jackson, Inc. were beginning to unravel. In the near term, a new team headed by two of Geffen's associates, lawyer Allen Grubman[14] and manager Sandy Gallin, took over Jackson's business—and with it, the LA Gear deal.

Before Branca was fired, Gallin had approached him to set up a meeting with Jackson, who'd just dismissed Dileo. Gallin (who has also managed Cher, Neil Diamond, and Dolly Parton) thought he might be a good fit for Jackson. The singer had considered a handful of others, but Gallin eventually won the job after bonding with the King of Pop over the scope of their shared dream of making Jackson as big in the film world as he was in music.

"What he thought he could become and what I thought he could become were very similar," says Gallin. "Michael thought of being the biggest, the best . . . to repeat the great success of *Thriller* and to be able to have more people attend your concerts, to be able to have the most successful short films at the time, to be able to do movies, and to succeed more than anyone else in any form of entertainment that he entered into, whether it was writing, producing, singing, acting, directing. It was innate to his personality."[15]

During the half decade Gallin would spend managing Jackson, he noticed something else besides boundless talent and ambition: as the singer underwent procedures to sculpt his physical features toward an impossible ideal of perfection, he became more and more drawn to painkillers like the ones initially prescribed to him after his Pepsi commercial accident years earlier. The manager didn't see it as a full-fledged addiction at that point, but it was certainly noteworthy.

"While I managed him, it wasn't anywhere near as serious as it became after I managed him, having nothing to do with me at all," says Gallin. "I think he got into it with his plastic surgeries . . . he could figure out a way to get what he wanted. It was very hard for doctors to say no to him."

Despite the managerial changes, Jackson's business career was chugging along at a healthy clip. To help promote Jackson's shoe, Saemann directed a commercial that features the King of Pop spinning through a dark, steamy street in his new kicks. His face appears for only about three seconds toward the end when, after destroying a street lamp with the sheer force of his mojo, Jackson looks up to find a young girl smiling and clapping from an upstairs window.[16]

Saemann and Jackson also developed a close working relationship. They'd go to record stores and sales meetings together; on one occasion, Jackson elevated the moods of seven hundred sales reps by dancing on a table. He and Saemann would even edit videos together late into the night. "He was no slouch," recalls the former LA Gear executive. "When Michael went to work on something, it might take two weeks to get ahold of him, but he'd give you five hours."[17]

Jackson, however, still hadn't completed his new album. Yetnikoff was gone, and his replacement wasn't going to push his biggest star too hard—not yet, anyway. Perhaps Branca or Dileo would have hurried him along, but they were out of the picture. Whenever Saemann broached the subject with Jackson, the response was the same. "I'm a creative guy," he'd say. "You can't force it."

In the end, LA Gear had to move forward with the launch of the sneaker line though neither the album nor the promised product tie-in had emerged. Retailers were expecting the shoes to be delivered on schedule—but they were also expecting the footwear to make an appearance in promotional material that accompanied

Jackson's new record. When that didn't materialize, the results were disastrous. The shoes sold hundreds of thousands of pairs, says Saemann, but there were also hundreds of thousands that had to be returned to the manufacturer after languishing too long on the shelves.

Jackson hadn't held up his end of the bargain, and LA Gear was suffering. The day Saemann introduced him at the press conference, the company's stock stood at $20.75 per share, down from a high of $50.38 the previous year.[18] By January 1991, the stock had plummeted to $2.88; it lost 21.5 percent on a single day, thanks to the announcement that the company expected to lose $4 million to $6 million in the fourth quarter.[19] Jackson's deal factored heavily into that figure.

In June of 1991, Saemann voluntarily resigned from the company "to pursue other business interests." Roy A. Disney's Trefoil Capital bought 30 percent of the slumping company around the same time.[20]

LA Gear would go on to sue Jackson in 1992; after the singer countersued, the two sides settled for an undisclosed sum. Saemann suspects the company let Jackson keep what they'd already paid him—the first half of the promised $20 million—but didn't have to fork over anything more. And despite the damage to Saemann's stock options and reputation, he still has some fondness for the singer.

"I enjoyed every minute around him; we talked as equals and friends," recalls Saemann. "But, genius or not, he didn't deliver."[21]

———

Back in 50 Cent's office, the rapper is done pacing. Now he's sitting down again, musing on his shared connections with Michael Jackson. There were plenty of those on the business front, given that the King of Pop proved it was possible for an entertainer to start his own clothing label, shoe line, and record company long before the birth of 50 Cent's G-Unit empire.

But he connects with Jackson on another level. Right or wrong, many people define both men by their most successful album—

Get Rich or Die Tryin' was the rapper's *Thriller*. Like Jackson, he had many other hits, but the album remained something of an albatross because of the inevitable comparisons it evoked whenever a new effort was released.

"[Reviewers] go, 'Yeah it's cool, but it's not as good as it was when you came the first time,'" he explains. "And you can't have a second chance at a first impression. No matter who you are."[22]

Despite spending more than a decade trying to top *Get Rich*, it's still his bestselling album and most critically acclaimed. 50 Cent doesn't seem too distressed, though; he's turned his attention to new business ventures like his SMS headphone line and SK Energy drink.

The specter of success took a seemingly heavier toll on Michael Jackson. One need only consider how much time and money he spent on subsequent albums to see how badly he yearned to top *Thriller*—a perfectionist's longing that caused him to drastically delay the launch of multiple works—sometimes at the expense of interconnected business ventures like the LA Gear shoe line.

He did all of this in a vain effort to achieve something that was, by definition, basically impossible: to make an album more successful than the most successful album of all time. And Jackson was spurred on over and over again by reviewers and listeners who continued to hold his work, both sonically and commercially, to the standard of *Thriller*.

"They just put you up against yourself," says 50 Cent. "If they give you an opponent, you can analyze and figure out their weaknesses and beat them. But if it's yourself, how do you win? How do you top that?"

Chapter 12

DANGEROUS VENTURES

Teddy Riley was already on the plane to California when his manager explained they'd be taking the last leg of their trip to Neverland via helicopter. The producer had seen a lot in his life despite being just twenty-three years old. After growing up in a Harlem housing project, he'd crafted tracks for the likes of Bobby Brown, Big Daddy Kane, and Keith Sweat, helping to establish the musical genre known as New Jack Swing along the way—but he'd never been in a chopper.

That was only the beginning of Riley's adventures with Michael Jackson. It was late 1990 and the singer still hadn't finished his follow-up to *Bad*, which he'd been working on since returning from his tour the previous year. He'd already completed a number of new songs including "Black or White," "Heal the World," and "Will You Be There," but didn't feel they were ready to be released; he didn't think he had enough material for a suitably revolutionary new album yet.

Riley touched down at Neverland armed with about seventy new tracks and a recommendation from Quincy Jones, who was out after producing Jackson's previous three albums.[1] Says sound engineer Bruce Swedien of the split: "I think Michael just wanted to take charge of his own life, and that's it."[2]

After signing a nondisclosure agreement with Neverland's security team, Riley was escorted to the main house and left alone in a room full of humanitarian awards and plaques commemorating Jackson's various recording milestones. There were other curiosities, too, including a gold-and-platinum chess piece that caught Riley's eye. He reached out to touch it—and suddenly felt a hand tap him on the side. He turned around and found himself face to face with Michael Jackson, who'd sneaked in through a secret door.

"It scared the heck out of me!" Riley recalls. "So that was my first time meeting him. . . . Michael is such a jokester. He just died laughing, fell on the floor. I was on the floor scared, he was on the floor laughing, and we just hit it off from there."[3]

Jackson then led Riley on a tour of his property. They stopped in one room that had two life-sized mannequins of the King of Pop, another filled with hundreds of red corduroy shirts, and a dark chamber where Riley was startled once again. This time, the culprit was a giant doll—used in the 1980 horror movie *Effects*—that popped out and growled at the producer, much to Jackson's amusement.

Then the singer took Riley to the guesthouse, where the producer would stay for the next few days with ten rooms all to himself on the shores of a tranquil pond. Inside, the building was a testing ground for future Jackson-branded products: every room had a carpet sporting the logo for Jackson's *Moonwalker* film. There were bowls filled with *Moonwalker* candy bars. The bathroom even had a *Moonwalker* toothbrush.

The two musicians talked for hours every day. Jackson gave the young producer insights on their industry, including his philosophy that "publishing is the real estate of the whole business." They covered other topics, too—life and love—Jackson even told Riley about a girl he was seeing at the time. Recalls Riley: "I guess he was just trying to feel me out to see if I was a trustworthy person."

After four days, Jackson was sold on having Riley craft tracks for his upcoming album, and arranged to have all of the producer's equipment packed up and sent across the country—five racks of samplers, a handful of synthesizers, and much more. As soon as Riley had set everything up, Jackson arrived to begin work.

"Oh my God, we are going to have so much fun," he said upon entering the studio. "Let's hear the music."

Riley first played the backing track for what would become Blackstreet's "Joy," and though Jackson seemed to like it, he ultimately passed. The producer continued to flip from demo to demo—skeletons of songs featuring drum machines and synthesizers, all waiting for lyrical flesh—hoping the King of Pop would bring some to life on *Dangerous*. But he gave Riley the "record company demo face" four songs in a row. In the middle of the fifth, Jackson stopped the track. Riley was convinced that he'd failed, and that he was about to be relieved of his duties.

"Play those chords of 'Remember the Time,'" said Jackson, referring to the last song. Riley obliged. "What is that chord called?"

"I don't know, 'cause I play everything by ear," the producer replied. "Maybe it's a C 9 augmented. Why'd you ask me what that chord is?"

"Because I've never had that chord or a chord like that in any of my music," said Jackson. "You just brought something to me that I never heard, never experienced in any of my records. Now I would like to write and do the melodies right now on that chord to see if it works with what I want to write to it."

They stayed in the room for about four hours until the song was finished. Then Jackson laid out the plan for the rest of the album.

"I take everything from the piano," he said. "Once we've got that, then we go and we make the record. You do what you do, and I write my melodies . . . we don't need anything but you and this piano and my melodies."

————

Time hadn't dampened Jackson's insistence on perfection or his relentless ambition, and with *Dangerous*, Jackson's goal was the same as it had been with *Bad*: 100 million copies sold. Says engineer Matt

Forger: "He realized that everything he released basically had to be perfect, because it was going to be compared to *Thriller.*"[4]

The same held true for the mega-deal that preceded the album. In March of 1991, Jackson scored a new agreement with Sony that promised him an advance of $5 million per record, a royalty of 25 percent of retail sales, and a share of profits through his own newly formed record label. He'd be encouraged to sign new acts as well; for his troubles, he'd get an up-front payment of $4 million, plus $1 million per year to run the label and $2.2 million annually for administration costs.[5]

In addition, the deal gave him the Hollywood opening he and manager Sandy Gallin had pursued since they'd started working together, calling for Jackson to earn $5 million for appearing in "a musical action adventure." The *Los Angeles Times* proclaimed the contract "the biggest ever awarded to an entertainer" and predicted it would net Jackson hundreds of millions of dollars.

"He always wanted better, more, bigger," says Gallin. "He was never satisfied. If he sold 3 million the first week, he should have sold 3.5 million. If the record was less than number one, he was never ever satisfied or happy."[6]

Dangerous finally made its debut on November 26, 1991. With tracks ranging from the guitar-heavy "Black or White" to the sugary "Heal the World," Jackson seemed to be trying to create something for everybody—which became the chief complaint for some reviewers. The *Los Angeles Times* called it "a messy grab-bag of ideas and high-tech non sequiturs,"[7] while the *New York Times* opined that the album "only reinforces Jackson's place as the most paradoxical superstar in pop history."[8]

It seemed that many critics were judging the album by its cover—both their preexisting mental image of Jackson and the collage art that physically adorned *Dangerous*. The cover featured Jackson's eyes peeking out from behind a gilded white mask; in the background, notable images include what appears to be Jackson's pet chimp wearing a crown, an elephant looming above Neverland-inspired gates, and famous circus act Tom Thumb standing on the head of P. T. Barnum. Said *Rolling Stone*: "The triumph of *Dangerous* is that it doesn't hide from the fears and contradictions of a lifetime spent under a spotlight."[9]

Though the album didn't meet Jackson's lofty sales expectations, it was a major hit, moving 600,000 copies in the US during its first week. *Dangerous* would go on to sell 40 million units worldwide.[10] Even as the album climbed the charts, a new reality was starting to take shape within Jackson's empire. Branca and Dileo were gone, Yetnikoff had been ousted, and it seemed that nobody in Jackson's modified inner circle was willing to tell him no—or even nudge him away from a bad decision, as Branca had with the Bela Lugosi tale that saved the "Thriller" video.

Jackson's spending showed no signs of slowing. New extravagances included tens of millions in renovations to Neverland, complete with a zoo and a railway line large enough for a full-size steam locomotive.[11] Because he'd averaged $58 million in annual earnings over the prior four years, his cash flow remained positive—for the time being, anyway. But the working relationships between the remaining employees of Michael Jackson, Inc. and its founder were faltering.

"When John Branca was involved, I would get phone calls from Michael, we would meet when he was back in Los Angeles or I'd be in Tokyo or London," says former ATV president Dale Kawashima, who left his job in December 1991. "But . . . I didn't have personal contact with Michael within the last year or so. It wasn't the same for me."[12]

The growing distance between Jackson and the decisions being made about his business was evident even to those who happened to be passing through his orbit for only a short while.

"I never saw him, with the exception of one time, ever get involved with anything businesslike," recalls Saul "Slash" Hudson, the longtime guitarist for Guns n' Roses whom Jackson had recruited to play on "Black or White." "The people around him seemed to be very eager to shelter him from all that."[13]

———————

Though *Dangerous* hadn't come anywhere close to topping *Thriller,* it still put Jackson back in the spotlight and helped him earn $35 million in 1991—an excellent showing, but noticeably lower than his peak during the *Bad* era. The international tour that followed was also shaping up to be a massive moneymaker. Gallin hoped to use the momentum to burnish the singer's image, which for some observers was still tainted by bizarre tabloid tales.

"He definitely had a strange image, almost like he was not from this planet or this world," recalls Gallin. "And . . . I thought people have to hear Michael talk, see that he is from this planet and that he's much more a human being and normal than they think he is."[14]

If the public couldn't be convinced of that, Gallin feared Jackson's commercial success—and, therefore, his own job—might be in jeopardy. He believed the best way to humanize Jackson was to put him in front of the largest television audience possible in two settings: an Oprah Winfrey special and a Super Bowl halftime show. When Gallin made the suggestions, Jackson initially resisted. But after assurances that he'd have creative control over both, he relented.

"Had he not wanted to, he would not have done it," says Gallin. "He was smart enough to know he had to reconnect with the American public."

The NFL was interested in bringing Jackson aboard for the same reason as Oprah: ratings. During the previous year's halftime show, a sizable chunk of viewers watching the game on CBS were so unenthused about the combination of Gloria Estefan, Brian Boitano, and Dorothy Hamill that they flipped to Fox to see a new episode of *In Living Color*.

The migration caused a ten-point dip in ratings during the biggest television event of the year, something that CBS and the NFL were desperate to avoid in the future.[15] To secure Jackson, the league agreed to cover the extravagant production costs—as it now does for all halftime acts[16]—and to contribute $100,000 ($160,000 in today's dollars) to his newly formed Heal the World charity.[17] Jackson and his touring band then rehearsed twenty-eight days in January at the Rose Bowl.[18]

On a sunny Sunday in Los Angeles, with the Dallas Cowboys leading the Buffalo Bills by a score of 28 to 10 halfway through Super Bowl XXVII, some 100,000 people waited at the Rose Bowl—and perhaps 1 billion more in front of televisions around the world—as Jackson prepared to take the stage. Suddenly, his image appeared in video form on one of the stadium's Jumbotrons, spinning around in a gold shirt and black pants as the organ blared a few notes from "Thriller."[19]

Then the stadium was filled with a noise that sounded like the flushing of a great cosmic airplane toilet, and Jackson's image disappeared into a vortex on the screen—only to emerge from a puff of smoke in human form atop the Jumbotron. Seconds later, the same thing happened on the screen on the other side of the stadium. And then, with the puzzled thousands cheering the ersatz Jacksons wildly, the whooshing sound returned. As fireworks crackled behind the stage at midfield, the real Michael Jackson erupted from its center as though shot by a cannon, landing on his feet, his motions looking as effortless as an Olympic gymnast sticking a jump.

Rather than launch immediately into a song, Jackson stood still as a statue for seventy-two seconds, an eternity on television. His first move was a slight turn of his head; after that, he waited another twenty seconds before slowly removing his sunglasses. Only then did he finally launch into his first song, "Jam," the beginning of an electrifying medley that included snippets of "Billie Jean," "Black or White," "We Are the World," and "Heal the World." There was moonwalking, crotch grabbing, and a finale that involved a chorus of children decked out in local attire from the countries of the world, sporting garb from sombreros to lederhosen.

Dallas would go on to slaughter Buffalo by a score of 52–17—the Cowboys would have amassed the highest point total of any Super Bowl winner had it not been for the infamous fumble by an end-zone-bound Leon Lett—and the game's viewers didn't stray from the halftime show this time. Despite the fact that the game was a blowout, the Super Bowl went on to draw a score of 43.9 on Nielsen's scale, an 8.6 percent increase from the previous year and the best since 1987.[20]

The NFL's executives quickly realized that a Super Bowl halftime show could be more than marching bands and figure skaters mixed with the occasional pop star. In subsequent years, it became a showcase for some of the biggest names in music, including U2, Paul McCartney, Prince, the Rolling Stones, Bruce Springsteen, Madonna, and Beyoncé.

Less than two weeks after the game, Oprah Winfrey made the trek to Neverland to film her live special, which was billed as Jackson's first televised interview in fourteen years. The singer strolled out in black pants and a red military-style shirt—and roundly dismissed some of the recent stories on topics from the Elephant Man's bones ("Where am I going to put some bones?") to his ever-lightening skin color ("I have a skin disorder that destroys the pigmentation") to the number of times he'd had plastic surgery ("You can count on two fingers").[21]

During the interview, Jackson also discussed his love life, saying that he was dating Brooke Shields, who accompanied him to the Grammys in 1984. Later, surprise guest Elizabeth Taylor described Jackson as "the least weird man I've ever known . . . highly intelligent, shrewd, intuitive, understanding, sympathetic, generous to almost a fault." Perhaps the most revealing moment of the interview came when Winfrey asked Jackson if he was happy with the way he looked now. "I'm never pleased with anything," he said. "I'm a perfectionist."

The show went a long way toward demystifying Jackson. There

were no hyperbaric chambers in his house, and Bubbles the chimp didn't make any cameos. Jackson came off as a shy, gracious, wealthy young man who lived an unusual but not deviant lifestyle; on camera, Neverland seemed like the sort of estate many regular people might daydream about owning.

When the ratings rolled in, the result for Winfrey was just as positive as it was for her subject. *Michael Jackson Talks to . . . Oprah Live* and her subsequent celebrity interview highlight reel became the second- and third-highest-rated segments of her career—only the 1988 weight-loss episode where Winfrey carted out sixty-seven pounds of actual fat on a red wagon performed better than the two related to Jackson.[22]

"He was unquestionably the biggest star in the world, the most talented," says Gallin. "Everybody wanted to be in business with him. . . . At that moment in time, something that Michael wanted to do, there would always be someone who wanted to finance it."[23]

———

Michael Jackson met thirteen-year-old Jordan Chandler in 1992 after his car broke down near a used-auto-rental outlet operated by the boy's stepfather.[24] Jackson later hosted Jordan, his sister, and his mother at Neverland on multiple occasions and even took them with him on trips abroad.

The Chandlers were one of many families he'd befriended, and Jordan one of many children he would entertain at his ranch. He'd host groups of youngsters ranging from terminally ill kids sent his way by the Make-A-Wish Foundation[25] to middle-schoolers Frank and Eddie Cascio, the sons of a hotel manager at New York's Helmsley Palace, where Jackson stayed when he was in the city.[26]

At Neverland, Jackson's young guests would sometimes spend the night; according to Frank Cascio, he'd give them his bed and sleep on the floor. To be sure, this wasn't normal behavior for an adult, let alone for the most famous musician in the world. Then again, nobody ever accused Michael Jackson of being normal. In 1992, though, nobody had accused him of much worse.

"When he was with children, he could be himself," wrote Cascio in his book, *My Friend Michael.* "He'd been in the spotlight his entire life and people looked at him differently because of that. But children didn't care who he was. I certainly didn't." Adds childhood pal Greg Campbell: "He liked to be around little kids, he always had that in him."[27] Oprah Winfrey noticed the same trait, telling the singer, "What's fascinating to me about you is that obviously you have this childlike aura about you, and I see children with you and they play with you like you're one of them."[28]

Jordan Chandler's biological father Evan, a man with the only-in-Los-Angeles occupation of dentist and screenwriter, seemed to share that attitude when his son began spending time with Jackson. Evan felt so comfortable with the singer that he asked him to pay for a renovation of his home. After an uneasy Jackson ignored the requests,[29] Chandler seemed to grow worried that he was being replaced as a father by Michael Jackson, of all people.[30]

As his son continued to spend time with Jackson, often having sleepovers (and sometimes sharing a bed), he started to wonder if something more sinister might be occurring. He hired an attorney who then contacted Beverly Hills psychiatrist Mathis Abrams and described the situation; without meeting with any of the parties involved, the doctor wrote a letter saying that it seemed there may have been sexual contact in the scenario described.[31]

Evan told his son's stepfather that he was pondering accusing Jackson of molestation. "If I go through with this, I win big . . . I will get everything I want," he said. "And [Jackson] will be destroyed forever."[32]

About two weeks later, while Evan was removing a problematic tooth from his son's mouth, Jordan suggested that he'd had sexual relations with Jackson (it's worth noting that, at the time of this initial admission, the boy was under the influence of an anesthetic called sodium amytal, which has been known to cause false memories in some patients).[33]

Rather than going directly to the police, Evan arranged a meeting at a Los Angeles hotel and made his next request of Jackson: $20 million to fund four of his screenplays (he had already cowritten the 1993 Mel Brooks flick *Robin Hood: Men in Tights*). If he didn't get the money, Chandler would publicly accuse Jackson of sexually abusing his son.[34]

Jackson asserted his innocence and rejected Chandler's demands; about two weeks later, the latter took his son to see Dr. Abrams in person. There, Jordan Chandler reportedly told the psychiatrist that he'd had sexual contact with Jackson. Dr. Abrams then notified the authorities.

As Jackson headed to Asia for the second leg of his tour, the biggest story of the decade was about to explode.[35]

––––––––

Around this time, Michael Jackson was involved in two film projects with an old colleague—Rusty Lemorande, who'd written and produced *Captain EO*.

Executives at some of the major Hollywood studios, impressed with Jackson's work on *EO* and in his revolutionary music videos, were finally coming to share the singer's belief that he could become a full-fledged movie star like Elvis Presley.

With backing from one of the major studios, Lemorande was working with Jackson on what he describes as "a supernatural musical film that featured fantastical characters and settings." By the summer of 1993, there was already a full-scale mock-up in the works.

"We put it up in a rented studio in East Hollywood," Lemorande recalls. "Draped all with black cloth, you could kind of go from room to room and experience this thing interactively. It was really enchanting, with black light and little tiny lights. There was a circus set, a highly detailed, magic circus train—interior and exterior—a miniature of an entire inner city block, and models of various fantasy characters that Michael would portray."[36]

Lemorande was on his way to the studio one day in August for final preparations before showing the elaborate setup to Jackson when he got some shocking news: Jackson was under investigation for child molestation. Suddenly, a production that looked like a lock to launch the next step in Jackson's film career—complete with ten musical numbers—was very much on the rocks.

Along with his *Captain EO* colleagues, Lemorande was surprised to hear of the allegations. Michael had children accompany him during much of the 3-D shoot, surrounded by an adult crew of nearly one hundred. Nothing seemed amiss. Besides, Lemorande figured, Jackson had withstood controversies before, like the one referenced in "Billie Jean." He assumed the legal process would ultimately bring out the truth.

In the meantime, though, Jackson was on tour and the film project would have to be shelved. Just as Lemorande began to anticipate the depressing process of closing down the studio, and then packing and storing the miniature wonderland, he got a call from one of Jackson's representatives, who asked Lemorande if there was any way he could pack up the sets and take them to the singer in Japan.

"A limited version, yeah," Lemorande replied. "Anything can be shipped."

"Well, how soon can you do it?"

Lemorande was given a sense that there was "an imminent concern" for Jackson's well-being—and that seeing the miniatures for the film project might help snap him out of a deep funk.

He landed in Tokyo a few days later. Lemorande spent hours unpacking boxes and rewiring miniatures, turning a hotel suite into a magical oasis filled with ten-inch-tall hand-painted maquettes. The moment Jackson walked in that night after his show, unannounced, the look on the singer's face said everything.

"He was like a little kid opening Christmas presents," Lemorande recalls. "Saying simple things like, 'This is wonderful, wow, this is what we're going to do.' Just very simple utterances of pleasure and satisfaction."

The room was kept dark to maintain the fantasy illusion, and Lemorande and Jackson toured the room with a flashlight. The singer held each figurine, lifting the arms and moving the legs like toys. Says Lemorande: "He really seemed a kid who was still playing out a childhood."

Jackson left the room with a smile on his face, perhaps convinced that he still had a future in Hollywood. As Lemorande turned off the lights and packed up the maquettes and displays, however, he couldn't help but feel they'd never see the light of day—and that the same held true for Michael Jackson's film career.

———

Back in the US, the headlines were already rolling in. "Peter Pan or Pervert?" blared the front page of the *New York Post*, while *Newsweek* asked, "Is He Dangerous or Off the Wall?"[37]

Evan Chandler filed a civil lawsuit for $30 million; at the same time, the district attorneys of Los Angeles and Santa Barbara counties launched criminal investigations. Police raided Neverland, Hayvenhurst, and a condo Jackson owned in Los Angeles, seizing notes and writings.[38]

Jordan Chandler described the singer's private parts in a sworn affidavit, and Jackson was forced to submit to a full body search when he eventually returned to the US. In front of a group of detectives and doctors, he had to stand naked and lift up his penis so that a photographer could shoot it from all angles. "None of the markings on Michael's body matched the boy's description," wrote Jermaine Jackson. "In fact, the imagination bore no resemblance to the reality."[39]

There were plenty of others who stood by Jackson: the rest of his family, the hordes of adoring fans, and even the Cascios—who were so convinced of his innocence that they permitted two of their sons to join Jackson on tour in Tel Aviv. That didn't seem inappropriate to Frank, then about the same age as Chandler.

"Let me be absolutely clear: odd as it may seem for an adult to have 'sleepovers' with a couple of kids, there was nothing sexual about them," wrote Cascio years later as an adult. "Nothing that was apparent to me then, as a child, and nothing that I can see now, as a grown man scrutinizing the past. Michael was truly just a kid at heart."[40]

The Cascios accompanied Jackson as the tour moved on to Switzerland and Argentina. The King of Pop helped the boys with their homework, taught them about the music business, and showed them a world far different from their New Jersey home. As the weeks went by, however, they began to notice something unusual. Every night, a doctor came to give Jackson "medicine"—which Frank would later identify as the painkiller Demerol.

The boys' host seemed to be relying on prescription drugs to put his mind and body at ease, and the side effects occasionally manifested themselves. One time while they were doing schoolwork, Jackson blurted out: "Mommy, I want to go to Disneyland and see Mickey Mouse." When Frank repeated the words back to him, Jackson said, "Sometimes the medicine makes me do that."

While on tour in the fall of 1993, Jackson called Branca—he wanted to rehire a familiar face to help navigate a treacherous situation and keep an eye on Michael Jackson, Inc. while its chairman was under fire. More specifically, Sony had offered to buy half of ATV for $75 million, and Jackson wanted to know what his onetime dealmaker thought. Branca's reaction: "Are you crazy, Michael?"[41]

Relieved, Jackson declined the offer and brought Branca back. The two agreed that, going forward, the lawyer would receive 5 percent of Jackson's earnings from ATV (years later, when the two parted ways once again, Branca would sell the interest back to Jackson for $12.5 million, a price he believes was about 40 percent below market value).

One of Branca's first actions was to replace powerhouse criminal attorney Bert Fields, whom he felt had bungled the matter by not settling privately for a much smaller sum early on, with Johnnie Cochran.[42] Fields insists he would have let the case go to trial: "I believed Michael was innocent and would be acquitted, and that a huge settlement would be perceived as an admission of guilt and would damage his career."[43]

Cochran reportedly took a different view, as did many of Jackson's advisors and friends—including Lisa Marie Presley, who'd grown close to him. Through a spokesperson, she declined to comment for this book; Cochran passed away in 2005, and his longtime colleague Carl Douglas did not respond to an interview request.

Those who spent time with Jackson say he was generally opposed to settling, but the option gained momentum in his camp as his emotional state deteriorated with every passing day on the road. The singer was in such bad shape by the time the tour rolled into Mexico City that his friend Elizabeth Taylor showed up to retrieve him. "Michael has to go away for a little bit," she told the Cascios. "He's not feeling well, and we're going to get him some help. After the show, he's getting on the plane and we're taking him to a safe place."[44]

Later that night, Taylor shepherded Jackson onto a private jet bound for London, where he quickly checked into rehab at Charter Nightingale Clinic, and not a moment too soon. When staff at the Hotel Presidente in Mexico City went to clean Jackson's five-room, $12,000-per-night suite, they reportedly discovered dented walls, vomit-stained carpets, and the words "I love you" scrawled on the furniture and walls. "He's threatening to kill himself," said Taylor shortly afterward. "And if he does, his blood will be on all of our hands."[45]

With Cochran still in charge of his legal team, Jackson agreed to settle with the Chandlers for about $20 million, the same sum he'd initially rejected.[46] Lost earnings and fees associated with canceling the rest of the Dangerous Tour likely cost him at least that much in the short term, and untold millions in the long term.

Many have since argued that settling was the wrong decision, and it certainly appears that way in hindsight. Indeed, the move made Jackson look guilty and opened the door to other accusations, namely the one that led to his 2005 child molestation trial. In that case, California law allowed prosecutors to bring in evidence of prior offenses, but nothing stuck—including testimony from Chandler's mother—and Jackson was cleared of all charges. But if what Taylor said was true, and if Jackson was indeed suicidal as a result of the charges, the picture becomes cloudier.

What of the Chandlers? Jordan quickly disappeared from public view. And in 2009, less than five months after Jackson's death, Evan was found dead in his New Jersey apartment with a bullet in his head and a gun in his hand. Reportedly, he was in poor health at the time and had been scheduled to see a blood doctor the day he died. Jersey City police spokesperson Stan Eason left little room for doubt about what had happened: "It's straightforward. Case closed. It's suicide."[47]

Chapter 13

HISTORY LESSON

After the Chandler settlement, Michael Jackson returned to Los Angeles ready to put the episode behind him. At least that's how it seemed to Branca when the two drove to Beverly Hills to look at a pair of mansions in the bluffs above Coldwater Canyon Park.

"This is going to be known as the Second Coming," Jackson said as they cruised into the hills. "Come on, we're going to go look at these houses!"[1]

This was a very different Jackson from the one who'd checked into rehab months earlier—desperation had given way to anger, which then became motivation. "I didn't feel like this was a guy on the verge," Branca recalls. "I felt this was a guy who was really pissed off."

The singer had many reasons to feel that way. He'd been accused of one of the most heinous crimes imaginable; as a consequence, his career as both a performer and a businessman seemed to be on the rocks. Some of his advisors were even recommending he start selling off the crown jewels of his empire. But Branca believed there were better options available for Michael Jackson, Inc.

———

In the winter of 1994, Dr. Robotnik crash-landed on Angel Island after a renegade hedgehog wrecked his Death Egg. Concerned for his safety, he enlisted the help of an angry echidna named Knuckles to defend him from the spiny crusader better known as Sonic—

169

and the rivals battled it out as Michael Jackson's music blared in the background.

At least, that's what a few video game enthusiasts concluded years after *Sonic the Hedgehog 3* for Sega Genesis became available in the United States. Jackson wasn't mentioned anywhere in the game, but the soundtrack to one of the levels did sound a lot like a sped-up version of his 1991 song "Who Is It." Following the 1995 debut of the track "Stranger in Moscow," some noticed a strong similarity to the game's end credits. Those claims were confirmed during the reporting of this book—both by Jackson's estate[2] and by Brad Buxer, who played in Jackson's touring band and worked on the game (and is named in its credits).[3]

The process began in early 1993, when Jackson came to Buxer and informed him that their next project would be composing music for *Sonic 3*. Though it's not uncommon for today's music stars to have a hand in video game soundtracks (electronic producer Skrillex has contributed remixes and original music to a handful of first-person shooters; rapper Jay Z executive-produced *NBA 2K13*), Jackson's foray into the game audio world was novel, just as it was when he starred in the 1989 Sega game *Moonwalker*. Both seemed a logical extension of Jackson's ambitions.

"I think he just wanted to do everything," says Buxer, who spent a month with Jackson crafting the tunes for Sega at Record One Studios in Los Angeles. "He always so much wanted to do movies and he was just interested in other platforms to get into musically."

The game ended up coming out months after the Chandlers went public with their accusations. Many observers still believe Jackson's name was removed from the credits because Sega didn't want to be associated with him at that point. In fact, under Jackson's contract, Sega didn't have the right to accord credit to the singer without his consent.[4]

Buxer believes it was Jackson who ultimately decided he didn't want his name on the game—because of its sound quality. The

Genesis console contained a sound chip that wasn't much better than the apparatus used in the ancient Pac-Man arcade games. Sega's programmers had spoken to Jackson prior to beginning work on the project, assuring him that the sound quality for this game would be better than their previous games (such as *Moonwalker*). But the final version of *Sonic 3* still wasn't good enough.

"He was a perfectionist when it came to almost everything," says Buxer. "And one of those things was sound quality. . . . He didn't want his name on it because he wasn't satisfied." Adds Matt Forger, who was also involved in the project: "Dealing with such requirements was something new to both MJ and Brad, as it was common practice to have unlimited resources when creating new music."[5]

Longtime associate Karen Langford gives yet another reason for the exclusion of his name: Sometimes the star didn't want to record music as Michael Jackson and deal with all the scrutiny that came along with it. From time to time, the King of Pop just wanted to have some fun.[6]

Jackson seemed to be enjoying himself outside the studio that year as well. In August of 1994, his mother received a call from her son that she took for one of his typical practical jokes. Michael told her that he'd just married Lisa Marie Presley. Her reply: "No, you did not."[7]

But he insisted they were in a hotel suite in the Dominican Republic, where they'd just been declared man and wife. They'd wanted a small, quiet ceremony so that the press wouldn't find out. Katherine didn't believe her son was telling the truth until Lisa Marie got on the line.

There were others who shared Katherine's initial skepticism. Some theorized the marriage was a plot dreamed up by the Church of Scientology, which reportedly counted Presley as a member, to recruit the world's biggest star[8] (subsequent stories say she defected[9]). Others suggested it was all a public relations move by Jackson; the *Los Angeles Times* summed it up with the headline "Jackson-Presley Union Sparks Shock, Doubt, Laughs."[10]

Some felt the union was very real. "I laughed at the media suggestions that they were 'faking it' because we all knew in the family the intensity of their relationship and how they always wanted to be together," Jermaine wrote. "Michael's joy couldn't have been faked."[11] Presley herself later discussed the relationship on Oprah Winfrey's talk show and confirmed that it was a "consummated" marriage.[12]

Still, there were other theories. Frank Cascio said Jackson told him he tied the knot "for business reasons." He'd just partnered with billionaire Prince Alwaleed Bin Talal—whom he'd met through Charles Bobbit, James Brown's longtime manager—to form a company called Kingdom Entertainment. According to Cascio, Jackson said the Saudi mogul preferred to do business with "family men," hence his decision to wed Lisa Marie.[13]

Jackson and Alwaleed later announced their venture at a packed press conference. They spoke of their desire to create a new media empire with plans to branch into what the prince called "diverse family entertainment," including feature films, hotels, animation, merchandizing, and theme parks. "Until recently, my hectic schedule and outstanding professional commitments left me little time to develop a specific strategy for a fully integrated entertainment company," Jackson explained. "All that began to change about eighteen months ago, when I first met my friend and partner."[14]

Alwaleed invested $20 million in MJJ Music, the joint venture record label formed by Jackson and Sony just a few years earlier. MJJ could also sign new artists—and did, adding girl group Brownstone, as well as 3T, an R&B trio comprised of Tito Jackson's sons that contributed the track "Didn't Mean to Hurt You" to the *Free Willy* soundtrack. The label's joint venture structure enabled Jackson to split its profits with Sony; for his own records, he also still received his industry-leading artist royalty.[15]

One of Jackson and Alwaleed's first dreams was to buy the financially troubled Marvel Comics. With his billionaire friend bringing the bulk of the financing, Jackson believed he could provide the creative brainpower needed to turn some of the company's more marketable names—Iron Man, Spider-Man, and all of the X-Men, to name a few—into Hollywood blockbusters.[16]

But complications arose due to Marvel's bankruptcy proceedings, and Jackson wasn't able to put a deal together.[17] Had he been able to follow through on his instincts and acquire a piece of the company, he would have shared in the profits of the superhero film boom—and, perhaps, in the $4 billion Disney paid for the company in 2009.[18] (Through a spokesperson who confirmed "several initial dealings" with Jackson in the mid-1990s, Alwaleed declined to be interviewed for this book.[19])

Meanwhile, Branca started looking for ways to create some liquidity for Jackson. To pay the Chandler settlement, the singer had taken out more cash on the credit line he'd opened to fund the initial ATV acquisition, and he needed to start generating more income to keep the debt levels from getting out of hand. After the battering Jackson's image took in the wake of the Chandler scandal, endorsement deals like the ones he'd signed with Pepsi and ventures like his clothing and shoe lines were no longer likely. And monetizing fame through agreements of that ilk was becoming less fashionable, at least in the music world, as the anti-establishment grunge movement—led by shaggy anti-corporate bands like Pearl Jam and Soundgarden—replaced the glamor and glitz of the late 1980s and early 1990s pop.

Behind-the-scenes deals like Jackson's proposed investment in Marvel made more sense for the time being, but Jackson's finances had been badly strained by the events of the previous year. Branca saw an opening with Sony, which was eager to bolster its publishing catalogue and was likely regretting the 1986 sale of CBS Songs for $125 million. He knew that the $75 million the company had offered for half of ATV was simply a starting point.

Branca began negotiating with Sony's chairman, Mickey Schulhof, to merge Jackson's catalogue with Sony's rather than sell it off altogether. This time, Jackson wasn't in the midst of a potentially career-threatening scandal, giving him the leverage to hammer out a deal with much more favorable terms. The agreement created a 50–50 joint venture called Sony/ATV; the company paid Jackson $115 million for the privilege of merging its less-valuable catalogue with his,[20] plus an annual guarantee just shy of $10 million that has since been negotiated upwards.[21]

More important, the deal established a partnership instead of a sale (in addition, Jackson maintained complete ownership of the copyrights held under Mijac Music, both his compositions and those by other songwriters). In just ten years, Michael Jackson, Inc. had netted over $100 million—and an extremely valuable joint venture— as a result of the ATV purchase.

Before finalizing the agreement with Sony, Branca called Marty Bandier, then chief of rival EMI Publishing, which had been handling the administration of the ATV catalogue, to see if he could get a better offer. But Sony's proposal was "an incredible deal,'" even according to Bandier.

"To sell your copyrights and keep half of them . . . that was a strategic deal that Sony made because they wanted, they understood that they needed to get back in the music publishing business," he says. "And they made a decision that they might overpay."[22] Adds Sony's Mottola: "It was a good deal for everybody involved; certainly it was an incredible deal for us."[23]

Bandier couldn't match the offer—that would have entailed giving Jackson half of EMI Publishing, which at that point was worth considerably more than either of the catalogues that formed Sony/ATV—and the two sides worked out a "reasonable" buyout of their agreement. Jackson and Branca also stipulated that Sony couldn't enter the music publishing business in any other form or capacity besides Sony/ATV, or force Jackson to sell his stake in the venture. That meant Sony was heavily incentivized to help Jackson realize his dream of having the world's top music publishing company.[24]

In the long term, the combined entity would grow to be worth billions. And in the short term, though Jackson was just two years removed from the worst ordeal of his personal and professional life, 1995 was shaping up to be one of the most lucrative years of his career.

———

In the mid-1990s, hip-hop was in the midst of a journey from the burned-out streets of the South Bronx to the top of the mainstream music world, and the genre found an unlikely champion in Michael Jackson.

Before recording his follow-up to *Dangerous*, the King of Pop had been paying close attention to the trends in popular music, as was his habit. A young rapper who went by the name Notorious B.I.G. had just released his debut, *Ready to Die*. Thanks to his knack for capturing the pace of life in Brooklyn's roughest neighborhoods with just the right mix of humor, bravado, and catchy samples, his singles were creeping up the *Billboard* charts. Jackson invited him to the recording studio.

"Michael was probably one of the most intuitive, up-to-date artists there was," recalls Sean "Diddy" Combs, whose Bad Boy Records had released B.I.G.'s debut. "[Jackson] knew hip-hop like he was born in the South Bronx in the eighties. He knew everything that was going on . . . and when I met him and he wanted to do something with Biggie, it wasn't anything surprising. Almost every dance he did, it was made up that week. He was strong enough and brave enough to recognize greatness in other forms, and he was great to recognize Biggie."[25]

The rapper appeared on the album that would become *HIStory: Past, Present and Future: Book I*, released in July 1995, as did NBA legend and occasional hip-hop artist Shaquille O'Neal. Their cameos offered moments of levity on an album that mostly focused on heavy subject matter—a rebuttal to the charges Jackson had faced, commentary on the scrutiny under which he lived, and a defense of his very humanity.

The double album consisted of one disc filled with his greatest hits, from "Billie Jean" to "Man in the Mirror," and another that contained fifteen new songs. None of the fresh material was produced by Quincy Jones or Teddy Riley (the latter initially considered giving Jackson the smash single "No Diggity," but at the behest of Interscope chief Jimmy Iovine, he decided to have his own group Blackstreet record it instead[26]). With only a few exceptions, Jackson was the sole credited songwriter and producer on *HIStory*'s new tracks, most of which were accordingly personal.

"Tired of injustice, tired of the schemes," he spits on "Scream," a duet with his sister Janet.[27] On the song "D.S.," in which he references a character named Dom Sheldon (a thinly veiled proxy for Tom Sneddon, the Santa Barbara district attorney who'd authorized the Neverland raid and the strip search of Jackson), the singer insists that "they wanna get my ass dead or alive."[28]

The album had plenty of other memorable moments, from the vulnerable, haunting "Stranger in Moscow" to the R. Kelly–penned "You Are Not Alone," a track whose sound would be replicated ad nauseam during the boy band craze of the late 1990s. But it was the raging rock ballad "They Don't Care About Us" that drew the most attention, at least at first, and not for the reasons Jackson wanted.

About a dozen lines into the song, he says, "Jew me, sue me, everybody do me / Kick me, kike me, don't you black or white me."[29] The *New York Times* called the lyrics "a burst of anti-Semitism" days before the album was released, and Jackson was slammed by scores of media outlets and organizations including the Anti-Defamation League (interestingly, the *Times* also opined that Jackson remained "one of the most gifted musicians alive").[30]

Jackson insisted that he'd been misunderstood, and apologized for any pain he'd caused. In a press release issued days later, ADL director Abraham Foxman said, "We have always believed that Mr. Jackson never intentionally meant to be offensive."[31]

The damage had been done, though, both externally and internally. Shortly after the *Times* review was published, Jackson asked Gallin, who is Jewish, to go on television and explain that he wasn't an anti-Semite. Gallin knew his client didn't have a bias against Jews, but didn't think getting on the talk show circuit was a good idea. He figured nobody knew who he was, and that they'd expect Jackson's manager to stand up for him anyway.

In fact, Jackson thought all his Jewish friends, including David Geffen and Steven Spielberg, would take to the airwaves to defend him. He soon found they shared Gallin's view. "I don't think they really thought he was anti-Semitic," says the manager. "But they weren't going to go on television. He wrote the lyric and he had to stop and explain it."[32]

This only made Jackson push Gallin harder, to no avail. "He tried to convince me to do it," Gallin recalls. "I knew it was the wrong thing to do, I wouldn't do it. He was very upset about all of this, and he thought that maybe I thought he was anti-Semitic. And he fired me."

Jackson immediately stopped talking to Gallin, and his relationships with Geffen and Spielberg suffered a similar fate. The firestorm came at a bad time for Sony, which had paid Jackson $50 million in advances for the album and reportedly spent $30 million on promotion (which included loading massive statues of Jackson onto barges and floating them down rivers in major European cities). They'd been hoping *HIStory* would sell 20 million copies.[33]

Despite the negative publicity, the album did eventually meet those lofty goals, making it the bestselling double-disc set of all time. And Jackson wanted a tour to match. As usual, his goal was perfection, and in an effort to prove to the world that he was back and bigger than ever, he was willing to spend just about anything to make that happen.

Jackson selected a stage setup so large that it couldn't fit into a 747; instead, his team had to use the world's largest plane, the Russian-made Antonov An-225.[34] The craft was initially designed to carry Soviet space shuttles on its back, boasting a payload capacity of 551,150 pounds (the equivalent of about ninety full-grown elephants[35]). Nearly the length of a football field, the An-225 was big enough to accommodate objects up to 230 feet long and 33 feet in diameter.[36] The planes were too big to land at many civilian airports, so Jackson often had to shell out $200,000 for landing fees at military fields.[37]

"There was always someone in Michael's life like [accountant] Marshall Gelfand who would say to him, 'Look what this is costing,'" says Branca. "And the response always was, 'I'm the artist here, I know what I'm doing, this is my vision, this is the way we're going to do it.'"

Then there were lodging fees for security guards, publicists, and managers; the latter group included Tarak Ben Ammar, a Tunisian businessman whom Prince Alwaleed had introduced to Jackson and who briefly served as his manager. Another figure who maneuvered his way into the singer's life around this time was Dieter Wiesner, a German operator with a penchant for tale-telling[38] who'd promised to help launch a Jackson-themed energy beverage called Mystery Drink. Though the product fizzled, Wiesner somehow gained the singer's trust and ended up as one of his advisors.[39]

The tour went on to gross $165 million,[40] but Jackson also had to cover the massive cost of loading his stage in and out of fifty-eight cities in thirty-five countries around the globe (he didn't play any shows in the continental United States). All in all, Jackson likely cleared only about $10 million to $20 million for the entire excursion—about 10 percent of the gross.[41] Most big pop tours take in closer to 30 percent. Profits weren't the only casualty of the *HIStory* album cycle: Jackson and Presley's relationship started to deteriorate not long after it began.

"Their worlds revolved around them—but that dynamic made it hard for them to take care of each other," wrote Frank Cascio, who'd remained friends with Jackson. In late 1995, the King of Pop and the King's daughter parted ways,[42] and Presley filed for divorce in January 1996. Around the same time, *Wiz* director Joel Schumacher received a phone call from Jackson. The two hadn't spoken much over the years, and now the singer was asking the director about landing the role of the Riddler in his 1995 film *Batman Forever*. "I didn't think that was an appropriate role for him," says Schumacher. "[But] he was always very sweet with me on the phone."[43]

When Jackson called again after the *HIStory* tour to see if he'd be interested in directing a film, Schumacher was more than willing to take a meeting. He joined the King of Pop in a very large conference room filled with a mix of security guards and creative types, and prepared to listen to a pitch.

Jackson had envisioned a film about a protagonist who lived in the shadows of an imaginary city. ("A little Dickensian," says Schumacher. "Although not period.") He would only come out at night, to help children—particularly the orphans, the rejects, the needy—but the rest of the townspeople thought he was a monster.

"[It] can be read as any kind of metaphor you want," says Schumacher. "I did not think I was right for that project but thanked him for thinking of me and gave him a hug. And never saw him again, except on television."

Jackson would go on to release the film, *Michael Jackson's Ghosts*, which he scored, produced, and wrote (along with Stephen King). He also played five different roles himself, including the villain—the town's chunky, pasty mayor—and the film's misunderstood protagonist, the Maestro. After a much-ballyhooed premier at the 1997 Cannes Film Festival, the production was released straight to television and video;[44] it seemed a different sort of specter continued to haunt Jackson.

"It was always his desire to be in the movies . . . but I do know

there was a doubt and a shadow cast upon Michael," Schumacher remembers. "And I don't know if that affected people's thinking [that]
he was bankable or viable."

In the late 1990s, Jackson added a new title to his résumé: father.
Shortly after splitting with Lisa Marie Presley in 1996, he married
Debbie Rowe, the longtime nurse of his dermatologist. That relationship ended in a generally amicable divorce in 1999, but resulted
in the birth of Jackson's first two children—Michael Joseph Jackson
Jr., in 1997, known as Prince, and Paris-Michael Katherine Jackson,
in 1998 (his third, Prince Michael Jackson II, known as Blanket, was
born in 2002 by a still-undisclosed mother).

There was more than grandiosity at play when Michael Jackson
named his sons. The singer's great-great-grandfather was a cotton
plantation slave in Alabama who passed on his name, Prince, to his
son and grandson. The latter moved north to Indiana to work as a
Pullman porter. "So the ridiculous moniker given by a white man
to his black slave, the way you might name a dog, was bestowed by
a black king upon his pale-skinned sons and heirs," explains writer
John Jeremiah Sullivan.[45]

In 1997, Jackson released *Blood on the Dance Floor: HIStory in the
Mix*, which included eight remixed tracks from his prior album and
five fresh songs. The effort earned praise from some and complaints
from others expecting a traditional full-length studio effort. Though
sales started slowly, the album would go on to move over 11 million
copies worldwide—making it the most successful remix album of all
time.[46]

Most of the new material was penned and produced by Jackson
himself, and the album's dark subject matter gave listeners a window
into the reality of his life. He sings prophetically about the allure of
painkillers like Demerol on "Morphine," and of marginalization and
alienation in "Is It Scary."

"The best writers write what they know, and this is what he knew, and this is what he experienced—this was his way of telling people what was happening to him," says sound engineer Matt Forger, adding: "He was often in pain due to various physical conditions and injuries. One can only imagine what this was like."[47]

By the late 1990s, Jackson was leaving more and more of his business to the new advisors who seemed to be popping up with the haphazardness and frequency of dandelions on a poorly maintained lawn. They ranged from sketchy (Dieter Wiesner, of Mystery Drink infamy) to random (Al Malnik, a Florida real estate mogul) to—occasionally—logical (music executive John McClain).

The latter did not grant an interview for this book and rarely speaks to the press, but former ATV president Dale Kawashima describes him as "a very smart, sharp person who actually knew Michael Jackson and the Jacksons as a kid growing up as a family friend."[48] McClain started out at A&M Records in the early 1980s and was the driving force behind Janet Jackson's 1986 breakout *Control*. He later moved on to Interscope, eventually convincing label boss Jimmy Iovine to go into business with Death Row Records and hip-hop legend Dr. Dre.[49]

At the dawn of the new millennium, McClain became one of Michael Jackson's managers alongside Trudy Green (who has also managed Aerosmith, Def Leppard, and others), but the singer still handled some moves himself. In 1999, he met with Kawashima to discuss reuniting to make some more publishing acquisitions, namely a catalogue owned by legendary songwriters Jerry Leiber and Mike Stoller. This wasn't the famous set of their own copyrights that included Elvis Presley's biggest hits ("Hound Dog," "Jailhouse Rock" and others, which Sony/ATV would buy in 2007 for $65 million). Rather, it was a catalogue of songs they'd purchased as investments, including hits like "Tie a Yellow Ribbon 'Round the Ole Oak Tree"[50] (named one of the one hundred biggest songs of all time by *Billboard*[51]).

Before Jackson left on a trip to Africa, where his itinerary included an audience with Nelson Mandela, he asked Kawashima to look into what it might take to buy the catalogue—and made sure to check in. "Dale, it's Michael Jackson calling," the King of Pop said a few days later in a voice message Kawashima played for me. "I'm in Africa right now. I hope you are getting the work done . . . don't forget our major goal, the acquisition." A couple of weeks later, Kawashima received another phone message from Jackson saying that he wouldn't be able to rehire him after all. It seemed the King of Pop was short on funds, and the deal fizzled.[52]

That same year, Jackson was performing a charity show in Munich when something reminiscent of his Pepsi commercial accident occurred. While singing "Earth Song" from the top of a hydraulic bridge onstage, the structure suddenly malfunctioned, sending it plummeting from a four-story height—with Jackson on board. A last-second emergency stop button triggered by a nearby engineer slowed his fall, and may have saved his life, but he still had a very rough landing.[53]

Incredibly, Jackson got back to his feet and completed his performance, only to pass out as soon as he arrived backstage. He was rushed to the hospital to treat a back injury that, according to Jermaine and others, troubled him for the rest of his life—and led him to seek more prescription drugs to relieve the pain. Perhaps more ominous, given the circumstances of Jackson's eventual demise, were his words to a band member who'd been with him that night in Germany: "Joseph always taught us that no matter what, the show must go on."[54]

Chapter 14

INVINCIBLE?

In a penthouse suite one hundred feet above the streets of Beverly Hills, Justin Bieber sits at the head of a glass table, musing on his recent successes. It's the spring of 2012—before any major publicity gaffes or run-ins with the law—and he has ridden the last crest of his cherubic adolescence to earnings of $108 million in two years.

He and manager Scooter Braun explain their guiding philosophies: don't endorse products you don't like, and include a charitable component in every deal. When I ask them if there's any artist Bieber is directly trying to emulate, both in terms of music and business, they share a knowing glance.

"For me, it's only one person," says Bieber. "Michael Jackson."[1]

From his early days, the Canadian singer has tried to model his career after the King of Pop's, part of the reason he picked Rodney Jerkins to produce a handful of tracks for his album *Believe*. The Grammy-winning hitmaker was among the principal architects of *Invincible*, Jackson's final studio album.

Having a manager who discovered him as a teenaged YouTube sensation didn't stop Bieber from getting into a great deal of trouble. By the time the King of Pop linked up with Jerkins, he had even less of a support structure in place.

"Michael had always felt like he had to look over his shoulder," says Jerkins. "There were a lot of trust issues."[2]

Jackson started working on *Invincible* in 1997, shortly after returning from the HIStory Tour. It seemed he'd have little trouble completing an album within the next couple of years, which would keep him on the same four-to-five-year cycle he'd followed during much of his solo career.

The studio experience had changed quite a bit over Jackson's twenty years as a solo artist. In the *Thriller* days, the record industry was totally reliant on magnetic tapes; by the mid-1990s, most acts recorded on analog tapes before transferring songs to digital hard drives. At the dawn of the new millennium, recording directly to computers became the standard, opening the door to nearly limitless options for sound manipulation.[3]

"Having more options and more possibilities doesn't reduce the time that you invest in something," says sound engineer Matt Forger. "It actually increases the time that you invest in something. So consequently, things just grew."

Jackson had another reason for wanting to take his time with the album. He believed he could get out of his latest Sony contract in 2000 and simply sell the new material to the highest bidder. Back when he signed his first solo contract with Sony's predecessor, CBS, Branca had insisted that the agreement be governed by California law, which would allow Jackson to terminate it after seven years if he saw fit. The singer assumed the same statutes held true.

As Jackson discovered in the mid-1990s, however, the contract had been reworked by one of Branca's replacements. Three albums were added to his original five-album deal, along with massive penalties for early termination—as much as $20 million for each album he didn't complete—which effectively nullified the benefits of the California law clause. Jackson eventually determined that he could leave the label only after delivering *Invincible* and a greatest hits album.

To make matters worse, Jackson's old ally Walter Yetnikoff was long gone, and Tommy Mottola had been running Sony's music division for nearly a decade. He helmed a label that was home to legacy acts such as Bruce Springsteen, Céline Dion, and Billy Joel while launching the careers of artists including Jennifer Lopez and Mariah Carey, whom he married in 1993 (and would divorce five years later). When it came to *Invincible*, he and Jackson clashed over recording budgets. "[I] considered an album that would cost $1 million like an overtly expensive, crazy, ridiculously expensive album," Mottola explains.[4]

Jackson's latest effort would end up costing far more. At one point during the recording process, he was running six studios simultaneously—each with its own producers and engineers—working around the clock, whether he was there or not. Says sound engineer Bruce Swedien, who worked on the album: "Anybody else would have settled for Michael's take number one. . . . He wanted to make it as perfect as he possibly could."[5]

Jackson had always admired the great draftsmen of the world. But even for Picasso, there would come a point when another brushstroke wouldn't improve a painting, and might even hurt it. In the current iteration of Michael Jackson, Inc., there were no longer any advisors who could tell Jackson when to stop trying to improve his musical canvases. "Not one central figure or anybody saying, 'No, I don't advise you to do this,'" recalls Mottola, who estimates that *Invincible* ended up costing Sony $30 million to $40 million. "Because if he said, 'No,' Michael would go to the next person who would say 'Yes.'"

By this point, Jackson's personal expenses might have made even Prince Alwaleed blush. Neverland had a hundred and twenty employees at its peak. There were bills for everything from flowers to flamingos, not to mention the additional staff needed to handle the busloads of underprivileged children whose visits continued even when Jackson wasn't around. Then there were the expenses for Jackson and his entourage. All in all, the singer's overhead was approaching $20 million per year in the early 2000s.

That was fine even half a decade earlier, when Jackson earned nearly $200 million in a span of two years. But as the new millennium dawned with *Invincible* still incomplete, there were five years between Jackson and his last studio album—and seven since he'd played a concert in the continental United States. He hadn't gotten an endorsement deal after the Chandler allegations, either, and his spending had overtaken his income.

Jackson would have been in immediate trouble if it weren't for his half of the Sony/ATV catalogue, which enabled him to continue to take out loans to support his lifestyle and provided some income as well. Coupled with continued sales of his own music, he was still pulling in low double-digit millions—and he remained quite cognizant of the value of his copyrights.

"I learned the publishing game by Michael," says Jerkins. "He taught me . . . how to locate the right catalogues to buy."[6]

———

Jackson finally completed *Invincible* after four years of recording, and Sony set the launch date for October 30, 2001. The year marked Jackson's thirtieth as a solo artist, and he decided to plan two anniversary concerts at Madison Square Garden to celebrate.

His friend David Gest, a concert promoter and sometime reality television star, agreed to produce the show; Frank Cascio, now an adult, had become Jackson's personal assistant and headed up the planning behind the scenes. The latter had developed some concerns that went beyond staging the show—he was worried that Jackson was relying increasingly on "medicine," his code name for prescription painkillers.[7]

Cascio had tried a number of times, unsuccessfully, to confront Jackson. He was so worried that, in September, he approached Randy, Tito, and Janet Jackson and explained the situation. They eventually tried to stage an intervention, but Michael insisted everything was fine. "My family talked to me about my medicine," he told Cascio. "They were out of line."

If something was wrong with Jackson, it wasn't readily apparent to the outside world at his anniversary concerts. Both shows featured a solo set by the King of Pop, a Jackson 5 mini-reunion, and performances by stars including Britney Spears, Usher, and Gloria Estefan. After the second show—on September 10—Michael retired to the Helmsley Palace hotel, while the brothers checked into the Plaza nearby. When they went to sleep that night, they had no idea they'd wake up in a different world.[8]

September 11 dawned cool and crisp in New York without a cloud in the sky, but by the middle of the day, the atmosphere was choked with thick black smoke billowing from the ruins of the World Trade Center. Almost immediately, Jackson started thinking about how he could release his song "What More Can I Give" as a charity single, aiming to raise money for the families of those who perished in the attacks. But according to Cascio, Sony was more concerned with Jackson's next album; the single was never officially released, escalating the tension between Mottola and Jackson.

Invincible debuted at number 1 on the *Billboard* charts the following month, selling 366,000 copies in its opening week—slightly less than *HIStory*, but enough to handily defeat new albums by Enrique Iglesias and the Backstreet Boys.[9] Initial reviews were mixed, typified by the *New York Times*, which both praised Jackson as the "skillful musician at work in the album's multitracked marvels" and concluded that "there's no joy or humor in it."[10] The numbers, however, said he was still the King of Pop.

Jackson had hoped to go on tour following the release of the album, but decided against it after the September 11 attacks (though he'd been offered $100 million to do so[11]). Had he performed even a handful of shows in the following year, he would have given *Invincible*—not to mention his own bank account—a much-needed boost.

In the months before the album's release, Jackson's relationship with Mottola soured further when the latter purportedly tried to impress someone by walking into one of the singer's recording sessions unannounced, only to find that Jackson wouldn't let him in. As the story goes, Mottola reacted by sending him a nasty fax.[12]

Perhaps because of the bubbling vendetta between Jackson and Mottola, perhaps because of the singer's decision not to tour, Sony stopped promoting Jackson's latest work after just two months. By contrast, they'd spent two *years* promoting *Dangerous* and *HIStory*. The label released only three singles and two videos (one of which Jackson didn't appear in because of his feud with Sony).

Jackson seemed to think Sony wanted his album to fail. If his cash flow issues worsened, he might have trouble making payments on a $200 million loan administered by Bank of America and secured by his stake in Sony/ATV.[13] So, in July 2002, Jackson went to New York to publicly express his dissatisfaction with his label. At a press conference in Harlem with activist Al Sharpton, he took the stage to speak about the plight of black artists in the music business, an exploitative history that he'd learned as a youngster and fought to avoid as an adult.

"Throughout the years, black artists have been taken advantage of, completely," he told the crowd. "It's time now that we have to put a stop to this incredible, incredible injustice."[14]

Jackson went on to cite examples from James Brown to Sammy Davis Jr., praising them as artists who inspired and paved the way for him. After a few moments, he went on the offensive. He singled out Sony and Mottola, calling the latter "a racist" and "very, very, very devilish." Later, he paraded around New York atop a double-decker bus, at one point holding up a sign that showed Mottola's face with devil horns drawn on in red.

When asked about his reaction to Jackson's theory that Sony was trying to ruin Jackson's career in order to gain full control of Sony/ATV, Mottola, who left the company in 2003, was predictably emphatic with his denials. "It's total bullshit," he said. "Why would any-one sabotage anything when you're there to make money? That's the same as people saying our government was part of the 9/11 con-spiracy. I mean, come on."[15]

Shortly after Jackson's barrage, Al Sharpton went on record say-ing he didn't believe Mottola was a racist, and that he hadn't known what the singer was going to say ahead of time.[16] Around the same time, Jackson received a call from Berry Gordy, who'd seen the media coverage of the comments. The Motown founder told Jack-son he shouldn't be playing "the race card" and advised him not to do it again.

"We've never done that," Gordy explained to his onetime protégé. "Our philosophy is there's music for all people, and it's not about white and black. And we can't [do that], especially you, be-cause you've never felt that way. You're angry now, you're bitter now. Think it over."[17]

"I agree with you," replied Jackson. "I don't have to think it over . . . I'm so glad you called me."

Jackson promised Gordy he wouldn't repeat the incident. But he'd never be able to shake the feeling that his catalogue—and the wealth it generated—made him a target on many different levels. That fear was likely the reason he agreed to have an attorney named David LeGrand investigate just about every one of his advisors in 2003, including John Branca.[18]

LeGrand wondered if Branca and Mottola were somehow con-spiring to defraud Jackson, funneling away his cash to offshore bank accounts. Though there wasn't any proof of such a scheme to begin with, the theory was enough for the singer, who sent Branca a one-page letter informing him that he and his firm had been terminated, effective immediately. Jackson gave no reason for the move, explain-ing only that LeGrand would be his new attorney.[19]

LeGrand then hired Interfor, a private intelligence company reportedly run by former Israeli Mossad agents, to look into the

matter. Though the agency did suggest it might be possible to un-
cover a potential offshore scheme if it had "additional time and a
proper budget," it was unable to find any signs of impropriety.[20]

In the end, the incident turned out to be nothing more than a
witch hunt. LeGrand was later asked under oath if he'd found any
fraud on Branca's part. His reply: "I was given no credible evidence
to support those charges."[21]

––––––––

As new operatives parachuted into the power vacuum at Michael
Jackson, Inc., the news emanating from the King of Pop's sphere
seemed to grow more bizarre by the day.

In April 2003, *Vanity Fair* reported that Seoul-based lawyer Myung-Ho Lee—yet another "business advisor"—had wired
$150,000 to Mali at Jackson's insistence. As the story goes, the recip-
ient of the payment was a voodoo chief named Baba, who arranged
for forty-two cows to be sacrificed in a ritual meant to curse Jackson's former pals Geffen and Spielberg.[22]

And then there was the "baby-dangling" incident, where Jackson
appeared at the window of a Berlin hotel and held one of his children out over the safety bars for a crowd of onlookers to see. The
spectacle prompted German authorities to launch an investigation,
and Jackson to issue a statement apologizing for his "terrible decision."[23] But was it a sign of madness or a strategic miscalculation?
"Michael Jackson is about as crazy as Colin Powell," photographer
Harry Benson told *Vanity Fair*. "He knows everything he is doing.
He holds his baby over the balcony and everybody goes crazy, but
he's in every newspaper around the world."

It seemed that Jackson had fallen back into his *Bad*-era overreli-
ance on the teachings of P. T. Barnum: that any publicity was good
publicity. The incident in Germany was not. It's certainly possible
that he planted the voodoo story; like the Elephant Man bones incident, however, it was too strange regardless of whether it was real.

And with no album or tour to promote, it was unclear what good the publicity would have done, anyway.

Even as the strange stories continued to trickle out, Jackson did seem to be focused on building businesses that could replace the physically grueling process of touring as a major income stream in the next phase of his career. This was a much wiser emulation of Barnum, who in *Humbug* described himself as "thoroughly disgusted with the life of an itinerant showman"; he preferred to have "a respectable, permanent business."[24]

To that end, Jackson had renewed his interest in buying Marvel. The US economy was in a rut after the tech bubble popped, and stocks were at their lowest levels in half a decade, meaning that some of the best entertainment companies could be had at bargain rates. Jackson's advisor Dieter Wiesner says he put together a consortium of investors—including banks in Germany, Switzerland, and the US—and they were ready to meet Marvel's $1.4 billion asking price. Jackson told him to start the bidding at $900 million.

"His plan was just unbelievable," Wiesner recalls. "He was saying, 'Dieter, we have to have all the rights. On the one side, I have this Beatles catalogue, I have this Mijac catalogue. On the other side, I will have this Marvel catalogue with forty-eight hundred different characters like Spider-Man, Incredible Hulk, all these things.' He knew exactly what he wanted to do."[25]

Wiesner says Jackson was also working on a multimillion-dollar deal to become the face of the new Mercedes-Benz SLR McLaren, a $500,000 supercar that boasted gull-wing doors and a 625-horsepower V-8 engine. His name would be inscribed on the inside of every door, and an animated King of Pop would moonwalk across the speedometer each time the car started. Wiesner also claims Jackson was doing creative consulting for various Las Vegas properties—and that the singer conceived both the volcano at the Mirage and the fountains at the Bellagio.

But in Wiesner, it seems Jackson might have found an advisor whose humbuggery could rival P. T. Barnum's. Representatives of Mercedes-Benz couldn't confirm that a project with the singer ever existed.[26] A spokesperson for MGM said that Jackson did have conversations with casino billionaire Steve Wynn, and did create music for a Siegfried and Roy show. The rest, however, was a mirage: "Michael was not involved with the fountains or the volcano in any way."[27]

The King of Pop had dismissed the close advisors who'd helped him build his empire, his court had been infiltrated by jesters, and his entire kingdom was now in jeopardy.

———

In 2002, Jackson received a request from a British filmmaker named Martin Bashir, who wanted to spend the better part of a year following the singer around Neverland to make a documentary called *Living with Michael Jackson*. Ten years earlier, Oprah Winfrey's interview had painted him in a reasonably positive light, and perhaps Jackson thought Bashir's work might have a similar effect.

But when the video aired in February 2003, it quickly became apparent that Bashir was seeking a different angle. His piece focused heavily on the King of Pop's changing physical appearance and his relationships with children. In one scene, Jackson discussed sharing a bedroom with Gavin Arvizo, a thirteen-year-old cancer survivor he'd invited to Neverland numerous times (the boy would stay in Jackson's bed while the singer slept on the floor nearby).[28]

Viewers assumed the worst, though, and Jackson's reputation was shattered once again. Hoping to stave off further devastation, Jackson rushed to create a way to show that Bashir had cherry-picked the most unflattering parts of his time at Neverland. With the help of the singer's own videographer, Hamid Moslehi, the "rebuttal video" aired on Fox weeks later; a collection of home videos followed in April (according to court documents later filed by Moslehi claiming he hadn't been paid, Jackson received $13 million for the two videos).[29]

The rebuttal seemed to reveal that Bashir had an agenda. On camera, the filmmaker called Neverland "a dangerous place for a vulnerable child to be." Off camera, he lavished praise upon Jackson: "Your relationship with your children is spectacular . . . it almost makes me weep when I see you with them." At one point, Bashir even asked the singer, "Do you sometimes despair at human nature? Can you ever do anything right?"[30]

For a few months, it seemed that Jackson's rebuttal had been sufficient, and that the scandal had blown over. But in the fall of 2003, about ten years after Jackson's settlement with the Chandlers, the Arvizos formally accused the singer of child molestation. The charges also included administering an intoxicating agent to a minor, false imprisonment, and extortion. The King of Pop was in Las Vegas when he heard that Neverland had been raided again. Unable to believe that the same nightmare was unfolding, he snapped— throwing chairs, knocking over tables, and generally smashing everything in sight.[31]

When Jackson recovered, he turned to his first choice for legal representation: Los Angeles lawyer Tom Mesereau, a Harvard grad with a shock of shoulder-length white hair and a reputation for doing pro bono work in the black community, particularly on cases that involved the death penalty. But he was busy preparing to defend Robert Blake in his murder trial and declined. When Mesereau withdrew himself from that case (due to "a falling out over some internal matters"), he received a call from Randy Jackson, who'd taken over as his brother's de facto business manager.

"Tom, we've always wanted you," Randy explained. "Johnnie Cochran always said you're the best . . . he said that if we were in trouble, he'd want you defending [Michael] and you were the one that could win."[32]

Mesereau agreed to speak with Randy and Michael in person,

and flew to Florida, where they'd been staying. The lawyer remembers Jackson being very quiet, sitting in the back of the room. His only questions had to do with who Mesereau was, how he lived his life, and how he approached his profession. Apparently the attorney's answers were enough for Jackson; Mesereau and his partner, Susan Yu, took over less than two weeks later.

One of the first things Mesereau noticed was the leadership structure of Michael Jackson, Inc., which was such a mess that the *Los Angeles Times* ran a feature trying to sort through the singer's long list of past and present advisors. Among them: Leonard Muhammad, who was known for running a series of allegedly deadbeat soap companies affiliated with the Nation of Islam until landing a role running Jackson's security and business operations, and Marc Schaffel, a director and producer of porn movies who had helped film two TV specials for Jackson.[33] Wiesner, meanwhile, had returned to Germany after the Nation of Islam became involved with Jackson's finances.

"I would have thought the world of Michael Jackson, when I met him, would be run like a major corporation," says Mesereau. "And I found out it wasn't true. This is a man who could wake up on any given morning and if he wanted to make millions of dollars somewhere in the world, he could do it. . . . If he wanted to go to any continent, any country, he could do it. So why does he have these mediocre advisors whispering in his ear?"

Mesereau plunged directly into his task. He moved to Santa Maria, where oral arguments began in early 2005. Not wanting to attract any attention from the legions of media members who'd flooded the town, he lived like a monk for six months, eschewing bars and restaurants and going to bed every night at eight o'clock. He spent most of his waking hours in a duplex that he called the War Room, accompanied by binders upon binders of material on the case.

As he grew to know Jackson better, Mesereau came to see that Jackson was much different from the caricature commonly portrayed in the press. He was thoughtful, kind, and incredibly well read—the singer frequented many of the same used book stores as Mesereau. Jackson also knew the cultural history of the United States all too well, and saw himself as a modern-day version of early twentieth-century boxing champ Jack Johnson: a black man who'd won a white man's game and was in danger of being taken down on false charges.

But Jackson also understood Mesereau's insistence on keeping the likes of Al Sharpton and Jesse Jackson from turning the case into a cause célèbre and potentially alienating a jury that didn't include a single black person. That didn't sit well with another member of Jackson's retinue—Raymone Bain, a boxing-agent-turned-music-publicist who'd taken over as his spokesperson; she had asked both men to come to the trial. Jesse Jackson showed up in Santa Maria; she told Mesereau it was a matter of protecting Michael's legacy.

"If Michael Jackson is convicted, his legacy is going to be dying in a California State prison," countered Mesereau. "We're not going to make a racial issue out of this." (Bain was relieved of her duties shortly thereafter.)[34]

The case against Jackson hinged not only on proving that the singer had plied Arvizo with alcohol and molested him. To nail him on charges of extortion, the prosecution tried to establish that the King of Pop was somehow so desperate financially that he would decide to hold an impoverished family hostage in order to extort cash from them—and called an expert witness who seemed to have little idea of what the Sony/ATV catalogue contained (he couldn't name any songwriters added in the past year), even though that was a crucial component of its future value.[35]

Jackson had always been hyper-aware of his catalogue's worth, and the trial only underscored this for him. He'd call Mesereau and Yu in the middle of the night to thank them for doing such a good job—and to beg them not to let anyone pay them off to deliberately lose his case.

"He *clearly* thought the catalogue made him a target," says Mesereau. "That various interests wanted his catalogue and would do anything to see him destroyed to get his catalogue, would want to see him in prison so he couldn't fend off lawsuits."

Jackson got up every morning at around four o'clock to get dressed and groomed before making the thirty-five-mile journey from Neverland to the courthouse. Rather than insist that Jackson don a Brooks Brothers suit and a tie, Mesereau told Jackson to wear whatever he pleased—to be himself. On Cinco de Mayo, for example, he wore a red, white, and green vest.

As the trial wore on, the prosecution tried to bolster its case by calling witnesses who claimed to have seen Jackson fondling other boys at Neverland. But when former Neverland employee Philip LeMarque testified that he'd seen Jackson grope Macaulay Culkin, he admitted upon further questioning from Mesereau that he'd investigated the possibility of selling the story to the tabloids—and was told he could get $100,000 if Jackson's hand was outside of Culkin's shorts, but $500,000 if it was inside.[36] Later on in the trial, Culkin took the stand and vehemently denied that Jackson had ever behaved inappropriately around him, calling the allegations of abuse "absolutely ridiculous."[37]

Chris Tucker and Jay Leno also showed up as witnesses for the defense. Mesereau remembers being impressed that both, as well as Culkin, made the trek to Santa Maria. He figured their agents, managers, and lawyers would advise them against testifying for the same reason his own friends had discouraged him from defending Jackson—"he's going down, he's going to prison, you're going to be ruined"—but their attitude, he says, was simple: "Michael needs us, we're there."[38]

A new picture of the Arvizos began to emerge. Both Leno and Tucker revealed that the family had contacted them numerous times through various charitable organizations; Leno noted that the child's remarks had seemed "scripted," while Tucker admitted to wiring the family $1,500 after they'd hounded him for a donation.[39]

Gavin's mother didn't do herself any favors. After revealing that she and her husband had been arrested in 2001 after Gavin stole merchandise from a J. C. Penney,[40] she admitted that she may have lied under oath in a civil suit in which she alleged she'd been assaulted in a public parking lot by the store's security guards (J. C. Penney had settled for upwards of $150,000).[41] It also emerged that she'd once said Jackson "helped cure her son from cancer," marveling at "what a beautiful friendship they have."[42]

Aside from the Arvizos, one of the prosecution's most prized witnesses was Debbie Rowe, who'd been working with the police. When she got up on the stand and anxiously looked over at Jackson, he turned to Mesereau, worried that the lawyer was about to demolish his ex-wife.

"I said, 'Michael, don't worry,'" recalls Mesereau. "He knew I knew what I was doing. I didn't use one binder. She was on our side, she was telling the truth; she was clearly sympathetic to him. She turned into one of our best witnesses. . . . She mentioned how people were taking advantage of him and what a good father he was."[43]

Some suspected Jackson was still relying heavily on painkillers. Randy Jackson would later explain that his brother was "an addict" who deflected half a dozen family interventions and nearly overdosed in 2005.[44] Mesereau says the singer was "always lucid, always delightfully nice to deal with," but that on verdict day, he looked "terrible."

Terrible, that is, until the jury read its decision: not guilty on all fourteen counts. Outside the courtroom, as the news began to reach the hordes of reporters and camera crews gathered outside, a group of Jackson's fans released a single white dove for each charge cleared.[45]

———

Jackson returned to Neverland with his family and a group of well-wishers who included his defense team.

"He just said, 'Thank you, thanks, thank you, thank you,'" Mesereau recalls. "He looked so old . . . not in a celebratory mood, not in an exuberant mood, just in a relieved, grateful, quiet kind of state."[46]

He and Yu stayed for a few hours, watching as Jackson met with some of the paralegals who'd worked day and night on the case for much of the past year. The singer hugged each one of them and thanked them for helping him and his children.

Before he departed, Mesereau offered Jackson one last piece of advice: leave Neverland for good. The local authorities had been humiliated, he warned, and they would soon be looking for another shot at him.

"Some child will wander through the fence," Mesereau told Jackson. "And they'll trump up some other phony case. . . . You've got to leave Santa Barbara County."

Chapter 15

THE PRODIGAL KING

After his acquittal in June 2005, Jackson searched desperately for an escape from the public eye—and found one in the Persian Gulf kingdom of Bahrain. He, his children, and their nanny, Grace Rwaramba, arrived as guests of Sheikh Abdullah, son of the country's king. Soon, Jackson and Abdullah were cooking up plans to start a music company called Two Seas Records together.

The sheikh gave Jackson the royal treatment, providing the singer with a grand home, land to build an even grander one, and three cars: a Bentley, a Maybach, and a Rolls-Royce.[1] That summer, Jackson seemed to be enjoying his new life; in August 2005, he was spotted in Dubai with Emirati racing star Mohammed Bin Sulayem;[2] by January, he'd reportedly agreed to advise a Bahraini company on creating amusement parks and music schools in the region.[3]

But the executive ranks of Michael Jackson, Inc. remained on shaky ground. It appeared that Jackson's former publicist, Raymone Bain, had been brought back to serve as his business manager. This despite the fact that she'd never managed a musician; her closest experience seemed to be suing boxing client "Marvelous" Marvin Hagler for $9.9 million over breach of contract and settling in 1990.[4] Even so, Jackson seemed enamored.

"I was impressed by her professionalism, her strategic thinking, and honesty," Jackson wrote to the *Washington Post* in a 2006 email, which—as the publication noted—sounded like a press release from Raymone Bain.[5]

Tom Mesereau discovered Bain had returned to Jackson's camp while working with his partner, Susan Yu, to help the singer tie up loose ends in the US (it was Bain who kept saying their check for the additional work was in the mail). Apparently, she and Jesse Jackson told the King of Pop they'd been humiliated by their lack of inclusion in the events surrounding his 2005 trial, and the reverend asked the singer to rehire her. Why it had to be as manager remains, like much of Jackson's life during his later years, a mystery.

Despite Jackson's fondness for Mesereau and Yu, the checks promised by Bain never arrived, and they reluctantly terminated their working relationship with the singer (a six-figure claim filed after his death was promptly paid by his estate).[6]

Bain later found herself on the other end of a payment dispute with Jackson and sued him for $44 million in unpaid fees in 2009; her claim was eventually rejected.[7]

———

While in Bahrain, Jackson was pulled into another international legal dispute. This time, it was a civil proceeding that stemmed from unpaid bills for an effort to refinance his ballooning debt a year earlier.

During his child molestation trial, he'd been hemorrhaging cash and wasn't bringing it in at anywhere near his peak rate. To finance his lifestyle, he had continued to borrow against his stake in the Sony/ATV catalogue, and he found himself needing to pay off a bloated $270 million Bank of America loan by the end of 2005 or risk losing his collateral.[8]

As he searched for a solution, a dizzying series of events unfolded: his brother Randy introduced him to California-based accountant Donald Stabler, who then brought in a financial company called Prescient Acquisition, which in turn brought Jackson to Fortress Investment Group, a private equity firm that specializes in distressed debt. The latter initially agreed to put up as much as $573 million, with the intention of actually buying Sony's share of the joint venture for itself *and* lending Jackson enough to pay off the debts on his half, after which he'd be left with additional millions to ease his liquidity crisis.

Around the same time, Jackson also turned to billionaire Ron Burkle for advice. The two had known each other since the late 1980s, when Burkle had flown thirty terminally ill children to Neverland via helicopter as part of a charitable event. They reconnected after bumping into each other at Johnnie Cochran's funeral in 2005; one of the first things Burkle noticed was that Jackson was crying.[9]

"I didn't know you were that close to Johnnie," he said.

"No, I'm in trouble," the singer replied.

"What kind of trouble are you in?"

"I'm just in big trouble. They're turning off the lights at Neverland."

Jackson met with Burkle afterward to discuss his financial situation, laying out the details as he understood them. The billionaire—who'd made his fortune buying and selling supermarket chains before investing in Spotify, SoundCloud, and Airbnb—listened closely and quickly realized Jackson's predicament.

"You're actually a really wealthy guy," he said. "But you can't pay for lunch."

"Will you help me?" said Jackson.

"Sure, I'll put you on the same plan that I'm on. My office will pay all your bills. But I don't want anything to do with any of your money. You sign all your checks."

Burkle lent Jackson a few hundred thousand dollars and told the singer not to let his brother or Stabler make him sign anything. When a dejected Jackson floated the idea of selling his half of Sony/ATV to Burkle, the mogul told him to keep it for his kids. Eventually, Jackson wrote a letter giving Burkle's company sole authority to make deals on his behalf. Burkle didn't charge Jackson for the assistance.[10]

Ultimately, Sony declined to sell its half of the catalogue, perhaps thinking it still had a chance of getting Jackson's half. Fortress ended up buying the Bank of America note, an outcome that seemingly had little to do with Prescient's involvement. The consequences of the convoluted series of events meant Jackson had effectively borrowed $330 million from Fortress, enabling him to pay off his Bank of America loan and postpone judgment day on his publishing assets.

But Stabler had promised Prescient a 9 percent finder's fee ($48 million) for setting up the Fortress deal, and the company argued that Jackson was still on the hook. The sum was a large one under any circumstance, especially for something as simple as an introduction to Fortress, a well-known (and sharp-elbowed) company in its sector.[11]

Before Jackson left for the Middle East, he and Burkle met with Prescient's legal team, which included veteran entertainment attorney Donald David (who has handled the postmortem interests of rapper Tupac Shakur). Burkle posited that Prescient had no case, and that Jackson hadn't authorized the agreement in question—a claim David disputed.

Throughout the meeting, it seemed there were two different Michael Jacksons inhabiting the same body. At some points, he fidgeted so much that he could barely stay in his seat. At others, he would slump down and gaze off into the distance. Says David: "It was like, even though it involved him, and it involved tens of millions of dollars, it was not something that was of immediate importance to him."[12]

Burkle and Jackson made an offer to settle for a price between $500,000 and $1 million, which Prescient rejected, deciding to take the matter to court.[13] By this point, however, Jackson had left for Bahrain, ditching Burkle's personal finance regimen in the process. "He just needed someone there to tell him no, and there wasn't anybody there to tell him no," the billionaire says. "And if you told him no, he handled it pretty well. But as soon as someone told him yes, he was gone."[14]

Once ensconced in Bahrain, Jackson returned to his free-spending ways. Instead of heading back to the US to give his deposition, he elected to fly his own legal team *and* the legal team of his foes to France, first class. He put all six of them up at the Hotel Plaza Athénée in Paris and had them driven in Mercedes limousines to a Westin hotel in Versailles for the proceedings. The total cost: $116,000.[15]

A decade earlier, that sum would have been a drop in the proverbial bucket. Jackson hadn't released a new studio album since 2001 and hadn't toured since 1997, yet he was still spending like it was 1988. According to an accountant who'd seen Jackson's budget about five years earlier, the singer's expenses totaled at least $20 million per year—including $5 million on security and maintenance for Neverland, $5 million on legal and professional fees, $7.5 million in personal expenses, and $2.5 million in miscellaneous costs. On top of that, he was paying $11 million a year in interest on his massive loans.[16]

Once in France for the deposition, Jackson's demeanor swung wildly from polite to glib, deeply knowledgeable to completely ignorant. At one point, he burst out laughing and called the entire case "ridiculous," then excused himself to go to the bathroom. He seemed flippant again when David asked him why he'd appointed Sheikh Abdullah to the board of a company that collected his publishing royalties.

"Who's asking?"[17]

"Me," countered David.

"Are you really?"

"Yes, I'm really asking because my client is really suing you for $48 million based on the agreement that I showed you."

"Oh, I know that. Interesting."

At other times, Jackson carefully evaded questions, using phrases like "I can't recall right now," "I couldn't precisely tell you," and "It's a bit foggy." Yet on occasion, he'd slip from the script and give a reasonably lucid explanation of a complex business topic. When asked to explain his publishing companies, for example, he said:

"They collect the royalties from BMI or ASCAP on the songs that are played on radio or TV or film, and the publishing company pretty much administers through mechanical royalties the songs. They pretty much distribute them to the public and collect the royalty. And it's a huge catalogue— so, that would entail a lot of work and a lot of people and a lot of trust—one of the biggest in the world. My songs were Mijac, my personal ones, separate company. And I have the Beatles and Elvis, and all the other artists from Sony are in Sony/ATV."

David also noticed that Jackson's voice would sometimes change from its usual high, soft register to a "normal adult male voice." Regardless of the singer's unpredictable behavior inside the courtroom and out, it seemed clear that this wasn't a simple case of an entertainer blithely frittering away a fortune, but something much more complex.

"He understood what he was doing in terms of his financial arrangements," says the attorney. "He may have made some bad financial decisions, but he clearly understood the consequences."[18]

As the proceedings unfolded, Jackson reluctantly revealed more and more about the state of his empire. He did at times seem to have a tenuous grasp on the identities and roles of those involved in his business, but his evasive manner at the deposition made it difficult to distinguish feigned unawareness from the real thing.

Asked about unofficial advisor Gaynell Lenoir, he said, "I'm not sure exactly what she was doing, but she was definitely around." When it came to explaining Randy Jackson's role in his business affairs, Michael's caginess was almost comical.

"In what way did you limit his authority?" David asked.[19]

"Oh, I don't know," Jackson replied. "And it wasn't me who did it."

"Well, who did it?"

"I don't know."

"Well, then, how do you know it was done?"

"Because I was talking to someone on the phone, and they mentioned it. I forget. I think it was a lawyer or something."

"So, an unnamed lawyer who you spoke to on the phone told you [he or she] had limited Randy's authority to act on your behalf?"

"It was something like that. Yeah."

"Do you remember when this happened?"

"I sure don't."

"Do you remember what firm the lawyer was with?"

"No."

"Do you remember anything about that conversation other than the fact that this unnamed lawyer said that to you?"

"That's all I can remember right now."

Even amid the absurdity, Jackson's testimony took a darker turn on occasion. When asked if he believed any of his employees might have stolen money from him so as to ensure that he wouldn't meet his obligations to Bank of America—thus forcing him to sell all or part of his publishing holdings to Sony—he replied in the affirmative. He wouldn't identify any by name, though, despite being pressed numerous times by David.

"It's the entertainment world, full of thieves and crooks," he offered. "That's not new. Everybody knows that. And they love entertainers, and they are around."

Jackson seemed to believe Stabler was in that group, but it was hard to tell from his responses whether that was the case—or if the singer was being cannily evasive in an effort to distance himself from the Prescient deal in hopes of avoiding a potential $48 million payment. When asked if he knew what the deal entailed, he hedged: "As we speak now? Yes. But at the time, I didn't think that. I didn't know the details of it."

Jackson also grudgingly recounted a moment when his brother Randy and Stabler brought him a document to sign at Neverland (he identified the agreement only as a "financial transaction worth mul-timillion dollars"). On Burkle's advice, he refused to sign it, angering Stabler, who allegedly left him an accusatory phone message shortly thereafter.

"You're with the Jews[20] now," said Stabler, who is African American. "You're not down with blacks anymore."

Jackson never spoke to the accountant again. But when asked if Stabler was still doing work for him, the singer replied, "I don't know."

Eventually, Jackson and his lawyers settled with Prescient for a low-seven-figure sum.[21] But it was the behavior of the King of Pop, not the financial result of the case, that left the deepest impression on Donald David.

"The fantastic range of emotions that he showed would not be atypical for a bipolar person," the lawyer recalls. "And if you're bipolar, sometimes you're manic and sometimes you're depressed. . . . I'm not a psychiatrist, I'm just a lawyer who deals with people. The problem is that the same mania that fuels the well-known buying cycle of manic-depressives also affects their [ability] to make good decisions about other things. And those other things may very well be business matters."[22]

For many great artists, the lines separating brilliance, insanity, and addiction are blurry. And though Jackson's mind may have been clouded during the deposition by cognitive issues—perhaps innate, perhaps drug-induced, perhaps both—that didn't stop David from seeing to the core of the man on the other side of the table from him.

"He was not a foolish man," he recalls. "People try to picture him as being childlike. It doesn't work with the guy I spoke to when I was deposing him."

By this point, Jackson could ill afford another big settlement. Though his career earnings had surpassed $1 billion and his net worth stood at $236 million, almost the entire sum was locked up in a handful of illiquid investments. According to a report prepared by the accounting firm Thompson, Cobb, Bazilio & Associates, Jackson's assets had a gross value of $567 million—led by his Sony/ATV stake ($390.6 million), Neverland ($33 million), and a collection of cars and antiques ($20 million)—but he had debts of $331 million. His cash reserves: just $668,215.[23]

Burkle had tried to suggest ways for Jackson to dig himself out. "'You have an option to make $100 million a year whenever you want,'" he explained. "[Michael] goes, 'I don't want to work, don't make me work.' I go, 'I'm not making you work. I'm just telling you there's only three things in life for you: don't spend so much money, sell things that I don't think you should sell, or go to work. You just have to pick one of the three.' He'd recoil at the thought of going to work, it just horrified him."[24]

To further complicate matters, Jackson had grown increasingly suspicious of everyone around him and believed that Sony—perhaps working secretly with people close to him—was trying to do more than just drive him into bankruptcy in hopes of winning full control of his catalogue. The last time Lisa Marie Presley spoke to her ex-husband was in 2005, and he revealed his deepest fear.

"He felt that someone was going to try and kill him to get ahold of his catalogue and his estate," she told Oprah Winfrey. "And I really didn't know what to do with that."[25]

Jackson's concerns may have been exacerbated by deteriorating relationships with his Bahraini business partners, who insisted upon being involved in every aspect of his life. Hip-hop legend Nas remembers calling Jackson around this time; when the singer picked up, there seemed to be someone else on the line with them.

"We just talked about having respect for each other's careers," Nas recalls. "I thought it was strange that there was an Arabic guy on the phone, 'cause anytime Mike needed to make reference to something he had going on, the guy would chime in. . . . I just thought, 'Wow, when you become that famous, when it becomes like that, it just seems scary, man. It made me concerned for him.'"[26]

In the summer of 2006, Jackson abruptly abandoned Bahrain—and his royal partner's plans for a record company—after signing a contract promising the prince half of everything he created going forward. When Jackson's erstwhile business partner later sued, the singer claimed he had no idea that was part of the deal but subsequently settled for $5 million.[27]

"The more money and the more power you have, the less likely you are to be smart," says Burkle. "Because fewer people are telling you when you're wrong. I think he would have benefitted from more people telling him he was wrong."[28]

———

If you take a map of Ireland and push a thumbtack into the island's geographical center, you'll likely puncture a spot somewhere near Rosemount, a village in the lowlands about two hours west of Dublin by car. That's where Michael Jackson and his children went after leaving Bahrain.

With a population in the hundreds, the town has room for only the essentials—gas station, church, pub. Outsiders rarely visit the lushly forested hamlet, which visitors learn from the looks they get when they walk into the Stile Bar. But if they pull up a stool, pretend to watch the television show *It's an Irish Thing* (think *I Love the 90s*, but for Ireland), get a pint of Guinness from bartender Tom Martin, and ask a few questions, they might be surprised to hear what the locals have to say about the King of Pop.

For half a year, he stayed at Grouse Lodge, a rural retreat with its own recording studio located about a mile up the road. He joined a long list of musicians who'd laid down tracks there, from R.E.M. to Snow Patrol, and for a moment, it seemed he'd found a place where he could live anonymously.

"He was literally near gone by the time we found out [he was here]," says Jackie Martin, Tom's wife.[29]

"He just stayed in the house," adds the bartender. "But the guy who drove him around in the minibus said he couldn't believe the hype about him. He found him a very genuine guy. Down to earth."[30]

That seemed to be the general perception of Jackson in Rosemount, and it came as something of a shock to the townspeople given what they'd heard about him previously.

"The media for years have been telling us that he was bleaching his skin, and he was doing this and that," says Jackie. "You're expecting somebody who was totally mental. But all he wanted was some peace and quiet to record his music."

Though it seemed Jackson had finally found the serenity he'd been seeking for years, his wanderlust took hold once again. Toward the end of 2006, he and his family left Ireland, eventually landing in a place that couldn't be more different from Rosemount: Las Vegas.

Chapter 16

THIS IS IT

In the fall of 2007, billionaire Tom Barrack received a call and an unusual request: would he be interested in coming to Las Vegas to have a meeting with Michael Jackson?

Barrack politely declined. The middle-aged, polo-playing, shiny-bald-headed founder of real estate investment firm Colony Capital—which manages $35 billion in assets around the world—was a great fan of the singer and owned a ranch near Neverland. But he didn't want to get wrapped up in the affairs of a music star.

"It's not my business," said Barrack. "I know nothing about it."[1]

"Well, he's got financial difficulties and he really just needs somebody impartial to talk to."

The voice on the other end of the line belonged to Jackson's latest business advisor, Dr. Tohme Tohme. Like many of the figures who materialized during Jackson's later years, he's still surrounded by a fair bit of mystery (nobody seems to know where he earned his doctorate, if at all, and he didn't reply to an email inquiry pressing the issue). Barrack describes him as "a business guy around town" who "would bring us transactions to look at." Initially, this one didn't entice Barrack.

"I'm not interested," he said.

A month later the billionaire traveled to Las Vegas on unrelated business. Jackson had relocated to the area with vague plans to launch a lucrative comeback residency on the Strip, but after a year, nothing had materialized.

Tohme heard Barrack was in town and called again.

"Can I come over and pick you up?" he asked. "I want to take you to see Michael. Just spend fifteen minutes with him and listen to what he has to say. He's up against a wall. He's in foreclosure on Neverland and he needs a financial surgeon to understand what his options are."[2]

Barrack paused. He still had misgivings, but Tohme's persistence had piqued his interest.

"Fine."

———

Jackson was living on a dusty residential street called Palomino Lane, a few miles beyond the glittering lights of the Strip, in an older part of Las Vegas. The house where he was staying wasn't quite Neverland, but some of its features were indeed fit for a king. Situated on a lot two or three times the size of the adjacent properties, it boasted a picturesque terra cotta roof, a turret topped by a blue-tiled dome, and tall security fence.[3]

When Tohme and Barrack arrived, the King of Pop himself met them at the front door. "Thank you so much for coming," he said. "Thank you, thank you, thank you!"[4]

They walked into his living room, remarkable only in the sense that it was utterly unremarkable in size and style. The noteworthy features were on the coffee table: two sets of financial documents—one for Neverland, one for Sony/ATV—each about the size of a phone book. Jackson's kids were playing nearby, and one of them asked him to make a peanut butter and jelly sandwich; he obliged. Then he moved on to business.

"I don't understand what's happening," he told Barrack. "All of a sudden I got to this place where they're saying Neverland will be foreclosed on Friday."

It was Monday. Jackson went on for about an hour and fifteen minutes, explaining his financial situation as best he could. As Barrack listened, he remembers "drinking the Kool-Aid." He was amazed by Jackson's "brilliant, unbelievable mind." The singer seemed completely lucid; there was no indication of drug use—though, as Barrack recalls, "everybody knew that he had a big pharmaceutical drug issue." Even so, the billionaire was hooked, and he decided to try and help Jackson.

"Let me take this stuff," he said. "I'll take a look at it and I'll get back to you in a day with just a point of view."

Barrack took the documents detailing Jackson's Neverland loans and his relationship with Sony/ATV back to his office in California. Along with his finance team, he began combing through the pages.

"It was an absolute nightmare," he recalls. "The long and the short of it is, for all sorts of reasons, MJ hadn't worked for over a decade. His income was primarily based on the Mijac portfolio—his own catalogue—and the Sony/ATV portfolio, which had been refinanced about three or four times."[5]

All in all, there was about $12 million more going out per year than there was coming in. Jackson hadn't toured since 1997, and his image and likeness earnings had dwindled to less than $100,000 per year.[6] He'd been able to live with the imbalance thanks to loans he'd taken out, largely against his Sony/ATV stake; by the end of 2007, the latter was thought to have a gross value of about $500 million. At that point, though, his total debts were approaching half a billion dollars, and there wasn't much left to mortgage. That was partly due to the relationships Jackson had with his advisors. Says Barrack: "Anyone that told Michael something he didn't want to hear, Michael got rid of."

To make matters worse, he kept spending money—$6 million on a single antiques shopping spree at the shops at Las Vegas' Venetian Hotel, for example.[7] And every time he took a loan out against his Sony/ATV stake, he needed Sony to guarantee it. In exchange, Barrack explains, the company would take a slightly larger interest in the residual payouts from the catalogue.

"Sony was doing a very good job of running the portfolio," says Barrack. "They were also accommodating Michael by letting him borrow money out of the portfolio. But at every instance that they did, they tightened the noose a bit. Not in a mean way, but in a normal business way."[8]

By the time Barrack arrived on the scene, the private equity fund Fortress held the $23 million note on Neverland. The property had already gone through the complete foreclosure process, paving the way for it to go on sale the Friday after Barrack first met with Jackson. Two days before that was set to happen, the pair spoke again.

"Here are the financial pieces," Barrack began. "You're spending $25 million a year . . . you're making $13 million. And that's getting worse because you have a due date on your Sony/ATV loan. Not only are you going to lose Neverland, but you're going to lose your catalogue. We can reshuffle some of these pieces, but at the end of the line, you're going to have to find a way to create some revenue . . . are you willing to start down that line?"

"Yeah," said Jackson. "I am."

The singer mentioned a few ideas to Barrack, speaking of 3-D films and holograms. Barrack countered by suggesting that Jackson consider trying to reestablish himself as a live performer, which could lead to a comeback tour. The Rolling Stones had just broken the record for gross ticket sales, pulling in over half a billion dollars for their 144-date excursion. Jackson could lift himself out of his financial mess with a tour less than half that size, and he could start even smaller.

"Even if it's you making an appearance on a late-night show and singing a song," said Barrack. "Even if it's you doing one two-day appearance at a Vegas show. Something that shows you're still Michael Jackson, that you still have the capability, that you're still coming back. And that will create an income stream that you can build."

Then Barrack presented the alternative.

"If you don't want to do that, if that's not where you're going, I have the names of five bankruptcy lawyers," he said. "And I suggest you get ahold of them as fast as you can, because *that's* where you're going."

According to Barrack, Jackson wasn't shocked by the assessment. He knew his finances had gotten out of control, and though he had an excellent grasp of the value of his assets and brand, the complex web of loans in which he'd become ensnared was beyond his expertise. (Says Barrack: "MJ realizing the value in the Beatles' catalogue is MJ's brilliance. MJ understanding a very complicated financing and distribution structure is quite another thing.")

But to Barrack, it seemed—as it had to fellow billionaire Ron Burkle—that Jackson genuinely wanted to get his financial life back in order. This time, however, he was willing to perform again.

"I think I can get there," Jackson told Barrack. "But it takes some time, and if I do it, I want to do it the right way."

"If you're interested in doing this, if you will promise me you'll work towards figuring it out, I will go buy the note from Fortress," the billionaire replied. "And that'll buy us some time to figure out a plan. But don't have me do this . . . unless you're really interested in building a program going forward to create some revenue for yourself."

"I'll do it," said Jackson. "I'll do it. Will you help me do it? Will you help me think through it? I need someone who's not invested."

Barrack agreed and bought the note from Fortress, with Jackson retaining partial ownership of Neverland. During the first half of 2008, they forged a partnership that called for Colony to manage the property, increasing its equity with every dollar spent. If Neverland was ever sold, the firm would get back the amount invested, plus a preferred return. (The long-term plan was to hold on to the ranch and possibly turn it into a school for the performing arts.)

The next step was to set up Jackson's comeback tour. Barrack put in a call to fellow billionaire Philip Anschutz, the owner of Anschutz Entertainment Group; he recommended that Jackson talk to Randy

Phillips, the head of his AEG Live division at the time. That conversation planted the seed that would eventually grow into plans for a string of performances at the O2 Arena in London and offer Jackson a chance to pull himself out of the hole into which he was slipping.

"Randy [Phillips] called and was very capable, confident, knew Michael and had worked with Michael before," remembers Barrack. "He said, 'This is a sensational opportunity for Michael, and I would love the opportunity to try and advise Michael and create a platform for him.' And that's how it all started."

———

While the wheels of Jackson's London shows slowly spun into motion, the singer kept his ears to the charts and his eyes on collaborating with some of the biggest names in the music business.

50 Cent remembers the King of Pop calling to tell him he'd been waking up to the rapper's "In Da Club" every morning—and wanted to work on a new song together. "He just said, 'I have a song, I think it's my new 'Thriller,'" 50 Cent recalls. "[Michael] had something that he thought would be interesting if I wrote with him on it. . . . I just didn't even know it was real when he said that."[9] (The rapper eventually laid a verse on the song, called "Monster," produced by Teddy Riley and released on the posthumous album *Michael*.)

By 2007, the trail blazed by Jackson's ill-fated clothing and footwear ventures was becoming crowded with entertainer-entrepreneurs—and this time, they were succeeding. Diddy's Sean John line was generating hundreds of millions of dollars in annual sales, and Jay Z's Rocawear became so successful that licensing giant Iconix bought the brand for $204 million.[10]

Around the same time, 50 Cent launched his G-Unit Clothing line, which racked up sales of $55 million in its first year. For his efforts, he earned an 8 percent royalty[11]—and gobs of praise from the financial press.[12] 50 Cent had been aware of Jackson's foray into the clothing world. He just didn't think of himself as being on a high enough level, at least initially, to do something similar. "He was so big in my mind that it was like, 'Fool, you ain't Michael Jackson!'" the rapper explains.[13]

The King of Pop also sat down with R&B singer-songwriter Ne-Yo, who has penned hits for Beyoncé, Rihanna, and Céline Dion, to create some new songs. "I learned a lot through the whole process," says Ne-Yo. "Mainly that simplicity is one of the most difficult things for an artist. And if you don't master simplicity, it's pretty much not gonna work. Every song I'd submit to him, he'd always go, 'I like where you're going, but it could be a little simpler, it's a little too thought-out. Music is supposed to just roll, it's not supposed to be forced.'"[14]

Jackson nearly collaborated with beatmaker Pharrell Williams, too. "The one time I did take a real shot at it, he didn't like it," says Williams, who has crafted tracks for artists from Jay Z to Gloria Estefan. "I was so happy that Michael Jackson [knew my name] . . . I never took it in a negative way. I was like, 'Okay, I gotta get better, I gotta get to the top of my game.'"[15]

Fellow superproducer Swizz Beatz remembers visiting Jackson in Las Vegas around the same time. He brought some "magic toys" for the singer's children, and remembers thinking that Jackson was a terrific father. During the visit, they discussed the idea of having Alicia Keys join them in the studio.

"I was going to bring my wife in to write, and we were going to do one big collaboration," the producer recalls. "He was a big fan of hers. I heard he had a crush on her, so I was like, 'Wow, MJ got a crush on my wife!' . . . It was getting ready to become a great recipe."[16]

Meanwhile, Jackson continued to generate entrepreneurial ideas of his own. In a series of notes handwritten to himself, he outlined plans to release one movie per year for the next five years, perhaps with the help of *American Idol* creator Simon Fuller. He also wrote of launching soda and cookie lines, all with the goal of becoming the "first multi-billionaire-entertainer-actor-director," maintaining an all-encompassing focus on being the best. "Chaplin Michelangelo Disney," he scribbled, without punctuation. "These men demanded perfection innovation always."[17]

Jackson thought he might start by convincing AEG to help him develop movies inspired by his time in the Gulf, namely the tales of Sinbad the Sailor and Ali Baba and the Forty Thieves. Why the focus on motion pictures? "If I don't concentrate [on] film," he wrote urgently, "no immortalization."

———

By 2009, Jackson hadn't toured in more than ten years, and *Invincible* was nearly a decade behind him. Not performing may have been even tougher on his psyche than on his bank account. "I'm not alive unless I'm onstage," he once told Walter Yetnikoff.[18]

Jermaine Jackson claims he noticed a change in his brother that occurred around this time: "I saw the performer's glint return to Michael's eyes . . . his life was back on track, his health was nearing peak fitness, and he was physically preparing for the greatest comeback ever seen. He was, for the first time in a long time, *just happy*."[19]

Perhaps he was at certain moments, but the undercurrents of insecurity and addiction that had long circled him were continuing to pull him down. Though Jackson was all smiles at a March 2009 press conference to announce This Is It—the concert series that would take place at London's 23,000-seat O2 Arena—he showed up ninety minutes late and seemed jittery. He appeared so unlike his usual self that some suggested it wasn't Jackson, but an impersonator.[20]

AEG's then-chief Randy Phillips would later recount that Jackson was "drunk and despondent" before the event, characterizing him as "an emotionally paralyzed mess, filled with self-loathing and doubt now that it is showtime. He is scared to death."[21]

Regardless of what was happening behind closed doors, the outside world's pent-up demand to see the King of Pop perform only seemed to be growing stronger. The ten concerts initially announced sold out in less than an hour; eventually AEG upped the total to fifty shows, all of which sold out or close to it. The concert promoter also entered negotiations with merchandiser Bravado to create Jackson-themed goods to sell at the shows.[22]

But as Jackson returned to California to ramp up his rehearsals, he felt ambivalent. On the one hand, he was elated to see fans all over the world express their support. On the other, it was a lot of performing for someone who'd been on the sidelines for over a decade.

"He wanted to do twelve and rest and then go do some more, but they kept adding dates," says Joe Jackson. "One day I had a meeting with one of the producers of the tour. And my question to him was, 'Why you all paying him American dollars when you should be paying him euros?'"[23] The answer: It would be highly unusual for AEG, an American company that does business in dollars, to pay Jackson in euros for shows in the UK, where the currency is pounds. (Joe didn't say which one of the producers he met with; given that he wasn't involved in the planning of This Is It, it seems unlikely he was in contact with AEG.)

For the fifty London dates, Jackson was expected to earn at least $50 million, with the potential to earn tens of millions more—if not hundreds of millions—through additional touring. As Barrack had predicted, the London shows would give Jackson a chance to prove he was ready for that.

By this point, Jackson and Branca hadn't spoken in years, and the lawyer wasn't sure if they'd ever work together again—until he got a call from Frank Dileo, who'd just rejoined Jackson's team. The singer wanted to reassemble the group responsible for running Michael Jackson, Inc. in its heyday.

"Don't just come in and say hi," Dileo said. "Michael wants ideas."[24]

Branca put together an agenda. Among the projects he had in mind: a live album, a world tour, a 3-D version of "Thriller," and a charity event involving the British royal family, Oprah Winfrey, and the newly elected president Barack Obama. Upon meeting with Branca, the singer signed a letter confirming he was bringing back his longtime right-hand man. The lawyer thought Jackson looked thin but reasoned that he always was—and that if the fifty-year-old could follow the example of "exercise fiend" Mick Jagger, he might even have another decade or two of touring left.

Meanwhile, Jackson seemed intent on micromanaging some aspects of This Is It, as he often did with performances in his earlier years. Michael Bush remembers Jackson asking him to make a costume that included baseball catcher leg protectors made of glass for the This Is It shows.

"There's no way you can wear those," Bush told him. "You'll hurt yourself . . . they'll break when you get down on your knees."[25]

"Bush, I've been in a bank," Jackson replied. "They have bulletproof glass. Make it out of that."

"Michael, bulletproof glass is three inches think."

"Oh," the singer said, pausing. Then: "I know you can do this for me."

Bush ended up designing the leg guards, making them out of Lucite. To the audience, it would look like they were glass, filling Jackson's requirement without risking damage to his body.

———

As the rehearsals for the This Is It shows wore on, however, many of those close to Jackson grew worried about his physical and mental health. Bursts of optimism and liveliness were mixed with feelings of fear and doubt—as well as bodily symptoms, including sensations of extreme coldness.

Kenny Ortega, the director who'd worked with Jackson on the Dangerous and HIStory tours, expressed his concerns in an email to AEG executive Paul Gongaware after Jackson missed a rehearsal on June 14:

Were you aware that MJ's doctor didn't permit him to attend rehearsals yesterday? Are Randy [Phillips] and Frank [Dileo] aware of this? Please have them stay on top of his health situation without invading MJ's privacy. It might be a good idea to talk with his doctor to make sure everything MJ requires is in place.[26]

The doctor in question was Conrad Murray, who had quit his medical practice two months earlier to serve as Jackson's personal physician. If This Is It was canceled or postponed because he couldn't get Jackson to rehearsals, that would leave Murray without a much-needed job to pay off the debts of $1 million he had racked up while running his now-defunct practice.

To help Jackson sleep, Murray had given him heavy doses of Propofol every night for two months. As Harvard sleep expert Dr. Charles Czeisler testified, though, Propofol is a surgical anesthetic and is not meant to be used for such long stretches of time. It interrupts normal sleep cycles and does not replace real sleep.

"The thing nobody was focusing on was the problem with the drugs and a whole world of enablers," says Burkle. "Somebody should have told him, 'No.' Somebody should have said, 'I'm not going to give you this medicine.'"[27]

Sure enough, by mid-June, Jackson's symptoms—inability to regulate body temperature, difficulty with balance, feelings of paranoia and anxiety—were, according to Czeisler, "consistent with what one might expect to see with someone who was suffering from total sleep deprivation over a chronic period of time."[28]

Some of Jackson's colleagues picked up on these effects. "There are strong signs of paranoia, anxiety, and obsessive-like behavior," Ortega wrote to AEG's executives on June 20. "I think the very best thing we can do is get a top psychiatrist to evaluate him ASAP. It's like there are two people in there."[29]

Hours after sending the emails, Ortega met with Phillips and

Murray at the house AEG was renting for Jackson in the Holmby Hills section of Los Angeles. The doctor said Jackson was physically and mentally capable of doing his job, and that Ortega should stick to his—and not try to be "an amateur doctor or psychologist."

Three days later, Jackson returned to rehearsals suddenly revitalized. It was as though he'd slept for the first time in two months. Murray had stopped using Propofol to knock Jackson out, and the singer had finally gotten some real, organic sleep. "He had a metamorphosis," Ortega said.

On June 24, 2009—just a few days before Jackson and his team were set to depart for London—Bush dressed Jackson for one of his last rehearsals at the Staples Center. Jackson seemed excited to get back on the stage, and when he left the arena that night, Bush thanked him for changing his life yet again. Jackson hugged him.

"I thought he was never going to let me go," Bush recalls. "He said, 'Oh, but you're changing mine again.'"[30]

———

The last time Tom Barrack talked to Jackson was in the spring of 2009. The singer was interested in making a down payment on a new home with cash advanced by AEG.

As much as Jackson loved Neverland, he felt the property had been tainted by the allegations leveled against him while living there. He couldn't bear to part with it, but he couldn't bear to go back, either. So he was eyeing two houses: a $55 million mansion in Bel Air and a $45 million estate in Las Vegas that had been owned by the Sultan of Brunei and his brother.[31]

He was particularly enamored of the latter, a 125,000-square-foot home with six guest houses, two of which had pools. There was also a 60,000-square-foot entertainment complex with an indoor Olympic-sized pool that featured a drop-down movie screen. (Burkle believes the desire to buy this house was part of the reason the singer was willing to keep adding shows to the calendar for This Is It.[32])

Jackson wanted to know if Barrack thought he should try to buy it immediately, or if he should wait.

"I told him in my opinion it was premature for him to be buried under a new load of debt," the billionaire recalls. "I recommended that he do nothing."[33]

Jackson put his plans on hold. And in the end, there was only one Neverland.

"Michael *was* Peter Pan, it *was* Neverland," says Barrack. "It was the only place I think that he actually found peace."

Chapter 17

POSTMORTEM PAYDAY

The reports started trickling in during the middle of the day on June 25, 2009: Michael Jackson was dead. The cause was acute Propofol intoxication; Jackson's death would later be ruled involuntary manslaughter, for which Conrad Murray would be sentenced to four years in jail. Jackson was fifty years old.

Not one for small exits, the King of Pop nearly took down the entire internet with him. TMZ was the first to report the news; when it began to experience outages, users shifted to celebrity blogger Perez Hilton's site, which also buckled under the unprecedented virtual weight. Soon the load had swamped Google, Twitter, and the website of the *Los Angeles Times*, while CNN's site reported a fivefold increase in traffic. Wikipedia went down—users made five hundred edits to Jackson's page in twenty-four hours—as did AOL Instant Messenger.

"Today was a seminal moment in internet history," said an AOL representative in a statement. "We've never seen anything like it in terms of scope or depth."[1] At *Forbes*, the entire newsroom dropped what it was doing to produce a package of stories on the financial impact of Jackson's death.[2]

Later that evening, candlelight vigils were held in Jackson's honor all around the world. In Gary, Indiana, supporters left flowers outside his childhood home; in front of London's O2 Arena, fans donned sequined military jackets and rhinestone-laden single white gloves in his honor. Outside the Apollo Theater in New York, fans moonwalked deep into the night.

Jackson's memorial service was held on July 7, 2009, at the Staples Center in Los Angeles, broadcast to a televised audience of 31.1 million Americans—just shy of the number that tuned in to watch President Ronald Reagan's burial in 2004, according to Nielsen Media Research.[3] Some estimates put the worldwide viewership in the neighborhood of 1 billion.[4]

Jackson's mother wanted her son interred at Neverland, but that required a permit and some legal wrangling. His billionaire backer Tom Barrack successfully lobbied California governor Arnold Schwarzenegger for an exemption. But local politicians were so concerned about the potential influx of visitors to Jackson's grave that they refused to issue the necessary documents.

"It would have been the perfect resting place," says Barrack. "Forget about the commercial aspects . . . that's where he found tranquility."[5]

As a substitute, Jackson's family selected Forest Lawn Memorial Park cemetery in Glendale for his burial, calling on Michael Bush to dress the King of Pop one last time. The designer crafted a replica of the pearl-encrusted military jacket Jackson wore to the Grammys in 1993, this time with extra rhinestones. Before the singer's body was moved to its final resting place, his parents placed a crown on top of his coffin. Grand as the departure was, the two Michaels once had a different sort of denouement in mind.

"Michael and myself were going to be at Caesars Palace, Michael's doing 'Billie Jean' with the walker, that's how it was supposed to end," says Bush. "And when they told us that Michael was gone, it was like, 'But we're not at Caesars yet!'"[6]

———

When John Branca heard the news that Jackson had died, his first reaction was disbelief. "It was completely unexpected, one hundred percent shocking," he says. "It was really not possible."[7]

Branca had left for a family vacation in Mexico just days earlier, planning to rest up before meeting Jackson in London to help launch his comeback. When he returned to Southern California, he asked his colleagues if they had a will for Jackson. They did—two, to be exact—and a different firm found another, from 1997 (the singer had continued to create new documents as his children were born), and Branca had been named as an executor on all three of them.

Along with John McClain, the music industry veteran and long-time Jackson associate who'd been named as a coexecutor on the most recent will (dated July 7, 2002), Branca submitted the document to probate court. Since he hadn't been involved with Jackson's affairs for the bulk of the past few years, he didn't know if a newer will existed. But as time went on and nothing surfaced, it became clear that the duo would be leading Michael Jackson, Inc. after its founder's death.[8] It also became clear that the estate was going to have more than its share of legal woes, starting with the claims of dozens of creditors.

These ranged from petty to outrageous: the State of California sought $1,647.24 for its franchise tax board, a company called Intermedia Productions claimed an amount "not yet determined . . . in excess of $1 million," and a man named Erle Bonner insisted Michael Jackson had stolen his cure for herpes—and filed a suit for $1,109,000,503,600.00.[9]

Katherine Jackson initially disputed the appointment of Branca and McClain but dropped her challenge when one of her lawyers indicated the pointlessness of trying to overturn a will that named her as a chief beneficiary.[10] That didn't stop a host of other Jacksons who'd been left out of the will, notably Joe and Randy, from continuing to publicly challenge the document and its executors.[11] Joe couldn't have liked the thought of his son's estate being run by Branca (the first person Michael hired after firing Joe) and McClain (whom Janet had selected to replace her father as manager right before her 1980s breakout).

Randy insisted the will was fake, arguing that Michael was in

New York on July 7, 2002, the date the document was marked signed in Los Angeles. Indeed, the King of Pop appears to have been in the Big Apple on July 6 to protest his treatment by Tommy Mottola, and on July 9 for meetings with Al Sharpton; a spokesperson for the latter confirms this.[12] But this sort of discrepancy wouldn't be enough to render the will invalid, according to attorney Andrew Katzenstein, who serves as a partner at law firm Proskauer and teaches the Estate and Gift Tax class at the University of Southern California.

It turns out the King of Pop's postmortem planning was remarkably consistent over the years. Branca is listed among the executors in his four latest wills: the two from 2002, one from 1997, and one from 1995. The documents are consistent in specifying the distribution of Jackson's assets: 20 percent to charity and the rest split between his children and a lifetime trust for his mother. Upon her death, any of her leftover funds would go into a trust for his kids.[13]

Even if the July 2002 will were somehow voided, "the last will prior would be given full force and effect," says Katzenstein.[14] In other words, nothing would change—the virtually identical March 2002 document would become the will of record; were that document to be invalidated, the prior will would be next in line, and so on.

As Jackson's family continued to sound off, Branca and McClain hunkered down and attacked their new task. The former says their first goal was to refinance Jackson's debt and lower the interest rates; the second was to create income; the third was to come up with new projects; the fourth was to perpetuate the singer's legacy. They would begin to accomplish all four within a matter of weeks—and just in time for Jackson's heirs, who appeared to be in danger of losing control of the Sony/ATV catalogue.[15]

"His creditors could say that, due to his passing, the owners of the estate have to make good on his debt in sixty days," said Chris White, an analyst at Wedbush Morgan, shortly after Jackson's death. "Then you'd have to put this joint venture on the block, and that would be a distressed sale."[16]

Essentially, there was a danger that creditors could force Jackson's estate to offload his holdings at a fire-sale price. By 2009—in the depths of the Great Recession—estimates of the gross value of Sony/ATV ranged from $750 million to $1.5 billion (it's now thought to be worth somewhere in the neighborhood of $2 billion). But a quick, mandatory sale might have fetched a sum on the lower end of that spectrum, leaving the estate with less than enough to pay back the singer's debts of over $400 million.

The estate was able to keep the Jackson's stake in the catalogue, however, thanks to moneymakers like concert flick *Michael Jackson's This Is It*. Just a few days after the King of Pop's death, Branca was shown video footage from Jackson's rehearsals and realized there was silver-screen potential. Even as the singer's family tried to stop the estate from turning the footage into a film, insisting Jackson wouldn't have wanted it released, Branca and McClain started shopping the idea of a documentary to the big movie studios.

Were Jackson alive, it's possible he would have quashed the film at the last minute, as he nearly did for the "Thriller" video—and he would have missed out on a major payday. Fox offered $25 million; then Warner, Sony, and Paramount jumped in. Branca and McClain raised the price to $35 million, then $50 million. When everyone went up to $50 million, they told Sony's executives they could have it for $60 million plus a hefty cut on the back end; Sony agreed. *This Is It* would go on to become the highest-grossing documentary ever, ultimately earning the estate about $200 million worldwide.[17]

The pact was one of many blockbusters racked up by the estate's executors, whose aggressive deal making could be the subject of an entire book in itself. Shortly after Jackson passed away, Branca and McClain landed a ten-project, ten-year deal with Sony worth $250 million—the most lucrative record deal of all time—to put out unreleased material and anniversary editions of Jackson's albums. The first product of the pact was a two-disc set called *This Is It*;

released in conjunction with the film of the same name, it became the third-bestselling album of 2009.

By the end of the year, Jackson had sold 8.3 million albums overall in the US—more than any other artist that year, nearly twice as many as the number two artist, Taylor Swift—and perhaps 15 million more worldwide. The estate scored another $20 million for a Jackson-themed video game, $10 million for a renegotiated deal with merchandizer Bravado to create T-shirts and the like, and a few million more for a rereleased version of the autobiography *Moonwalk*.

The estate trimmed the rate on a $75 million loan associated with the Mijac catalogue from a whopping 17 percent (courtesy of his late-career mess of advisors) to a much more manageable 6 percent before paying it off altogether in late 2011. Branca and McClain also negotiated the rate on the Sony/ATV loan from 5.8 percent to 2.9 percent,[18] eventually upping the estate's annual guarantee from the catalogue to around $25 million as the publishing company continued to grow.[19]

According to court documents, the estate had pulled in gross receipts of $265 million through October 31, 2010, adding another $48 million by year's end. Of the former sum, about $160 million was paid out, divided between creditors ($48 million), debt service ($38 million), Jackson's family ($5 million), the entire mortgage on the Hayvenhurst property where his mother lived ($4 million, which saved the house from foreclosure), and others.[20]

Still, the estate's management team has had its share of critics, particularly among Jackson's siblings. In the summer of 2013, Randy once again questioned the legitimacy of his brother's will and called for Branca and McClain to resign immediately in a letter also signed by siblings Janet, Rebbie, and Jermaine (who'd described McClain in a book he'd released just a year earlier as "a friend for life . . . almost an adopted brother"[21] and ultimately rescinded his signature).

They accused the coexecutors of taking advantage of their elderly mother and exploiting Michael for financial gain, and seemed particularly incensed that a judge in 2009 had authorized the executors to receive a 10 percent commission on the estate's earnings.[22] There's little doubt that Randy would have liked to be the one getting a cut, as it appears he did for the role he played toward the end of his brother's financial career (a 2006 court document that lists Michael's outstanding bills at the time includes a debt of $1,650,000 to Randy).[23]

A bizarre series of events followed. Katherine went missing, and many news outlets reported that she'd been kidnapped by members of her own family. It turned out that she'd been taken by some of her children to a spa in Arizona, where she stayed for a number of days, unaware of her grandchildren's desperate attempts to reach her after she left the Calabasas home where she'd been living with them.[24]

Katherine eventually returned to California and wrote that, while in Arizona, her cell phone had been taken away, her room phone was dead, and her television didn't work despite her repeated requests to have it fixed. Tito's son TJ Jackson, who'd been named temporary guardian of Jackson's children in Katherine's absence, was appointed coguardian and said that his grandmother had been lured to the spa by someone pretending to be a doctor. Her lawyers suggested that the events may have been a plot by her children to "gain control over Mrs. Jackson as a means to get at funds."[25]

Michael Jackson knew all too well how his family operated. His parents had brushes with bankruptcy, and many of his brothers encountered serious financial difficulties throughout their lives. Jermaine was threatened with jail time over unpaid child support in October 2013—around the same time he reportedly bought a Ferrari.[26] Given his family's history of that sort of behavior, his decision to exclude all but his mother from the will seems understandable.

Jackson's siblings ended the ordeal further than ever from their brother's assets: they hadn't been able to convince Katherine, the only immediate family member of theirs with legal standing in the dispute, to challenge the executors. Perhaps it's because she real-

ized their 10 percent fee wasn't so pricey compared to what managers of other major acts charge. "Most managers want 15 percent,"
says Chuck Leavell, who plays keyboards for the Rolling Stones.[27]
Longtime U2 manager Paul McGuinness reportedly received a 20
percent cut of the band's proceeds; Elvis Presley famously paid his
manager 50 percent of his earnings.

"The bottom line is these guys did an amazing job and created
amazing results for the estate," says Katzenstein of Branca and Mc-
Clain. "The judge looked at that and said, 'You know what? You're
entitled to your fee.'"[28] New cash continued to flood the estate's coffers, and by the end of 2012, all of Jackson's personal debts had been
paid off (though a low-nine-figure business loan remains attached to
his ATV stake).

In a move separate from the estate but with implications for the
entire Jackson family, Katherine Jackson launched a wrongful death
suit in 2013 against AEG Live. The trial centered on the question
of whether or not the concert promoter (as opposed to Jackson)
had hired Murray, the doctor who administered the fatal dose of
Propofol, and whether he was unfit to care for Jackson. An affirmative answer on both counts would have meant a hefty payday for the
Jacksons; some speculated the total could exceed $1.5 billion.[29]

During the five-month trial that followed, the King of Pop's final
days were relived in salacious detail. A parade of expert witnesses
testified about his doctor-shopping and use of prescription painkillers; his family's lawyers produced callous emails from AEG executives referring to Jackson as "the freak"; at the lowest point, pictures
of Jackson's naked corpse were shown.

In October 2013, the jury decided in favor of AEG, determining
that although the company had hired Murray, he wasn't unfit to care
for the singer. The decision eliminated the possibility of a massive
windfall for Jackson's brothers, sisters, and father. They would have
had access to the funds paid by AEG via Katherine—either directly,
in the form of handouts, or by inheriting her share whenever she

passes away. Though she's free to give them money that she receives from her son's estate, his will didn't provide for them, so his postmortem success won't spill over to them when she's gone.

The estate's funds won't be distributed to Jackson's children's trusts until all pending litigation is complete and all claims are settled. (In October 2013, the IRS levied a whopping $702 million tax bill stemming from a dispute over Jackson's worth at the time of his death.[30] The estate maintains it's in compliance with tax laws and has appealed the move; legal action figures to drag on for quite some time.) But the kids remain financially well positioned. Their expenses are covered—including luxury housing in an exclusive neighborhood on the outskirts of Los Angeles, vacations with friends in tow, private school tuition, and charitable contributions in their names.[31]

Of course, there's more to life than the trappings of success, and Jackson's death has clearly taken a toll on his children. His daughter, Paris, was hospitalized in June 2013 after an apparent suicide attempt. But she seems to have recovered; Jackson's oldest son, meanwhile, already has a budding entertainment career—he made his acting debut in a recent episode of *90210*.

––––––––

Despite the unsavory details dredged up by the trial, Jackson's legacy seems to be healthy. The estate pulled in an estimated $130 million in 2013, up slightly from 2012, and the singer's image appears to be at its best state in decades. In 2012, Pepsi paid the estate $6 million to put Jackson's face on one billion Pepsi cans—the King of Pop's first major endorsement deal since the 1993 allegations.[32]

The partnership was on display at New York's Gotham Hall on a late-summer evening in 2012 for the launch of *BAD 25*, an anniversary album that featured remastered and remixed versions of Jackson's 1988 classic (a Spike Lee documentary on the original aired in November 2012). Spotlights flooded the red carpet (which was actually blue, representing Pepsi) as news cameras from all the major networks rolled. A handful of stars, including singer-songwriter Ne-Yo and superproducer Swizz Beatz, had gathered to reminisce on the King of Pop—and imagine what might have happened had Jackson gone on to launch his comeback tour.

"It would have still been going on, one hundred percent," said Swizz Beatz. "Come on, man, like, our generation being able to be at an MJ concert? Even if he just stood there and the songs played and he didn't even move, it would still be like, 'Yo, that's MJ right there!'"[33]

The producer was working with Jackson on new music shortly before the singer's death and remembers him talking about improving his diet and preparing to showcase some new dance moves and songs.

"Man, all he kept saying was, 'This is it, this is it, this is it,'" Swizz Beatz remembered. "I didn't literally know that that was going to be it. I thought it was going to be it in the literal sense of about to take over the world."

Jackson's postmortem *This Is It* may not have been the same as a sold-out concert series, but it proved to be a crucial step for his legacy. The amount of cash generated helped his estate keep assets like the Mijac catalogue and his share of Sony/ATV for his heirs. And it reaffirmed the public's interest in the King of Pop—so much so that major brands felt comfortable shelling out millions to renew their associations with him.

It wasn't just *This Is It*, though, that rocketed Jackson to arguably his highest level of popularity in a quarter of a century. His death itself, one of the most significant news events of the social media era, served to turn the eyes of millions of people to him. And instead of seeing the scandals, the plastic surgeries, the P. T. Barnum–inspired eccentricities (real or constructed), they saw the King of Pop in his prime. He has since been crowned by a new generation of fans— the ones who, along with the loyal old guard, have sent Jackson's YouTube Vevo views past 1.3 billion since 2009 (on par with Taylor

Swift and Katy Perry, and twice as many as Justin Timberlake). By the end of 2013, he boasted 65 million Facebook likes, more than Justin Bieber or Lady Gaga.

The resurrected Michael Jackson, Inc. wasn't constrained by the struggles that plagued its founder toward the end of his career: in the last eight years of his life, Jackson did not release a new studio album or go on tour. Within just three years of his death, however, he would accomplish both feats, and the financial results were staggering.

Chapter 18

IMMORTAL

It's about ten minutes before the start of the Michael Jackson *One* show in Las Vegas, and already the tabloid media's presence can be felt. On the sides of the theater, floor-to-ceiling screens display headlines created specially for the performance: "Squirrel Saves Woman," "Bubbles' Mystery Friend Revealed," "Woman Teleports to Cirque Show."[1]

John Branca is sitting fifteen rows from the stage, grinning as he surveys the headlines. He's in town for the debut performance at the Mandalay Bay Resort and Casino, in a theater renovated exclusively for *One*, and he's got every reason to be excited. The show is partly his brainchild, a joint venture between the Michael Jackson estate and Cirque du Soleil.

Suddenly, a dozen figures wrapped in red trench coats—the ersatz paparazzi injected into the show to give the audience a taste of Jackson's life—start marching up the aisle, bristling with microphones and cameras, faces obscured by dark fedoras and sunglasses. One points in Branca's direction, cueing a rush toward their target. "Paparazzi's coming to get you," says his friend Johnny Lockwood.

But they're after someone sitting the next row up. They jostle each other to get closer to the unsuspecting audience member, each motion punctuated by an exaggerated click of their shutters. One of them almost hits Branca in the face with a boom microphone, then scampers off, followed by the rest of the faux newshounds. Was it worse with Michael himself?

"Yeah," says Branca. "They'd knock you over."

————

The roots of *One* trace back to late 2009, when Branca entered into preliminary talks with Guy Laliberté, the fire-breathing billionaire circus performer who founded Cirque du Soleil. The subject was a new spectacular called *Michael Jackson The Immortal World Tour*.

Cirque had launched tribute shows before, including the Beatles-themed *Love!* and, later, *Viva Elvis*. Branca wanted to start with something similar; if it proved to be successful, the estate could launch a traveling arena show, entertaining ten thousand to twenty thousand fans per night. There was one problem: the fire-breathing billionaire was in outer space.

At age fifty, Laliberté had decided he needed a new challenge in life, so he shelled out over $20 million to make a trip to the international space station with a private interstellar travel company called Space Adventures. Branca had to wait nearly a month for him to return. When they finally met in Montreal, the attorney noticed Laliberté was chain-smoking cigarettes.

"Guy, did they let you smoke like that in the space capsule?"[2]

"No, they didn't let me have cigarettes," he sighed.

Soon the topic turned to business.

"Michael was the greatest entertainer that ever lived," Branca began. "We need a live show."

"We need two shows."

"I agree," said Branca. "But we have to do the one in Las Vegas."

"No, we need [first] a traveling concert show."

Branca was impressed by Laliberté's passion. After weeks of back-and-forth, they began to negotiate a joint-venture deal to launch *Immortal* as a world tour, with a permanent show in Las Vegas to follow.

He suggested some character sketches: one to represent Jackson himself; a mime to reflect Jackson's admiration for Marcel Marceau; perhaps Bubbles the chimpanzee as well. He also helped pick the songs and gave input on just about every aspect of the show, kicking off a deep and lucrative collaboration between the estate and Cirque.

Following its Montreal debut in October 2011, the show swung through Canada and the northern US before stopping for nearly a month of performances at Sin City's Mandalay Bay Events Center during December. The mini-residency was accompanied by a make-shift museum for the Michael Jackson faithful—complete with some of his iconic military-inspired jackets, one of his trademark rhine-stone gloves, and one of his vintage Rolls-Royce sedans.

One of the most fascinating parts of the exhibit was a reconstruc-tion of Jackson's Neverland library. Karen Langford, whose duties with the estate include overseeing its archives, remembers picking through the 30,000-square foot Southern California warehouse in which Jackson's books were stored, trying to decide which ones should make the cut. There were so many that she could have laid them end-to-end from one side of the building to the other—and back—with lots more left.

"In just this particular warehouse, there is one wall that is floor to ceiling—three stories tall—that has boxes and boxes of nothing but books," she says. "It's massive. And I promise you that he looked at every one of them."[3]

During the month in Vegas, *Immortal* drew over 150,000 people to the Mandalay Bay Events Center; the packed house on *Immortal's* first night included entertainers CeeLo Green, Jay Z, and Beyoncé. They looked on as a troupe of acrobats floated over the stage, con-torted themselves into refrigerator-sized books, and popped out of coffins to a soundtrack of Jackson's finest works.

"We have all done our best to make this a celebration of his essence in his absence," said the show's musical director, Greg Phillinganes—who started working with Jackson back in the late

1970s—shortly after the show's debut. "His passion for humanity . . . his commitment to excellence, his flair for the big show, we've tried to incorporate all those factors."[4]

Some media outlets lavished praise on *Immortal* (*Billboard* gave the show its Creative Content Award and MTV called it "a high-energy tribute to the legend"[5]), while others were ambivalent ("The Cirque show breathlessly flies [but] there is cheese," noted the *New York Times*[6]). A few were downright negative ("It takes only a few consecutive duds to damage a legacy, and if *Immortal* is the best they can do, the show's title will end up sounding sadly ironic," concluded the *Los Angeles Times*[7]).

But the ticket sales story was clear: *Immortal* was the highest-grossing concert tour in North America during the first six months of 2012, topping major pop acts like Taylor Swift. The totals look even more impressive over time. By the end of 2013, the show had racked up gross ticket sales of more than $350 million, making it one of the ten top-grossing concert tours in history.

The economics of the aerial extravaganza compare favorably to those of an actual Jackson tour. An artist's cut on a big arena show like *Immortal* is typically about 30 percent to 35 percent. If the show grosses $1.5 million on a given night, that leaves $250,000 for the estate after splitting proceeds with Cirque. Had Jackson launched an arena tour, his gross would likely have been higher—let's say $2.5 million. But he spared no expense on his shows (remember the Russian military airplanes?) and took home only about 10 percent of the $165 million he grossed on his last tour. A 10 percent cut of $2.5 million per night is $250,000, about what his estate gets for *Immortal*.

Of course, the estate and Cirque have to pay down about $50 million in startup costs over the life of the show, and Jackson might have gone on to play 80,000-seat stadiums (though that would have required a hefty setup fee, too). But judging by this back-of-the-envelope math, the Cirque show's impact on the bottom line of

Michael Jackson, Inc. is similar to what a successful tour by the living King of Pop might have achieved.

In death, however, Jackson was able to do something he never could have been able to do in life: perform shows in two different locations at the same time.

Planning for the *One* show began just as *Immortal* was getting started. Branca went to see the other Cirque shows in Las Vegas two or three times apiece and attended the Beatles' *Love!*—his chief competition—seven or eight times. He brought that knowledge to subsequent planning sessions for *One*.

"I said the whole show has to be an immersion," says Branca. "The audience has to feel like they're in the show."[8]

That meant plenty of extravagances. In addition to the creative components—plot, music, acrobatics—Cirque's latest joint venture with the Jackson estate required its own permanent home in Las Vegas. After *The Lion King* ended its run at Mandalay Bay in 2011, the space underwent an extensive renovation and returned two years later as the Michael Jackson *One* Theater.

The 1,804-seat venue was fitted with banks of speakers arranged in different programmable zones. Each member of the audience would also be surrounded by sound from three individual speakers (two behind the head, one blasting from the front). Branca also suggested building three floor-to-ceiling video screens on either side of the stage and having acrobats dance up the walls during "Billie Jean" (initially he wanted them to moonwalk across the ceiling, but that proved to be logistically impossible). The estate and Cirque brought on Jamie King, who had danced with Jackson on the Dangerous Tour, to write and direct the show (he helmed *Immortal* as well).

"I started my career with Michael and spent two years on the road onstage by his side," says King. "This was the education of a lifetime because I learned everything about performance from the greatest live performer ever. You can have the best technology in the world, the best stage and sound design and the sets, but unless you have a real understanding of how to deeply impact the audience, nothing else matters."[9]

As such, King aimed to capture Jackson's spirit in *One* through four objects: his dancing shoes, his sunglasses, his black fedora, and his sequined glove. The show's dancers gain mystical powers from each as they move from one scene to the next, each segment resembling a live music video acted out in gravity-defying detail.

The sequences reflect the diverse subject matter of the Jackson songs they accompany. For the introspective "Stranger in Moscow," a lone acrobat ascends a silk rope, performing midair flips and twists so effortlessly that it seems he's surrounded by water; at the end of the sequence, snowflakes fall from the ceiling, somehow winking off into oblivion before they hit the seats. During the jarringly sensual "Dirty Diana," a lady in red executes a similar feat on a giant stripper pole.[10]

And, after hints of his spirit appear throughout the first half of the show, a life-sized representation of Jackson appears toward the end. The phantom King of Pop—a hologram-like illusion—performs "Man in the Mirror" before transforming into a Jackson 5–era version of himself, and finally evaporating to tremendous applause. Though it's far from the genuine article, the spectral Jackson helps bring the singer to a new generation of fans.

"Kids who didn't grow up with Michael are now discovering Michael through these two shows, *Immortal* and *One*," says King. "His spirit is still with us and his music will live forever."[11]

It seems Jackson's earning power will, too. Even as *Immortal* continues to crisscross the globe, *One* has been drawing near-capacity crowds at an average ticket price of about $140. That translates to gross ticket sales of nearly $10 million per month,[12] or roughly $3 million for the estate after taking out expenses and Cirque's share (costs are much lower for a resident show than a traveling one). As such, it could add another $30 million to $40 million to the estate's bottom line per year.

In the five years since Jackson's death, the estate's earnings are already more than halfway to his $1.1 billion solo career tally, and at the current pace should pass that mark within ten years of his passing—about one-third of the time it took for Jackson to reach it in life (though it may take at least another ten years for the estate to match his inflation-adjusted $1.9 billion career total).

"The cash flow on an annual basis is tremendous," explains Donald David, one of the lawyers who handled the postmortem finances of Tupac Shakur. "Sure, it's going to decline eventually, but it's going to be a huge amount in the foreseeable future. [Jackson's] kids are going to have grandkids before that money's gone."[13]

Jackson's estate has pulled nine figures in each full year since his death. Is it possible that its annual take will eventually head south of the $100 million mark? Sure. *Immortal* will run its course, and *One* won't always be the shiny new toy in Vegas. Even Jackson's Sony/ATV earnings could take a hit if Paul McCartney regains some of his songwriting copyrights over the next decade due to the quirks of US copyright law, as some have predicted.[14] Under that scenario, however, he'd recover only his half of the Lennon-McCartney songs, and only in the United States.

On the publishing front, the Beatles' songs are just one very profitable piece of an immense puzzle for Jackson's postmortem empire. A consortium of investors led by Sony/ATV (and Jackson's estate) bought EMI Publishing for $2.2 billion in 2012, boosting the size of the company's catalogue to 2 million songs—a total that makes Sony/ATV the world's largest publishing company.[15]

That's one of the many goals Jackson was unable to accomplish toward the end of his time on Earth but did, finally, from beyond the grave. He was also able to get out on the road, release new music, and start picking up endorsement deals again. The massive sums of cash generated have secured the very assets he so often worried about losing. Were it not for the demons, internal and external, that marred his final years—and had he been surrounded by a better and more consistent team in his later years—his story might have had a different ending.

————

Backstage after the debut of *One*, the dancers and acrobats are elated. Vegas veteran Robin Leach, in the audience that night, would later call the show "Cirque's best spectacular in its nearly thirty-year history."[16]

More important, the performers had made a terrific impression on their fire-breathing billionaire boss.

"Guys, you were fantastic," says Laliberté, looking dapper in dark jeans, sneakers, and a crushed-velvet blazer. "I think it will be here for a long, long time."[17]

Laliberté, however, will not.

"Okay," he says with a shrug. "Flying to Cannes."

He bids the dancers adieu, then ambles over to Branca. They exchange a few words and back-slaps, and go their separate ways. As far as the lawyer is concerned, they're just getting started.

"I'm making it up," Branca begins, imagining what the Cirque du Soleil partnership might look like a few years down the line. "*Immortal* has now been certified as one of the three biggest rock tours of all time. Joins U2 and the Rolling Stones!"[18]

As for the *One* show? Vegas spectacles, much like pop superstars, tend to have short lifespans. For every ongoing show like the Beatles-themed *Love!* there's a *Viva Elvis*, which lasted less than three years. Still, Branca is optimistic.

"*Mystère* is going on nineteen years," he says. "That was [Cirque's] first one. Eighteen years and it's still running eighty percent of capacity. The Beatles show is six years."

Whenever *Immortal* wraps up, Branca wants to see the final performance in Vegas in the theater next door to *One*.

"Under one roof you've got *One* at the Michael Jackson theater, you've got the *Immortal* show at Mandalay Bay, so people can come down and buy two nights," he says. "I mean, come on. No artist has ever had two shows under one roof."

Two concerts centered on the same person at the same time in the same place, setting a precedent for the entire industry? Sounds relentlessly ambitious, with boldness bordering on narcissism, a dream that can only be realized by studying the greats and becoming greater. Sounds like an artist powerful enough to earn more than $700 million from beyond the grave—more than any living solo act over the past five years. Sounds like Michael Jackson.

———

Back in Gary, Indiana, the sun is setting over 2300 Jackson Street, and in just the past half hour, three carloads of people have stopped to make a pilgrimage to the King of Pop's childhood home.

One car contained a family of four, all of whom filed out and quietly paid their respects. Another, full of grown men, stopped across the street, its inhabitants reluctant to get out. A third produced a trio of women who spoke excitedly to each other in German.

"Did you come all the way from Germany for this?" I asked one.

"No," she said, "That would be crazy!"

"She probably would," her friend countered.[19]

They're just a few examples of Michael Jackson's global reach. For every record Jackson sells in the US, he still moves two abroad. It's conceivable that a slice of this fan base would make the trek to Gary to see a memorial grander than the house at Jackson Street, which could bring a much-needed influx of cash to a struggling city. But funding would have to come from outside.

"We are certainly open to ideas," Mayor Freeman-Wilson told me earlier in my visit to Indiana. "Particularly ideas from people with money. . . . Am I open to it, would we embrace a concept from people who have the money to implement it? Absolutely. Our partnership would probably incorporate providing land for something like that. . . . The greatest entertainer of all time is a Gary native. That's a real source of pride for us."[20]

For now, groundskeeper Greg Campbell remains focused on the monument at hand. He's been sweeping the concrete path in front of the house since I arrived, showing no signs of stopping. He's keeping it immaculate for the hundreds of daily visitors who've shown up at the house following Jackson's death—in particular, for one guest who's been on the scene nearly every day.

"The amazing thing about this, man, when we first started working over here, there was a bird," he says. "And he would always come over the front sidewalk and just look. Then when I'd leave and be walking all over the city somewhere, that same bird would be following me."[21]

Campbell smiles.

"He'd come and just stare at the house," he says. "So I'm thinking that might be Michael's reincarnation."

Regardless of where the King of Pop's spirit resides, one thing's for sure: Michael Jackson, Inc. is alive and well.

ACKNOWLEDGMENTS

On a steamy June afternoon in 2012, I found myself standing on the stage at New York's Apollo Theater—alone with a rare, tangible piece of Michael Jackson's legacy. I had just interviewed four of his brothers, but now the auditorium was empty, except for the small slab of wood sitting atop a faintly glimmering pedestal. It was the same piece of the lucky Tree of Hope that the members of the Jackson 5 had rubbed before their first gig at the Apollo nearly half a century earlier.

I glanced over my shoulder and back across the darkened seats. Nobody else in sight. Tentatively, I crept toward the pedestal, waiting for an *Indiana Jones*–style booby trap. But there were no blow-darts, no boulders falling from the rafters as I ran my hand over the talisman and hoped for some luck on my authorial journey.

Apart from the obvious obstacle of never having an opportunity to interview Michael Jackson, the conception of this book was much the same as my experience with the Tree of Hope that day in Harlem. The idea of a business-focused biography of Michael Jackson was sitting there on a pedestal for me; all I had to do was walk up and put my hand on it. But it took quite a while to germinate, and, as with most books, the process was far from easy. I couldn't have done it without the help of a number of people along the way.

For planting the seed, I'd like to thank Donald David, a trusted source and an attorney who once found himself on the other side of the negotiating table from Michael Jackson. For helping it grow, I'm so grateful to my agents: Ed Victor, for his sage advice, and William Clark, for finding a great home for this book. Many thanks to Leslie Meredith at Simon & Schuster's Atria for her keen editorial eye, words of encouragement, and tacos along the way—and to Donna Loffredo, Yona Deshommes, and the rest of the team as well.

I decided to keep my day job while writing *Michael Jackson, Inc.*, and I was able to do double duty because of the support I received from everyone at *Forbes*—for that, I'm especially grateful to Dan Bigman, Randall Lane, and Lewis D'Vorkin. Thanks also to Sue Radlauer for her sleuthing skills, Abe Brown for helping me scale a paywall, Hannah Elliott and Morgan Brennan for some deeply helpful introductions, and everyone on the Forbes softball team for their eternally solid (and liquid) companionship.

I will always be thankful to Mary Ellen Egan and Stewart Pinkerton for giving me my start at the magazine, to Lea Goldman for asking me one day if I liked hip-hop, to Neil Weinberg and Matt Schifrin and a host of others for their faith in me. For their constant support outside of work, many thanks to Ezra Markowitz, Melissa Ocana, Madeline Kerner, Lara Berlin, Rob LaFranco, Charlie Warner, Julia Bradford, the Mosses, and the Commish.

It wouldn't be fair to single out sources; there are more than a hundred of them, and they all deserve my gratitude for their generosity with their time and memories—this book wouldn't have been possible without them. I hope I'll get a chance to thank each one of them individually.

This book was mostly written at home in New York, but I churned out a significant chunk while staying with friends, family, and strangers during numerous reporting trips (and on more than a few "vacations"). So, big thanks to Jon Bittner and Rebecca Blum in Rhode Island; James, Mary Beth, Neil, Bridget, and Irma O'Malley in Texas; Joel, Maggie, Joslin, Jaden, and Addison Peck in Illinois (Lee and Naomi, too); Bebe, Alec, and Lee Seymour on Cape Cod; various innkeepers in Ireland; the Peter Pan Bus; airplanes; Gus La Rocco and Terry Fixel in Florida (and Sam La Rocco for her thoughts on chickens). Thanks also to Marcus Leonard—for accompanying me to scenic Gary, Indiana, and to the city's only bar—and to Matt Lachman, the most gracious host in all of Los Angeles and an excellent editorial sounding board and friend to boot.

I was able to (mostly) maintain my sanity while writing this book because of dear friends who lured me out of my apartment from time to time. There were delicious dinners with Jon Bruner, Bethany Kerner, Andrew Cedotal, Nicole Villeneuve, Mike Seplowitz, and Dan Hammond; *moules frites* with Choppy; Roma Pizza with Dan Adler and Kelly Reid; beers and burgers with Borbay; and bowties and booze with Mike Safir and Peter Schwartz.

Major thanks to those who read early drafts of this book, particularly the aforementioned Andrew and Neil, Richard Hyfler, and the artist formerly known as Nick Messitte-Greenberg. His willingness to deliver utterly unvarnished, deeply vulgar, and incredibly constructive criticism proved invaluable. I might have had to stop sleeping altogether if it weren't for the incredible contributions of researcher Natalie Robehmed, who helped out with tasks that ranged from mundane (fact-checking) to arcane (tracking down *Billboard* charts from magazine issues older than either of us). I look forward to reading her books someday.

Special thanks to my parents, all three of them. In addition to giving birth to me, Suzanne O'Malley showed me what it meant to be a reporter. Dan Greenburg taught me that if you love what you do, you never have to work a day in your life. When it came to writing, he always emphasized the art of revision; the same can be said for Judith Greenburg, whose edits I liken to visiting a verbal ENT (at some point, a whole lot of really terrible stuff that you created gets extracted, it kind of hurts, and then you wonder how the hell it got there in the first place). Thank you for everything!

Most of all, I would like to thank Dr. Danielle La Rocco. When we started dating in 2008, she knew she was getting roommates—Bruner, Choppy, Adler (and possibly Claude)—but didn't know she'd end up living with Jay Z and Michael Jackson, too. The latter's ghostly moonwalk followed Danielle and me through a year in which we adopted a digitally challenged kitten, endured a hurricane, and moved to a new apartment.

The King of Pop even followed us to Ireland, where we discussed my book with the drunkest man in the world at a tiny pub in the town of Moate, down the road from the place Jackson stayed for a few months in 2006. When "Billie Jean" erupted from the speakers twice in a row, I became convinced the only explanation was supernatural. As it turned out, a mischievous bartender had overheard our conversation and decided to mess with us. Had it not been for Danielle, I would never have figured this out. I was so impressed, I proposed to her the next day.

BOOKS FOR FOOD

Every time someone buys a copy of this book, a person in need will receive a free meal through the United Nations' World Food Programme.

Why? Michael Jackson donated tens of millions of dollars to various charities over the course of his life and left 20 percent of his financial legacy to good causes. I figured it would only be fitting to make a contribution from my author royalties.

I chose the WFP because hunger affects one in seven people on the planet and kills more people per year than AIDS, tuberculosis, and malaria combined. When you're hungry, your body compensates for the lack of nutrition by slowing down. That makes studying or working difficult and weakens the immune system, particularly for children, who can become more vulnerable to common ailments. This isn't an expensive problem to solve: the WFP provides nutritious meals for just $0.25 apiece.

I was also inspired by 50 Cent, who took a similar approach in 2011 when he released his SK Energy beverage (which retails for $3, roughly the same as the standard author's cut per book). "This is the most important project I've participated in," he told me shortly after the launch. Since then, he's donated over 4 million meals; his goal is 1 billion. Perhaps more significantly, he believes his actions will convince beverage giants like Coca-Cola and Pepsi to include a unit-based donation for all their products.

So I'll contribute a meal for every copy of my book sold, as measured by Nielsen BookScan at the end of each year, and I'll cross my fingers that other creative types—and the companies who publish their works—will do the same.

To learn more, or to donate directly to the World Food Programme, visit www.wfp.org.

MICHAEL JACKSON'S CAREER EARNINGS

From the moment Michael Jackson's adult solo career began in earnest in 1979 through his death in 2009, he earned a whopping $1.1 billion dollars. In the five years since then, his estate has collected over $700 million more. Adjusted for inflation, his lifetime earnings stand at $1.9 billion; add in his postmortem paychecks in today's dollars, and the total rises to $2.6 billion. Here's the year-by-year breakdown.

YEAR	ANNUAL EARNINGS	ANNUAL EARNINGS ADJUSTED FOR INFLATION*
1979	$4 million	$13 million
1980	$9 million	$26 million
1981	$5 million	$13 million
1982	$6 million	$15 million
1983	$43 million	$101 million
1984	$91 million	$205 million
1985	$37 million	$80 million
1986	$20 million	$43 million
1987	$67 million	$138 million
1988	$125 million	$247 million
1989	$37 million	$70 million
1990	$34 million	$61 million
1991	$35 million	$60 million
1992	$64 million	$107 million
1993	$34 million	$55 million

1994	$19 million	$30 million
1995	$118 million	$181 million
1996	$71 million	$106 million
1997	$42 million	$61 million
1998	$18 million	$26 million
1999	$17 million	$24 million
2000	$18 million	$24 million
2001	$34 million	$45 million
2002	$19 million	$25 million
2003	$21 million	$27 million
2004	$20 million	$25 million
2005	$23 million	$28 million
2006	$19 million	$22 million
2007	$18 million	$20 million
2008	$13 million	$14 million
2009	$10 million / **$75 million**	**$93 million**
2010	**$245 million**	**$262 million**
2011	**$145 million**	**$151 million**
2012	**$115 million**	**$117 million**
2013	**$130 million**	**$130 million**

Lifetime earnings estimates generated by the author throughout the process of researching *Michael Jackson, Inc.* These figures represent pretax earnings before paying out managers, agents, and lawyers, as well as housing, travel, staff, and other expenditures. Estimates do not reflect Sony/ATV profits automatically reinvested into the company. (These *are* included in the slightly higher figures the author helped develop for *Forbes* after Jackson's death.) The figures above do include Jackson's annual eight-figure guaranteed share of Sony/ATV profits that weren't reinvested. **Figures in boldface** represent postmortem income.

MICHAEL JACKSON'S ATV MEMO

The soon-to-be King of Pop passed this note to his lawyer, John Branca, during a meeting in 1985. Jackson eventually acquired the company in question—and his stake is worth about $1 billion today. (*Courtesy of the Michael Jackson Estate*)

NOTES

INTRODUCTION

1. Walter Yetnikoff, interview by author, New York, New York, March 2013.
2. John Branca, interview by author, Beverly Hills, California, February 2013.
3. Michael Jackson, unpublished memo (circa 1985); see appendix.
4. Sheryl Crow, telephone conversation with author, September 2013.
5. Sandy Gallin, telephone conversation with author, August 2013.
6. Curtis "50 Cent" Jackson, interview by author, New York, New York, March 2013.
7. Chris "Ludacris" Bridges, interview by author, New York, New York, June 2012.
8. Pharrell Williams, telephone conversation with author, November 2012.
9. Berry Gordy, interview by author, New York, New York, February 2013.
10. Kevin Liles, interview by author, New York, New York, August 2012.
11. Josh Altman, telephone conversation with author, October 2013.
12. Tom Barrack, telephone conversation with author, August 2013.
13. Karen Langford, telephone conversation with author, October 2013.
14. Fred "Fab 5 Freddy" Brathwaite, interview by author, Brooklyn, New York, January 2013.
15. Neil Harris, *Humbug: The Art of P.T. Barnum* (Chicago: University of Chicago Press, 1973), 4.
16. Nic Kynaston, ed., *Guinness World Records 2000* (London/New York: Guinness World Records Ltd, 1999), 88.
17. Walter Yetnikoff, interview by author, New York, New York, March 2013.
18. Joel Schumacher, telephone conversation with author, October 2012.
19. Liv Buli, electronic message to author, February 2013.
20. The Nielsen Company, "2009 Year-End Music Industry Report," January 6, 2010. http://www.businesswire.com/news/home/20100106007077/en/2009-U.S.-Music-Purchases-2.1-2008-Music.
21. Michael Jackson, interview with Oprah Winfrey, *Michael Jackson Talks to . . . Oprah Live*, 1993, http://www.youtube.com/watch?v=wN1dTHdckzg.
22. Berry Gordy, interview by author, New York, New York, February 2013.

CHAPTER ONE: STEELTOWN DREAMING

1. Author's observation, Gary, Indiana, July 2012.
2. Greg Campbell, interview by author, Gary, Indiana, July 2012.
3. Keith Jackson, interview by author, Gary, Indiana, July 2012.
4. Joe Jackson, interview by author, Las Vegas, Nevada, August 2012.
5. Keith Jackson, interview by author, Gary, Indiana, July 2012.
6. Mayor Karen Freeman-Wilson, interview by author, Gary, Indiana, July 2012.
7. Michael Jackson, *Moonwalk* (New York: Harmony Books, 1988), 26.
8. Joe Jackson, interview by author, Las Vegas, Nevada, August 2012.
9. Jermaine Jackson, *You Are Not Alone* (New York: Touchstone/Simon & Schuster, 2011), 22–23.
10. Joe Jackson, interview by author, Las Vegas, Nevada, August 2012.
11. Jermaine Jackson, *You Are Not Alone*, 13.
12. Ibid, 33–34.
13. Joe Jackson, interview by author, Las Vegas, Nevada, August 2012.
14. Jermaine Jackson, *You Are Not Alone*, 40.
15. Michael Jackson, *Moonwalk*, 28–29.
16. Greg Campbell, interview by author, Gary, Indiana, July 2012.
17. Keith Jackson, interview by author, Gary, Indiana, July 2012.
18. Michael Jackson, *Moonwalk*, 32.
19. Joe Jackson, interview by author, Las Vegas, Nevada, August 2012.
20. Author's observation, Gary, Indiana, July 2012.
21. Author's note: Unfortunately, this website is about as well maintained as the building to which it's dedicated. Around the time of my visit to Gary, the URL directed me to a page occupied by a blue-and-yellow cartoon alligator and the words "HostGator: *Start a Website Today!*"
22. Jermaine Jackson, *You Are Not Alone*, 61.
23. Joe Jackson, interview by author, Las Vegas, Nevada, August 2012.
24. Michael Jackson, *Moonwalk*, 34.
25. Joe Jackson, interview by author, Las Vegas, Nevada, August 2012.
26. Jermaine Jackson, *You Are Not Alone*, 50.
27. Michael Jackson, *Moonwalk*, 37.
28. Gordon Keith, telephone conversation with author, July 2012.
29. Catherine Sinclair, interview by author, Gary, Indiana, July 2012.
30. Greg Campbell, interview by author, Gary, Indiana, July 2012.
31. Jermaine Jackson, *You Are Not Alone*, 59.
32. Keith Jackson, interview by author, Gary, Indiana, July 2012.
33. Michael Jackson, *Moonwalk*, 29.
34. Joe Jackson, interview by author, Las Vegas, Nevada, August 2012.
35. Jake Austen, "The Jackson Find," *Chicago Reader*, September 10, 2009, http://www.chicagoreader.com/chicago/the-jackson-find/Content?oid=1191672.

36. Gordon Keith, telephone conversation with author, July 2012.

37. Jermaine Jackson, *You Are Not Alone*, 77.

38. Gordon Keith, telephone conversation with author, July 2012.

39. Joe Jackson, interview by author, Las Vegas, Nevada, August 2012.

40. Jermaine Jackson, *You Are Not Alone*, 68.

41. Michael Jackson, *Moonwalk*, 43.

42. Smokey Robinson, *Smokey: Inside My Life* (New York: McGraw-Hill, 1988), 175.

43. Jermaine Jackson, *You Are Not Alone*, 69–74.

44. Ibid.

45. Joe Jackson, interview by author, Las Vegas, Nevada, August 2012.

46. Tito Jackson, interview by author, New York, New York, June 2012.

47. Apollo Theater website, "Amateur Night History and Legacy," Apollo Theater, http://www.apollotheater.org/amateur-night-history-legacy.

48. Jermaine Jackson, interview by author, New York, New York, June 2012.

49. Marlon Jackson, interview by author, New York, New York, June 2012.

50. Jermaine Jackson, interview by author, New York, New York, June 2012.

51. Jackie Jackson, interview by author, New York, New York, June 2012.

52. Jermaine Jackson, interview by author, New York, New York, June 2012.

53. Tito Jackson, interview by author, New York, New York, June 2012.

CHAPTER TWO: MOTOWN UNIVERSITY

1. Berry Gordy, interview by author, New York, New York, February 2013.

2. Smokey Robinson, *Smokey: Inside My Life*, 175.

3. Author's note: Suzanne de Passe had numerous scheduling conflicts that prevented her from being interviewed for this book.

4. Berry Gordy, interview by author, New York, New York, February 2013.

5. Author's note: At least two Jackson biographers have said that Berry Gordy was not present for the Jackson 5's initial Motown audition, but signed him after watching their audition tape. However, both Gordy and one of his representatives say he watched the performance in person; Jermaine Jackson also writes that the Jacksons performed in front of Gordy at their first audition (*You Are Not Alone*, 92).

6. Berry Gordy, interview by author, New York, New York, February 2013.

7. Michael Jackson, *Moonwalk*, 63.

8. Berry Gordy, interview by author, New York, New York, February 2013.

9. Michael Jackson, *Moonwalk*, 75.

10. J. Randy Taraborrelli, *Michael Jackson: The Magic and the Madness* (New York: Birch Lane Press, 1991), 47.

11. Bernie Resnick, electronic message to author, July 2013.

12. Berry Gordy, interview by author, New York, New York, February 2013.

13. Gordon Keith, telephone conversation with author, July 2012.

14. Joe Jackson, interview by author, Las Vegas, Nevada, August 2012.

15. Berry Gordy, interview by author, New York, New York, February 2013.

16. Michael Jackson, *Moonwalk*, 67–69.

17. Berry Gordy, interview by author, New York, New York, February 2013.

18. Joe Jackson, interview by author, Las Vegas, Nevada, August 2012.

19. Berry Gordy, interview by author, New York, New York, February 2013.

20. Jackson 5, *Diana Ross Presents the Jackson 5*, Motown, 1969.

21. Joe Jackson, interview by author, Las Vegas, Nevada, August 2012.

22. Berry Gordy and Nansci Neiman, electronic message to the author, March 2013.

23. Langdon Winner, "Diana Ross Presents the Jackson 5," *Rolling Stone*, March 7, 1970, http://www.rollingstone.com/music/albumreviews/diana-ross-presents-the-jackson-5-19700307.

24. Keith Jackson, interview by author, Gary, Indiana, July 2012.

25. Berry Gordy, interview by author, New York, New York, February 2013.

26. Jermaine Jackson, *You Are Not Alone*, 107.

27. Berry Gordy, interview by author, New York, New York, February 2013.

28. Michael Jackson, *Moonwalk*, 81.

29. Jermaine Jackson, *You Are Not Alone*, 153–155.

30. Michael Jackson, *Moonwalk*, 106.

31. Jermaine Jackson, *You Are Not Alone*, 167.

32. Michael Jackson, interview with Oprah Winfrey, *Michael Jackson Talks to . . . Oprah Live*, 1993, http://www.youtube.com/watch?v=wN1dTHdckzg.

33. Michael Jackson, *Moonwalk*, 106–108.

34. Neil Weinberg, interview by author, New York, New York, January 2013.

35. Michael Jackson, *Moonwalk*, 114.

36. Emanuel Legrand, "International Publishing for Non-Publishers," Midem Academy 2013, 4, http://www.midem.com/RM/RM_MidemEvent/documents/pdf/library/academics/midem-academy-emmanuel-legrand-international-publishing-non-publishers.pdf.

37. Berry Gordy, interview by author, New York, New York, February 2013.

38. Joe Jackson, interview by author, Las Vegas, Nevada, August 2012.

39. Michael Jackson, *Moonwalk*, 115.

40. Berry Gordy, interview by author, New York, New York, February 2013.

41. Jermaine Jackson, *You Are Not Alone*, 185.

42. Berry Gordy, interview by author, New York, New York, February 2013.

CHAPTER THREE: EPIC CHANGES

1. Walter Yetnikoff, interview by author, New York, New York, March 2013.

2. Jermaine Jackson, *You Are Not Alone*, 177.

3. Joe Jackson, interview by author, Las Vegas, Nevada, August 2012.

4. Berry Gordy, interview by author, New York, New York, February 2013.

5. Smokey Robinson, *Smokey: Inside My Life*, 212.

6. Jermaine Jackson, *You Are Not Alone*, 178.

7. Ibid., 185.

8. Michael Jackson, *Moonwalk*, 117–120.

9. Walter Yetnikoff, interview by author, New York, New York, March 2013.

10. Michael Jackson, *Moonwalk*, 128–129.

11. Walter Yetnikoff, interview by author, New York, New York, March 2013.

12. IMDB staff, "The Wiz," IMDB, http://www.imdb.com/title/tt0078504/.

13. Michael Jackson, *Moonwalk*, 133.

14. Berry Gordy, interview by author, New York, New York, February 2013.

15. Joel Schumacher, telephone conversation with author, October 2012.

16. Susan Blond, electronic message to author, October 2013; interview by author, New York, New York, August 2012.

17. Joel Schumacher, telephone conversation with author, October 2012.

18. Michael Jackson, *Moonwalk*, 136, 142, 150.

19. Quincy Jones, *Q: The Autobiography of Quincy Jones* (New York: Doubleday, 2001), 232.

20. Bruce Swedien, telephone conversation with author, November 2012.

21. Matt Forger, electronic message to author, June 2013.

22. Keith Jackson, interview by author, Gary, Indiana, July 2012.

23. Bruce Swedien, telephone conversation with author, November 2012.

24. Roger Ebert, "The Wiz," *Chicago Sun Times*, October 28, 1978.

25. *Globe and Mail* staff, "Film Drops a Great Yellow Brick," *Globe and Mail*, October 28, 1978.

26. Adam Lee Davies, Tom Huddleston, David Jenkins and Anna Smith, "Cinema's 50 Greatest Flops, Follies and Failures," *TimeOut London*, http://www.timeout.com/film/features/show-feature/10340/.

27. IMDB staff, "The Wiz," IMDB, http://www.imdb.com/title/tt0078504/.

28. Joel Schumacher, telephone conversation with author, October 2012.

29. Berry Gordy, interview by author, New York, New York, February 2013.

30. Stephen Holden, "Michael Jackson: *Off the Wall*," *Rolling Stone*, November 1, 1979, http://www.rollingstone.com/music/albumreviews/off-the-wall-19791101.

31. Walter Yetnikoff, interview by author, New York, New York, March 2013.

32. Smokey Robinson, *Smokey: Inside My Life*, 212.

33. Michael Jackson, *Moonwalk*, 152.

34. Walter Yetnikoff, interview by author, New York, New York, March 2013.

CHAPTER FOUR: EMPIRE BUILDING

1. John Branca, interview by author, Beverly Hills, California, August 2012.

2. Karen Langford, telephone conversation with author, July 2013.

3. John Branca, interview by author, New York, New York, November 2012.

4. Berry Gordy, interview by author, New York, New York, February 2013.

5. John Branca, telephone conversation with author, April 2013; Entertainment Law Initiative speech, Beverly Hills, California, February 2012.

6. John Branca, interview by author, Beverly Hills, California, August 2012.

7. Guardian staff, "Fatboy Slim's 'Praise You' Voted Best Video," *The Guardian*, July 31, 2001, http://www.guardian.co.uk/uk/2001/jul/31/2.

8. Michael Jackson, *Moonwalk*, 176.

9. Michael Jackson, "Learning from the Past," unpublished notes (circa 1987), dictated to author by Karen Langford via telephone, July 2013.

10. Michael Jackson, *Moonwalk*, 147, 176.

11. Matt Forger, telephone conversation with author, November 2012.

12. Michael Jackson, *Moonwalk*, 180.

13. Matt Forger, telephone conversation with author, November 2012.

14. Quincy Jones, *Q: The Autobiography of Quincy Jones*, 236–237.

15. Matt Forger, telephone conversation with author, November 2012.

16. Bruce Swedien, telephone conversation with author, November 2012.

17. Michael Jackson, *Moonwalk*, 198.

18. Matt Forger, telephone conversation with author, November 2012.

19. Quincy Jones, *Q: The Autobiography of Quincy Jones*, 238–239.

20. Bruce Swedien, telephone conversation with author, November 2012.

21. John Branca, interview by author, Beverly Hills, California, August 2012.

22. Freddie DeMann staff member (name unknown), telephone conversation with author, July 2013.

23. Ron Weisner, telephone conversation with author, September 2013.

24. John Branca, interview by author, Beverly Hills, California, August 2012.

CHAPTER FIVE: KISSING THE MONSTER

1. Walter Yetnikoff, interview by author, New York, New York, March 2013.

2. John Branca, interview by author, Beverly Hills, California, August 2012.

3. Walter Yetnikoff, interview by author, New York, New York, March 2013.

4. Michigan.gov staff, "US Motor Vehicle Sales," Michigan.gov, date unknown, http://www.senate.michigan.gov/sfa/Publications/Issues/MOTORVEH/MOTORVE1.html.

5. Christopher Connelly, *"Thriller,"* *Rolling Stone*, January 28, 1983, http://www.rollingstone.com/music/albumreviews/thriller-19830128.

6. Billboard staff, *"Thriller,"* *Billboard*, December 11, 1982, http://www.billboard.biz/bbbiz/others/thriller-937199.story.

7. John Rockwell, "Michael Jackson's *Thriller*: Superb Job," *New York Times*, December 19, 1982, http://www.nytimes.com/1982/12/19/arts/michael-jackson-s-thriller-superb-job.html.

8. Walter Yetnikoff, *Howling at the Moon* (New York: Broadway Books, 2004), 153–154.

9. Jay Cocks, "Sing a Song of Seeing," *Time*, December 26, 1983.

10. Michael Jackson, *Moonwalk*, 200.

11. Fred "Fab 5 Freddy" Brathwaite, interview by author, Brooklyn, New York, January 2013.

12. Walter Yetnikoff, interview by author, New York, New York, April 2013.

13. Paul Grein, "Chartbeat," *Billboard*, February 26, 1983.

14. Paul Grein, "Jackson and Q in View; The British Are Coming," *Billboard*, March 5, 1983.

15. Billboard staff, "'Billie Jean' Gets Her MTV," *Billboard*, March 26, 1983.

16. Walter Yetnikoff, interview by author, New York, New York, April 2013.

17. Michael Jackson, *Moonwalk*, 204.

18. John Kellogg, interview by author, Boston, Massachusetts, January 2013.

19. Berry Gordy, interview by author, New York, New York, February 2013.

20. Michael Jackson, "Motown 25 Performance of Billie Jean," unpublished notes (circa 1983), dictated to author by Karen Langford via telephone, July 2013.

21. Michael Jackson, interview with Oprah Winfrey, *Michael Jackson Talks to . . . Oprah Live*, 1993, http://www.youtube.com/watch?v=wN1dTHdckzg.

22. Michael Jackson, spoken interlude, *Motown 25: Yesterday, Today, Forever*, 1983.

23. Michael Jackson, "Motown 25 Performance of Billie Jean," unpublished notes (circa 1983), dictated to author by Karen Langford via telephone, July 2013.

24. Walter Yetnikoff, interview by author, New York, New York, April 2013.

25. Michael Jackson, *Moonwalk*, 213.

26. Jay Cocks, "Sing a Song of Seeing," *Time*, December 26, 1983.

27. Joseph Vogel, *Man in the Music* (New York: Sterling, 2011), 67–68.

28. Kevin Liles, interview by author, New York, New York, August 2012.

29. Christopher "Ludacris" Bridges, interview by author, New York, New York, June 2012.

30. Matt Forger, telephone conversation with author, November 2012.

31. John Branca, interview by author, Beverly Hills, California, August 2012.

32. Myrna Oliver, "Milton Rudin; Hollywood Attorney," *Los Angeles Times*, December 16, 1999, http://articles.latimes.com/1999/dec/16/news/mn-44506.

33. John Branca, interview by author, Beverly Hills, California, August 2012.

34. Walter Yetnikoff, interview by author, New York, New York, April 2013.

35. Nancy Griffin, "The 'Thriller' Diaries," *Vanity Fair*, July 2010, http://www.vanityfair.com/hollywood/features/2010/07/michael-jackson-thriller-201007?printable=true&currentPage=2.

36. Walter Yetnikoff, interview by author, New York, New York, March 2013.

37. Bob Pittman, electronic message to author, January 2013.

38. Walter Yetnikoff, interview by author, New York, New York, March 2013.

39. Berry Gordy, interview by author, New York, New York, February 2013.

40. John Branca, telephone conversation with author, April 2013; interview by author, Beverly Hills, California, August 2012.

41. Michael Jackson, "Thriller" music video, 1983, http://www.youtube.com/watch?v=sOnqjkJTMaA.

42. Gayle Gaviola, electronic message to author, September 2013.

43. John Branca, interview by author, Beverly Hills, California, August 2012.
44. Walter Yetnikoff, interview by author, New York, New York, March 2013.
45. Tom O'Neil, "Flashback: Michael Jackson's Historic Grammy Triumph for 'Thriller,'" *Los Angeles Times*, June 26, 2009.
46. Walter Yetnikoff, interview by author, New York, New York, March 2013.
47. Walter Yetnikoff, *Howling at the Moon*, 159.
48. Jessica Erskine, electronic message to author, September 2013.
49. Ronald Reagan, speech introducing Michael Jackson, 1984, http://www.youtube.com/watch?v=XEmj9MTqoGk.
50. John Branca, interview by author, Beverly Hills, California, August 2012.
51. Author's note: In our March 2013 interview, Yetnikoff didn't recall giving Jackson his masters back. Then again, he admits his memory of the 1980s is spotty, as evidenced by the following interchange that occurred when we discussed the *Motown 25* special.

    Yetnikoff: It probably did spike sales . . . what year was that?
    Greenburg: 1983.
    Yetnikoff: I was drunk.

CHAPTER SIX: THE BUSINESS OF VICTORY

1. Charles Sullivan, interview by author, New York, New York, September 2012.
2. John Branca, interview by author, Los Angeles, California, February 2013.
3. Joe Jackson, interview by author, Las Vegas, Nevada, August 2012.
4. Michael Jackson, *Moonwalk*, 238.
5. Jermaine Jackson, *You Are Not Alone*, 243.
6. Charles Sullivan, interview by author, New York, New York, September 2012.
7. Ben Sisario, "Frank Dileo, Michael Jackson's Manager, Dies at 63," *New York Times*, August 24, 2011, http://www.nytimes.com/2011/08/25/arts/music/frank-dileo-michael-jacksons-manager-dies-at-63.html.
8. Robert Hilburn, "The Long and Winding Road," *Los Angeles Times*, September 22, 1985.
9. John Branca, interview by author, Beverly Hills, California, August 2012.
10. Jermaine Jackson, *You Are Not Alone*, 247.
11. Charles Sullivan, interview by author, New York, New York, September 2012.
12. Edward C. Baig, "The Can-Do Promoter of the Jacksons Tour," *Fortune*, August 20, 1984.
13. Cynthia Minor, telephone conversation with author, October 2012.
14. John Branca, interview by author, New York, New York, November 2012.
15. Jermaine Jackson, *You Are Not Alone*, 245.
16. Michael Jackson, *Moonwalk*, 236.
17. Karen Langford, telephone conversation with author, July 2013.
18. Michael Jackson, *Moonwalk*, 237–238.

19. Susan Blond, interview by author, New York, New York, August 2012.

20. Jermaine Jackson, *You Are Not Alone*, 247.

21. Charles Sullivan, interview by author, New York, New York, September 2012.

22. Bruce Swedien, telephone conversation with author, November 2012.

23. Author's note: Over the course of his career, Jermaine Jackson actually released three self-titled albums—*Jermaine*, *Jermaine* (yes, again) and *Jermaine Jackson*—as well as another called *My Name Is Jermaine* (at least there was only one *Precious Moments*).

24. Walter Yetnikoff, interview by author, New York, New York, April 2013.

25. Jermaine Jackson, *You Are Not Alone*, 256.

26. Cynthia Minor, telephone conversation with author, October 2012.

27. Michael Jackson, *Moonwalk*, 245.

28. Cynthia Minor, telephone conversation with author, October 2012.

29. Michael Cohl, telephone conversation with author, September 2013.

30. Jermaine Jackson, *You Are Not Alone*, 259, 263.

31. Cynthia Minor, telephone conversation with author, October 2012.

32. Walter Yetnikoff, interview by author, New York, New York, April 2013.

33. Michael Jackson, *Moonwalk*, 242.

34. Cynthia Minor, telephone conversation with author, October 2012.

35. Jermaine Jackson, *You Are Not Alone*, 273.

36. Charles Sullivan, interview by author, New York, New York, September 2012.

37. Michael Cohl, telephone conversation with author, September 2013.

38. Charles Sullivan, interview by author, New York, New York, September 2012.

39. Karen Langford, telephone conversation with author, July 2013.

40. Charles Sullivan, interview by author, New York, New York, September 2012.

41. Linda Moss, "Jeans to Jackson," *Crain's New York Business*, June 2, 1986.

42. Monte Burke, "Unlikely Dynasty," *Forbes*, September 19, 2005.

43. Charles Sullivan, interview by author, New York, New York, September 2012.

44. Monte Burke, "Unlikely Dynasty," *Forbes*, September 19, 2005.

45. Charles Sullivan, interview by author, New York, New York, September 2012; electronic message to author, June 2013.

CHAPTER SEVEN: BUYING THE BEATLES

1. Marty Bandier, interview by author, New York, New York, January 2013.

2. John Branca, interview by author, Beverly Hills, California, August 2012.

3. Michael Jackson, *Moonwalk*, 189.

4. John Branca, interview by author, Beverly Hills, California, August 2012.

5. Karen Langford, telephone conversation with author, July 2013.

6. Les Bider, telephone conversation with author, October 2013.

7. John Branca, interview by author, New York, New York, November 2012; telephone conversation with author, April 2013.

8. Andrew Ross Sorkin, "Berry Gordy Sells EMI a Stake in Catalogue of Motown Songs," *New York Times*, July 2, 1997.

9. Berry Gordy, interview by author, New York, New York, February 2013.

10. John Branca, interview by author, Beverly Hills, California, August 2012.

11. Louis Kraar, "Australia's Acquisitive Recluse," *Fortune*, August 19, 1985, http://money.cnn.com/magazines/fortune/fortune_archive/1985/08/19/66315/index.htm.

12. Yoko Ono, interview by author, New York, New York, April 2013.

13. John Branca, interview by author, Beverly Hills, California, August 2012. Author's note: Eastman doesn't remember any such conversation. "Michael Jackson's people never called me," he told me when reached for comment via telephone.

14. Marty Bandier, interview by author, New York, New York, January 2013.

15. Joe Jackson, interview by author, Las Vegas, Nevada, August 2012.

16. Marty Bandier, interview by author, New York, New York, January 2013.

17. Walter Yetnikoff, interview by author, New York, New York, March 2013.

18. Tom Barrack, telephone conversation with author, August 2013.

19. Michael Jackson, unpublished memo (circa 1985); see appendix.

20. John Branca, interview by author, Beverly Hills, California, August 2012.

21. Marty Bandier, interview by author, New York, New York, January 2013.

22. Ibid.

23. John Branca, interview by author, Beverly Hills, California, August 2012.

24. Marty Bandier, interview by author, New York, New York, January 2013

25. J. Randy Taraborrelli, *Michael Jackson: The Magic and the Madness*, 337.

26. Paul McCartney, interview with David Letterman, *The Late Show*, July 15, 2009, http://www.youtube.com/watch?v=f4cVsqUF7GQ.

27. John Branca, interview by author, New York, New York, November 2012.

28. Marty Bandier, interview by author, New York, New York, January 2013.

29. John Branca, interview by author, New York, New York, November 2012; telephone interview by author, October 2013; telephone conversation with author, April 2013.

30. Dale Kawashima, telephone conversation with author, December 2012.

31. Marty Bandier, interview by author, New York, New York, January 2013.

32. Walter Yetnikoff, interview by author, New York, New York, April 2013.

33. Marty Bandier, interview by author, New York, New York, January 2013.

CHAPTER EIGHT: DANCING WITH THE STARS

1. Author's observation, Anaheim, California, February 2013.

2. Author's note: this figure includes the cost of upgrading theaters to accommodate *Captain EO*.

3. John Branca, electronic message to author, February 2012.

4. Rusty Lemorande, interview by author, Anaheim, California, February 2013.
5. Michael Jackson, *Moonwalk*, 258.
6. John Branca, interview by author, Los Angeles, California, February 2013.
7. Rusty Lemorande, interview by author, Anaheim, California, February 2013.
8. Michael Bush, interview by author, New York, New York, November 2012.
9. Matt Forger, electronic message to author, September 2013.
10. Rusty Lemorande, interview by author, Anaheim, California, February 2013.
11. Michael Jackson, *Moonwalk*, 258.
12. Rusty Lemorande, interview by author, Anaheim, California, February 2013.
13. Michael Bush, interview by author, New York, New York, November 2012.
14. Matt Forger, telephone conversation with author, November 2012.
15. Rusty Lemorande, interview by author, Anaheim, California, February 2013.
16. Walter Yetnikoff, interview by author, New York, New York, April 2013.
17. Vincent Canby, "'Big Screen' Takes on New Meaning," *New York Times*, April 19, 1987, http://www.nytimes.com/1987/04/19/movies/big-screen-takes-on-new-meaning.html?pagewanted=all&src=pm.
18. Chris Kohler, "Michael Jackson's Revived *Captain EO* Is Still Wired, Slightly Tired," *Wired*, March 22, 2010, http://www.wired.com/underwire/2010/03/captain-eo-tribute/.
19. Rusty Lemorande, interview by author, Anaheim, California, February 2013.

CHAPTER NINE: GOOD AND BAD

1. Michael Levine, interview by author, Beverly Hills, California, August 2012.
2. John Branca, interview by author, Los Angeles, California, February 2013.
3. RIAA staff, Gold and Platinum database, various searches, http://www.riaa.com/goldandplatinumdata.php.
4. Joseph Vogel, *Man in the Music*, 97; electronic message to author, June 2012.
5. Michael Jackson, "Thoughts on Work and Secrecy," unpublished notes (circa 1985), dictated to author by Karen Langford via telephone, July 2013.
6. Neil Harris, *Humbug: The Art of P.T. Barnum*, 4.
7. Ibid, 57.
8. Michael Levine, interview by author, Beverly Hills, California, August 2012.
9. John Antczak, "Superstar Buying Oxygen Therapy Device; Physician Warns Against It," Associated Press, September 16, 1986.
10. United Press International staff, "Michael Jackson Told to Avoid Oxygen Unit," *San Francisco Chronicle*, September 20, 1986.
11. Michael Levine, interview by author, Beverly Hills, California, August 2012.
12. J. Randy Taraborrelli, *Michael Jackson: The Magic and the Madness*, 361–363.
13. Neil Harris, *Humbug: The Art of P. T. Barnum*, 27.
14. Jon Wiener, "Beatles Buy-Out," *New Republic*, May 11, 1987, http://www.newrepublic.com/article/music/beatles-buy-out.
15. Marty Bandier, interview by author, New York, New York, January 2013.
16. John Branca, interview by author, Los Angeles, California, February 2013.

17. Paul McCartney, interview with David Letterman, *The Late Show*, July 15, 2009, http://www.youtube.com/watch?v=f4cVsqUF7GQ.

18. Jonathan Takiff, "Commercial Viewers Getting a Different Look at Beatles," *Houston Chronicle*, June 13, 1987.

19. Patrick Goldstein, "Revolting Trend in TV Commercials?" *Los Angeles Times*, May 10, 1987.

20. Jon Wiener, "Beatles Buy-Out," *New Republic*, May 11, 1987, http://www.newrepublic.com/article/music/beatles-buy-out.

21. Alan Light, "Changes in Mellencamp Country," *New York Times*, January 22, 2007, http://www.nytimes.com/2007/01/22/arts/music/22mell.html.

22. Joseph Vogel, electronic message to author, June 2012.

23. John Branca, interview by author, Beverly Hills, California, August 2012.

24. Matt Forger, telephone conversation with author, November 2012.

25. Bruce Swedien, telephone conversation with author, November 2012.

26. Bea Swedien, telephone conversation with author, November 2012.

27. John Branca, interview by author, Los Angeles, California, February 2013.

28. Karen Langford, electronic message to author, October 2013.

29. Fred "Fab 5 Freddy" Brathwaite, interview by author, Brooklyn, New York, January 2013.

30. Jon Pareles, "Pop: Michael Jackson's 'Bad,' Follow-Up to a Blockbuster," *New York Times*, August 31, 1987, http://www.nytimes.com/1987/08/31/arts/pop-michael-jackson-s-bad-follow-up-to-a-blockbuster.html.

31. Richard Cromelin, "Michael Jackson Has a Good Thing in 'Bad,'" *Los Angeles Times*, August 31, 1987, http://www.latimes.com/la-archive-bad-review-aug31,0,7199736.story.

32. Davitt Sigerson, *"Bad,"* *Rolling Stone*, October 22, 1987, http://www.rollingstone.com/music/albumreviews/bad-19871022.

33. Joseph Vogel, *Man in the Music*, 93.

34. Paul Richter and William K. Knoedelseder Jr., "Sony Buys CBS Record Division For $2 Billion After Months of Talks," *Los Angeles Times*, November 19, 1987.

35. Walter Yetnikoff, interview by author, New York, New York, April 2013.

36. Michael Jackson, *BAD 25* liner notes, MJJ Productions/Epic, 2012.

37. Bruce Swedien, telephone conversation with author, November 2012.

38. Michael Cohl, telephone conversation with author, September 2013.

39. Michael Bush, interview by author, New York, New York, November 2012.

40. Dale Kawashima, telephone conversation with author, December 2012.

41. Jon Bon Jovi, telephone conversation with author, August 2012.

42. Sheryl Crow, telephone conversation with author, September 2013.

43. Michael Levine, interview by author, Beverly Hills, California, August 2012.

44. James Baldwin, *The Price of the Ticket* (New York: Macmillan, 1985), 689.

CHAPTER TEN: OFF TO NEVERLAND

1. Author's observation, Neverland Valley Ranch, Santa Ynez, California, August 2012.
2. Tom Barrack, telephone conversation with author, August 2012.
3. Author's observation, Neverland Valley Ranch, Santa Ynez, California, August 2012.
4. John Branca, interview by author, Beverly Hills, California, August 2012.
5. Don Kaplan, "Liz & Jacko: Hollywood's Odd Couple," *New York Post*, March 24, 2011.
6. Elizabeth Taylor, interview with Oprah Winfrey, *Michael Jackson Talks to . . . Oprah Live*, 1993, http://www.youtube.com/watch?v=wN1dTHdckzg.
7. Michael Jackson, *Moonwalk*, 281.
8. John Branca, interview by author, Beverly Hills, California, August 2012.
9. Les Bider, telephone conversation with author, October 2013.
10. Karen Langford, telephone conversation with author, July 2013.
11. RIAA staff, "Moonwalker," RIAA searchable database, http://www.riaa.com/goldandplatinumdata.php?resultpage=1&table=SEARCH_RESULTS&action=&title=moonwalker&artist=michael%20jackson&startMonth=1&endMonth=1&startYear=1958&endYear=2009&sort=Artist&perPage=25.
12. Karen Langford, electronic message to author, August 2013.
13. Shaye Areheart, interview by author, New York, New York, September 2013.
14. John Branca, telephone conversation with author, October 2013.
15. Ken Tucker, "Firing Your Father Isn't Easy," *New York Times*, June 5, 1988, http://www.nytimes.com/1988/06/05/books/summer-reading-firing-your-father-isn-t-easy.html.
16. Shaye Areheart, interview by author, New York, New York, September 2013.
17. Walter Yetnikoff, interview by author, New York, New York, April 2013.
18. Priscilla Giraldo, electronic message to author, October 2012.
19. David Geffen, electronic message to author, April 2013.
20. Karen Langford, electronic message to author, August 2013.
21. Walter Yetnikoff, interview by author, New York, New York, April 2013.
22. AllMusic staff, "Original Soundtrack: *Days of Thunder*," AllMusic.com, date unknown, http://www.allmusic.com/album/days-of-thunder-mw0000308768/awards.
23. Tom Mesereau, interview by author, Los Angeles, California, August 2012.
24. Donny B. Lord, telephone conversation with author, March 2013.
25. Melanie Cohen, "Custody of Jackson Children May Be Marred by Bankruptcy Filing," *Wall Street Journal*, July 1, 2009, http://blogs.wsj.com/bankruptcy/2009/07/01/custody-of-jackson-children-may-be-marred-by-bankruptcy-filing/.

26. Joe Jackson, interview by author, Las Vegas, Nevada, August 2012.

27. Josh Altman, telephone conversation with author, October 2013.

CHAPTER ELEVEN: NEW SHOES

1. Curtis "50 Cent" Jackson, interview by author, New York, New York, March 2013.

2. Walter LaFeber, *Michael Jordan and the New Global Capitalism* (New York: W. W. Norton & Company, 2002), 60–65.

3. Russell Simmons, electronic message to author, July 2013.

4. Sandy Saemann, telephone conversation with author, July 2013.

5. Walter LaFeber, *Michael Jordan and the New Global Capitalism*, 65.

6. John Branca, interview by author, Beverly Hills, California, August 2012; telephone conversation with author, April 2013.

7. Sandy Saemann, telephone conversation with author, July 2013.

8. Michael Jackson, LA Gear press conference, 1992, http://www.youtube.com/watch?v=ZPlKYYQa8Ow.

9. John Branca, interview by author, Los Angeles, California, February 2013.

10. Walter Yetnikoff, telephone conversation with author, November 2013.

11. John Branca, interview by author, Los Angeles, California, February 2013.

12. Walter Yetnikoff, telephone conversation with author, November 2013.

13. Michael Jackson, memo to Gary Stiffelman (circa 1990).

14. Author's note: When reached via telephone, Grubman declined to be interviewed for this book.

15. Sandy Gallin, telephone conversation with author, August 2013.

16. Michael Jackson, LA Gear commercial, 1990, http://www.youtube.com/watch?v=oNueHwzCS2M.

17. Sandy Saemann, telephone conversation with author, July 2013.

18. Bruce Horovitz, "Michael Jackson Starts Selling LA Gear's Soles," *Los Angeles Times*, August 6, 1990, http://articles.latimes.com/1990-08-06/business/fi-189_1_michael-jackson.

19. Michael Lev, "Shares of LA Gear Drop on News of Loss," *New York Times*, January 22, 1991, http://www.nytimes.com/1991/01/22/business/company-news-shares-of-la-gear-drop-on-news-of-loss.html.

20. Stuart Silverstein, "LA Gear's No. 2 Executive, Sandy Saemann, Is Leaving," *Los Angeles Times*, June 13, 1991, http://articles.latimes.com/1991-06-13/business/fi-776_1_stock-market.

21. Sandy Saemann, telephone conversation with author, July 2013.

22. Curtis "50 Cent" Jackson, interview by author, New York, New York, March 2013.

CHAPTER TWELVE: DANGEROUS VENTURES

1. Author's note: According to Riley, Jones had removed himself from consideration for the role of producer. ("I'm tired, Michael," he had supposedly told the King of Pop. "I need to rest on this one, but I got your man.") Bruce Swedien and others, however, insisted that the decision was Jackson's.
2. Bruce Swedien, telephone conversation with author, November 2012.
3. Teddy Riley, telephone conversation with author, July 2013.
4. Matt Forger, telephone conversation with author, November 2012.
5. Alan Cintron and Chuck Philips, "Michael Jackson Agrees to Huge Contract with Sony," *Los Angeles Times*, March 21, 1991, http://www.latimes.com/la-me-jacksontimeline-sony,0,6376836,print.story.
6. Sandy Gallin, telephone conversation with author, August 2013.
7. Chris Willman, "Michael Jackson's *Dangerous*," *Los Angeles Times*, November 24, 1991, http://www.latimes.com/la-archive-dangerous-review-nov24,0,5763920.story.
8. Jon Pareles, "Michael Jackson in the Electronic Wilderness," November 24, 1991, http://www.nytimes.com/1991/11/24/arts/recordings-view-michael-jackson-in-the-electronic-wilderness.html?pagewanted=all&src=pm.
9. Alan Light, "Michael Jackson: *Dangerous*," *Rolling Stone*, January 1, 1992, http://www.rollingstone.com/music/albumreviews/dangerous-19920101.
10. Joseph Vogel, *Man in the Music*, 149, 131.
11. Karen Langford, telephone conversation with author, July 2013.
12. Dale Kawashima, telephone conversation with author, December 2012.
13. Saul "Slash" Hudson, interview by author, New York, New York, September 2012.
14. Sandy Gallin, telephone conversation with author, August 2013.
15. New York Times staff, "Super Bowl XXVII; Overnight TV Rating Higher," *New York Times*, February 2, 1993, http://www.nytimes.com/1993/02/02/sports/super-bowl-xxvii-overnight-tv-rating-higher.html.
16. Brian McCarthy, electronic message to author, January 2013.
17. Greg Aiello, electronic message to author, January 2013. Author's note: Aiello said the NFL didn't have a record of the payment; as for the reported figure, he was "confident that it is accurate."
18. Brad Buxer, electronic message to author, August 2013.
19. Michael Jackson, Super Bowl XXVII Halftime Show, 1993, http://www.youtube.com/watch?v=1T5cB6yyivY.
20. New York Times staff, "Super Bowl XXVII; Overnight TV Rating Higher," *New York Times*, February 2, 1993, http://www.nytimes.com/1993/02/02/sports/super-bowl-xxvii-overnight-tv-rating-higher.html.
21. Michael Jackson, interview with Oprah Winfrey, *Michael Jackson Talks to . . . Oprah Live*, 1993, http://www.youtube.com/watch?v=wN1dTHdckzg.
22. Oprah.com staff, "25 Highest-Rated *Oprah Show* Episodes," Oprah.com,

April 29, 2011, http://www.oprah.com/own-where-are-they-now/25-most-watched-oprah-show-episodes/26.

23. Sandy Gallin, telephone conversation with author, August 2013.

24. Jermaine Jackson, *You Are Not Alone*, 315.

25. Elizabeth Taylor, interview with Oprah Winfrey, *Michael Jackson Talks to . . .Oprah Live*, 1993, http://www.youtube.com/watch?v=wN1dTHdckzg.

26. Frank Cascio, *My Friend Michael* (New York: William Morrow/Harper-Collins, 2011), 12, 17.

27. Greg Campbell, interview by author, Gary, Indiana, July 2012.

28. Oprah Winfrey, monologue, *Michael Jackson Talks to . . . Oprah Live*, 1993, http://www.youtube.com/watch?v=wN1dTHdckzg.

29. Jermaine Jackson, *You Are Not Alone*, 317.

30. Frank Cascio, *My Friend Michael*, 42.

31. Mary A. Fischer, "Was Michael Jackson Framed?" *GQ*, October 1994.

32. Jermaine Jackson, *You Are Not Alone*, 318.

33. J. Randy Taraborrelli, *Michael Jackson: The Magic and the Madness*, 485.

34. Jermaine Jackson, *You Are Not Alone*, 318.

35. Mary A. Fischer, "Was Michael Jackson Framed?" *GQ*, October 1994.

36. Rusty Lemorande, interview by author, Anaheim, California, February 2013.

37. Newsweek staff, "Michael's World," *Newsweek*, September 5, 1993.

38. Jermaine Jackson, *You Are Not Alone*, 319–320.

39. Ibid.

40. Frank Cascio, *My Friend Michael*, 37, 63–35.

41. John Branca, interview by author, Beverly Hills, California, August 2012; electronic message to author, February 2012.

42. Author's note: Branca says he fired Fields; Fields says he resigned.

43. Bert Fields, electronic message to author, September 2013.

44. Frank Cascio, *My Friend Michael*, 67.

45. J. Randy Taraborrelli, *Michael Jackson: The Magic and the Madness*, 525, 530.

46. Jermaine Jackson, *You Are Not Alone*, 328.

47. Bill Hutchinson, "Evan Chandler, Dad of Boy Who Accused Michael Jackson of Molestation, Commits Suicide in New Jersey," *New York Daily News*, November 17, 2009, http://www.nydailynews.com/entertainment/gossip/evan-chandler-dad-boy-accused-michael-jackson-molestation-commits-suicide-new-jersey-article-1.417751.

CHAPTER THIRTEEN: HISTORY LESSON

1. John Branca, interview by author, Beverly Hills, California, August 2012.

2. Karen Langford, electronic message to author, August 2013.

3. Brad Buxer, electronic message to author, August 2013.

4. Karen Langford, electronic message to author, October 2013.

5. Matt Forger, electronic message to author, September 2013.

6. Karen Langford, electronic message to author, August 2013.

7. Jermaine Jackson, *You Are Not Alone*, 334–335.

8. Richard N. Lelby, "One Theory on Michael-Lisa: It's All a Plot," *Seattle Times*, August 9, 1994, http://community.seattletimes.nwsource.com/archive /?date=19940809&slug=1924408.

9. Tony Ortega, "Lisa Marie Presley Says 'So Long' to Scientology," *The Village Voice*, May 13, 2012, http://blogs.villagevoice.com/runninscared /2012/05/lisa_marie_presley_says_so_long_to_scientology.php.

10. Anne Bergman, "Jackson-Presley Union Sparks Shock, Doubt, Laughs," *Los Angeles Times*, August 3, 1994, http://articles.latimes.com/1994-08-03/enter-tainment/ca-22934_1_michael-jackson.

11. Jermaine Jackson, *You Are Not Alone*, 335.

12. Episode Unknown, *Oprah*, CTV, date unknown, http://www.youtube.com /watch?v=paqnj3dDUOY.

13. Frank Cascio, *My Friend Michael*, 84.

14. Michael Jackson and Prince Alwaleed Bin Talal, press conference, 1997, http://www.youtube.com/watch?v=6LxRAweU7Fs&feature=related.

15. John Branca, interview by author, Beverly Hills, California, February 2013.

16. Sandy Gallin, telephone conversation with author, August 2013.

17. Karen Langford, telephone conversation with author, July 2013.

18. Brooks Barnes and Michael Cieply, "Disney Swoops into Action, Buying Marvel for $4 Billion," *New York Times*, August 31, 2009, http://www .nytimes.com/2009/09/01/business/media/01disney.html.

19. Heba Fatani, electronic message to author, September 2013.

20. Marty Bandier, interview by author, New York, New York, January 2013.

21. Karen Langford, electronic message to the author, October 2013.

22. Marty Bandier, interview by author, New York, New York, January 2013.

23. Tommy Mottola, telephone conversation with author, December 2012.

24. Marty Bandier, interview by author, New York, New York, January 2013.

25. Sean "Diddy" Combs, telephone conversation with author, June 2013.

26. Teddy Riley, telephone conversation with author, July 2013.

27. Michael Jackson, "Scream," *HIStory: Past, Present and Future, Book I*, Epic, 1995.

28. Michael Jackson, "D.S.," *HIStory: Past, Present and Future, Book I*, Epic, 1995.

29. Michael Jackson, "They Don't Care About Us," *HIStory: Past, Present and Future, Book I*, Epic, 1995.

30. Jon Pareles, "Michael Jackson Is Angry, Understand?" *New York Times*, June 18, 1995, http://www.nytimes.com/1995/06/18/arts/pop-view-michael-jackson-is-angry-understand.html?pagewanted=all&src=pm.

31. Abraham Foxman, "ADL Welcomes Michael Jackson's Decision to Remove Anti-Semitic Lyrics From Song," Anti-Defamation League release, June 22, 1995, http://archive.adl.org/PresRele/ASUS_12/2471_12.asp.

32. Sandy Gallin, telephone conversation with author, August 2013.

33. Jon Pareles, "Michael Jackson Is Angry, Understand?" *New York Times*, June 18, 1995, http://www.nytimes.com/1995/06/18/arts/pop-view-michael-jackson-is-angry-understand.html?pagewanted=all&src=pm.

34. Karen Langford, telephone conversation with author, July 2013.

35. Author's note: For all the circus planners out there, that's ninety female Asian elephants.

36. Popular Mechanics staff, "Extreme Machines Antonov An-225 Is the World's Biggest Plane," *Popular Mechanics*, January 1, 2003, http://www.popularmechanics.com/technology/aviation/news/1280771.

37. John Branca, interview by author, Beverly Hills, California, May 2013; telephone conversation with author, October 2013.

38. Author's note: Wiesner claims to have worked for candy maker Haribo and airline Lufthansa, but only the latter was able to confirm that he'd actually been an employee.

39. Dieter Wiesner, telephone conversation with author, September 2013.

40. *Katherine Jackson et al. vs. AEG Live*, July 29, 2013.

41. John Branca, interview by author, Beverly Hills, California, February 2013.

42. Frank Cascio, *My Friend Michael*, 87–88.

43. Joel Schumacher, telephone conversation with author, October 2012.

44. Karen Langford, electronic message to author, October 2013.

45. John Jeremiah Sullivan, *Pulphead Essays* (New York: Farrar, Straus and Giroux, 2011), 109–110.

46. Joseph Vogel, *Man in the Music*, 208.

47. Matt Forger, telephone conversation with author, November 2012; electronic message to author, September 2013.

48. Dale Kawashima, telephone conversation with author, December 2012.

49. Chuck Philips, "Back in the Club," *Los Angeles Times*, March 26, 1998, http://articles.latimes.com/1998/mar/26/business/fi-32786.

50. John Branca, telephone conversation with author, October 2013.

51. Billboard staff, "Hot 100 55th Anniversary: The All-Time Top 100 Songs," Fred Bronson, August 2, 2013, http://www.billboard.com/articles/list/2155531/the-hot-100-all-time-top-songs?list_page=5.

52. Michael Jackson, telephone message, date unknown, 1999.

53. Jermaine Jackson, *You Are Not Alone*, 357–358.

54. Ibid.

CHAPTER FOURTEEN: INVINCIBLE?

1. Justin Bieber, interview by author, Los Angeles, California, April 2012.

2. Rodney Jerkins, interview by author, Los Angeles, California, April 2012.

3. Matt Forger, electronic message to author, September 2013; telephone conversation with author, November 2012.

4. Tommy Mottola, telephone conversation with author, December 2012.

5. Bruce Swedien, telephone conversation with author, September 2013.

6. Rodney Jerkins, interview by author, Los Angeles, California, April 2012.

7. Frank Cascio, *My Friend Michael*, 215–216.

8. Jermaine Jackson, *You Are Not Alone*, 353–354.

9. Joe D'Angelo, "Michael Jackson Proves *Invincible* on *Billboard* Albums Chart," November 7, 2001, http://www.mtv.com/news/articles/1450569/michael-jackson-debut-at-1.jhtml.

10. Jon Pareles, "To Regain Glory, the New Michael Imitates the Old," *New York Times*, October 28, 2001, http://www.nytimes.com/2001/10/28/arts/music-to-regain-glory-the-new-michael-imitates-the-old.html.

11. *The People of the State of California vs. Michael Joe Jackson*, Supreme Court of the State of California, No. 1133603, April 8, 2005.

12. Ron Burkle, interview by author, New York, New York, October 2013.

13. Ryan Nakashima and Alex Veiga, "Jackson Lived Like King but Died Awash in Debt," Associated Press, June 26, 2009.

14. Michael Jackson, speech in New York, 2002, http://www.youtube.com/watch?v=tBv3GzD97FY.

15. Tommy Mottola, telephone conversation with author, December 2012.

16. Jennifer Vineyard, "Michael Jackson Shocks Al Sharpton by Calling Tommy Mottola a Racist," MTV.com, July 8, 2002, http://www.mtv.com/news/articles/1455976/michael-jackson-calls-tommy-mottola-racist.jhtml.

17. Berry Gordy, interview by author, New York, New York, February 2013.

18. *The People of the State of California vs. Michael Joe Jackson*, Supreme Court of the State of California, No. 1133603, May 13, 2005.

19. Michael Jackson, letter to John Branca, February 2003, http://www.scribd.com/doc/43788480/You-Re-Fired.

20. Interfor staff, report on "MJ Business Associates," 2003, http://www.scribd.com/doc/102043792/Interfor-Report-John-Branca.

21. *The People of the State of California vs. Michael Joe Jackson*, Supreme Court of the State of California, No. 1133603, May 3, 2005.

22. Maureen Orth, "Losing His Grip," *Vanity Fair*, April 2003, http://www.vanityfair.com/fame/features/2003/04/orth200304.

23. Billboard Staff, "German Police Review Jackson's Baby Dangling," *Billboard*, November 20, 2002, http://www.billboard.com/articles/news/73382/german-police-review-jacksons-baby-dangling.

24. Neil Harris, *Humbug: The Art of P.T. Barnum*, 27.

25. Dieter Wiesner, telephone conversation with author, September 2013.

26. Christine Chase, electronic message to author, September 2013.

27. Jenn Michaels, electronic message to author, September 2013.

28. *Living with Michael Jackson*, Martin Bashir, 2003.

29. *Hamid Moslehi vs. MJJ Productions et al.*, Central District of California, Western Division, No. 0410234, http://www.thesmokinggun.com/file/hero-videographer-sues-jackson.

30. *Living with Michael Jackson*, Martin Bashir, 2003.

31. Frank Cascio, *My Friend Michael*, 278–279.

32. Tom Mesereau, interview by author, Los Angeles, California, August 2012.
33. Jeff Leeds, "Advice from a Team in Turmoil," *Los Angeles Times*, January 13, 2004, http://articles.latimes.com/2004/jan/13/entertainment/et-leeds13.
34. Tom Mesereau, telephone conversation with author, September 2013.
35. *The People of the State of California vs. Michael Joe Jackson*, Supreme Court of the State of California, No. 1133603, May 3, 2005.
36. *The People of the State of California vs. Michael Joe Jackson*, Supreme Court of the State of California, No. 1133603, April 8, 2005.
37. *The People of the State of California vs. Michael Joe Jackson*, Supreme Court of the State of California, No. 1133603, May 11, 2005.
38. Tom Mesereau, interview by author, Los Angeles, California, August 2012.
39. *The People of the State of California vs. Michael Joe Jackson*, Supreme Court of the State of California, No. 1133603, May 24, 2005.
40. *The People of the State of California vs. Michael Joe Jackson*, Supreme Court of the State of California, No. 1133603, April 18, 2005.
41. *The People of the State of California vs. Michael Joe Jackson*, Supreme Court of the State of California, No. 1133603, April 15, 2005.
42. *The People of the State of California vs. Michael Joe Jackson*, Supreme Court of the State of California, No. 1133603, May 19, 2005.
43. Tom Mesereau, interview by author, Los Angeles, California, August 2012.
44. Nancy Dillon, "Michael Jackson Nearly Overdosed," *New York Daily News*, August 10, 2013, http://www.nydailynews.com/entertainment/gossip/michael-jackson-overdosed-family-staged-10-drug-interventions-brother-article-1.1423100.
45. CourtTV, Michael Jackson trial coverage, 2005, http://www.youtube.com/watch?v=RtIEgIqRz0g&list=FLA7-TRMHUbDN1CaMKgAWclQ&index=30.
46. Tom Mesereau, interview by author, Los Angeles, California, August 2012.

CHAPTER FIFTEEN: THE PRODIGAL KING

1. *Prescient Acquisition Group et al. vs. Michael J. Jackson et al.*, No. 05 CV.6298, June 12–13, 2006.
2. BBC Staff, "Michael Jackson Surfaces in Dubai," BBC.com, August 30, 2005, http://news.bbc.co.uk/2/hi/4196746.stm.
3. Habib Toumi, "Jackson Settles Down to His New Life in the Gulf," Gulf-News.com, January 23, 2006, http://gulfnews.com/news/gulf/bahrain/jackson-settles-down-to-his-new-life-in-the-gulf-1.222403.
4. Teresa Wiltz, "Keeper of the Famed," *Washington Post*, October 8, 2006, http://www.washingtonpost.com/wp-dyn/content/article/2006/10/07/AR2006100700991.html.
5. Author's note: Bain did not respond to interview requests for this book.
6. Tom Mesereau, telephone conversation with author, September 2013.
7. Kim Masters, "Michael Jackson's Strange Final Days Revealed in

Dueling Lawsuits," *The Hollywood Reporter*, July 19, 2012, http://www .hollywoodreporter.com/news/michael-jackson-manager-tohme-lawsuit-351241?page=2.

8. *Prescient Acquisition Group et al. vs. Michael J. Jackson et al.*, No. 05 CV.6298, June 12–13, 2006.
9. Ron Burkle, interview with author, New York, New York, October 2013.
10. Ibid.
11. Author's note: Don Stabler did not reply to interview requests for this book.
12. Donald David, interview with author, New York, New York, August 2013.
13. Ibid.
14. Ron Burkle, interview with author, New York, New York, October 2013.
15. Donald David, interview with author, New York, New York, August 2013.
16. *The People of the State of California vs. Michael Joe Jackson*, Supreme Court of the State of California, No. 1133603, May 3, 2005.
17. *Prescient Acquisition Group et al. vs. Michael J. Jackson et al.*, No. 05 CV.6298, June 12–13, 2006.
18. Donald David, interview with author, New York, New York, August 2013.
19. *Prescient Acquisition Group et al. vs. Michael J. Jackson et al.*, No. 05 CV.6298, June 12–13, 2006.
20. Author's note: Burkle is not Jewish, so it's not exactly clear who's being referred to here.
21. Ron Burkle, interview with author, New York, New York, October 2013.
22. Donald David, interview with author, New York, New York, August 2013.
23. Frank James, "Michael Jackson's 2007 Net Worth: $236 Million," NPR .com, June 30, 2009, http://www.npr.org/blogs/thetwo-way/2009/06/michael_jackson_2007_net_worth.html.
24. Ron Burkle, interview with author, New York, New York, October 2013.
25. Lisa Marie Presley, interview with Oprah Winfrey, 2005, http://www .oprah.com/oprahshow/The-Last-Time-Lisa-Marie-Presley-Spoke-to-Michael-Jackson-Video.
26. Nasir "Nas" Jones, telephone conversation with author, April 2013.
27. Tom Barrack, telephone conversation with author, August 2013.
28. Ron Burkle, interview with author, New York, New York, October 2013.
29. Tom Martin, interview by author, Rosemount, Ireland, May 2013.
30. Jackie Martin, interview by author, Rosemount, Ireland, May 2013.

CHAPTER SIXTEEN: THIS IS IT

1. Tom Barrack, telephone conversation with author, August 2013.
2. Ibid.
3. Author's observation, Las Vegas, Nevada, September 2013.
4. Tom Barrack, telephone conversation with author, August 2013.
5. Ibid.
6. Karen Langford, electronic message to the author, October 2013.

7. Ron Burkle, interview with author, New York, New York, October 2013.

8. Tom Barrack, telephone conversation with author, August 2013.

9. Curtis "50 Cent" Jackson, interview by author, New York, New York, March 2013.

10. New York Times staff, "Jay Z Cashes In with Rocawear Deal," *New York Times*, March 6, 2007, http://dealbook.nytimes.com/2007/03/06/jay-z-cashes-in-with-200-million-rocawear-deal/.

11. Lea Goldman, "Capitalist Rap," *Forbes*, July 3, 2006.

12. Author's note: This writer included.

13. Curtis "50 Cent" Jackson, interview by author, New York, New York, March 2013.

14. Shaffer "Ne-Yo" Smith, interview by author, New York, New York, August 2012.

15. Pharrell Williams, telephone conversation with author, November 2012.

16. Kasseem "Swizz Beatz" Dean, interview by author, New York, New York, August 2012.

17. Michael Jackson, notes to self, published by *New York Post* in September 2013, http://pagesix.com/2013/09/12/michael-jackson-planned-to-immortalize-himself-in-films/.

18. Walter Yetnikoff, interview by author, New York, New York, April 2013.

19. Jermaine Jackson, *You Are Not Alone*, 390.

20. Paul Harris, "The Square Chin. The Deep Voice. But Was It Really Michael Jackson?" *Daily Mail*, March 13, 2009, http://www.dailymail.co.uk/tvshowbiz/article-1161879/The-square-chin-The-deep-voice-But-really-Michael-Jackson.html.

21. *Katherine Jackson et al. vs. AEG Live*, June 5, 2013.

22. Karen Langford, telephone conversation with author, October 2013; electronic message to author, October 2013.

23. Joe Jackson, interview by author, Las Vegas, Nevada, August 2012.

24. John Branca, interview by author, Beverly Hills, California, May 2013.

25. Michael Bush, interview by author, New York, New York, November 2012.

26. Kenneth Ortega, electronic message to AEG executives, June 14, 2009.

27. Ron Burkle, interview with author, New York, New York, October 2013.

28. *Katherine Jackson et al. vs. AEG Live*, June 21, 2013, http://www.scribd.com/doc/149594512/Jackson-V-AEGLive-Transcripts-June-21st-Dr-Charles-Czeisler-Sleep-Medicine-Harvard-Medical-School.

29. Kenneth Ortega, electronic message to AEG executives, June 20, 2009.

30. Michael Bush, interview by author, New York, New York, November 2012.

31. Tom Barrack, telephone conversation with author, August 2013.

32. Ron Burkle, interview with author, New York, New York, October 2013.

33. Tom Barrack, telephone conversation with author, August 2013.

CHAPTER SEVENTEEN: POSTMORTEM PAYDAY

1. Linnie Rawlinson and Nick Hunt, "Jackson Dies, Almost Takes Internet with Him," CNN.com, June 26, 2009, http://www.cnn.com/2009/TECH /06/26/michael.jackson.internet/.
2. Author's observation, New York, New York, June 2009.
3. Jill Serjeant and Eric Walsh, "Michael Jackson Memorial Draws 31.1 Million US TV Viewers," Reuters, July 9, 2009, http://www .reuters.com/article/2009/07/09/us-jackson-television-sb-idUS-TRE56774W20090709.
4. P. J. Huffstutter and Richard Fausset, "Around the World, a Shared Moment of 'Missing Michael,'" *Los Angeles Times*, July 8, 2009, http:// articles.latimes.com/2009/jul/08/nation/na-jackson-moment8.
5. Tom Barrack, telephone conversation with author, August 2013.
6. Michael Bush, interview by author, New York, New York, November 2012.
7. John Branca, interview by author, Beverly Hills, California, May 2013.
8. Karen Langford, telephone conversation with author, October 2013.
9. Author's observation of files at Los Angeles Superior Courthouse, Los Angeles, California, September 2013.
10. John Branca, telephone conversation with author, October 2013.
11. Author's note: Randy Jackson's attorney did not reply to requests to interview his client for this book.
12. Rachel Noerdlinger, electronic message to author, October 2013.
13. Author's observation, Los Angeles, California, August 2013.
14. Andrew Katzenstein, telephone conversation with author, August 2012. Note: Portions of this interview and associated topics appear in my story "The Scandalously Boring Truth About Michael Jackson's Will," Forbes .com, August 17, 2012, http://www.forbes.com/sites/zackomalleygreen burg/2012/08/17/the-scandalously-boring-truth-about-michael-jacksons-will/.
15. John Branca, interview by author, Beverly Hills, California, May 2013.
16. Chris White, telephone conversation with author, June 2009. Note: Portions of this interview and associated topics appear in my story "Michael Jackson's Estate Sale," Forbes.com, June 25, 2009, http://www.forbes.com /2009/06/26/michael-jackson-beatles-business-media-estate.html.
17. John Branca, telephone conversation with author, October 2013; interview by author, Beverly Hills, California, May 2013.
18. Karen Langford, telephone conversation with author, October 2013.
19. John Branca, telephone conversation with author, October 2013.
20. Response to Probate Notes, Superior Court of the State of California, No. BP 117 321, September 8, 2011, http://www.scribd.com/doc/68019500/ Report-of-Status-of-Administrations-and-Petition-for-Settlement.
21. Jermaine Jackson, *You Are Not Alone*, 144.

22. Author's note: The 10 percent cut encompasses all executor fees and does not apply to Jackson's Sony/ATV earnings.
23. *Ayscough & Marar vs. Michael J. Jackson et al.*, No. YC052627, July 25, 2006.
24. Los Angeles Times staff, "Katherine Jackson Shocked to Learn Reports of Her Kidnapping," *Los Angeles Times*, August 2, 2012, http://latimesblogs. latimes.com/lanow/2012/08/katherine-jackson-shocked-to-learn-reports-of-her-kidnapping.html.
25. Ibid.
26. Evelyn Diaz, "Jermaine Jackson Faces Jail Time Over Unpaid Child Support," BET.com, October 23, 2013, http://music.msn.com/music/article .aspx?news=835561.
27. Chuck Leavell, electronic message to author, September 2013.
28. Andrew Katzenstein, telephone conversation with author, September 2013.
29. Ben Sisario, "Jury Clears Promoter in Death of Michael Jackson," *New York Times*, October 2, 2013, http://www.nytimes.com/2013/10 /03/business/media/concert-promoter-found-not-liable-in-death-of-michael-jackson.html?hp&_r=1&.
30. Patrick Temple-West, "US Agency Says Michael Jackson Estate Owes $702 Million in Taxes," Reuters, August 23, 2013, http://www.reuters .com/article/2013/08/23/entertainment-us-usa-tax-jackson-idUSBRE-97M0YN20130823.
31. Estate of Michael Jackson, record of disbursements (November 2010 through Decmber 2011).
32. Karen Langford, telephone conversation with author, July 2013.
33. Kasseem "Swizz Beatz" Dean, interview with author, August 2012.

CHAPTER EIGHTEEN: IMMORTAL

1. Author's observation, Las Vegas, Nevada, May 2013.
2. John Branca, interview by author, Beverly Hills, California, May 2013.
3. Karen Langford, telephone conversation with author, July 2013.
4. Greg Phillinganes, telephone conversation with author, December 2011. Note: Portions of this interview and associated topics appear in my story "Why Michael Jackson Is the Top Touring Act in America, Again," Forbes.com, December 11, 2011, http://www.forbes.com/sites/zackomal leygreenburg/2011/12/12/why-michael-jackson-is-the-top-touring-act-in-america-again/.
5. Uptin Saiidi, "Michael Jackson Lives On in '*Immortal*' Tour," MTV, April 3, 2012, http://www.mtv.com/news/articles/1682347/michael-jackson-immortal-cirque.jhtml.
6. Andy Webster, "Singing Pageant of Pop, with a Circus Atmosphere," *New York Times*, April 2, 2012, http://theater.nytimes.com/2012/04/03/theater/ reviews/michael-jackson-the-immortal-world-tour-cirque-du-soleil.html? _r=0.

7. Randall Roberts, "Theater Review: Cirque du Soleil's *'Immortal,'*" *Los Angeles Times*, December 5, 2011.

8. John Branca, interview by author, Beverly Hills, California, May 2013.

9. Jamie King, electronic message to author, October 2013.

10. Author's observation, Las Vegas, Nevada, May 2013.

11. Jamie King, electronic message to author, October 2013. Author's note: A small portion of this interview also appeared in my Forbes.com piece "Michael Jackson *One*: The Latest Piece of a Postmortem Empire," October 23, 2013, http://www.forbes.com/sites/zackomalleygreenburg/2013/10/23/michael-jackson-one-the-latest-piece-of-a-postmortem-empire/.

12. Karen Langford, electronic message to author, October 2013.

13. Donald David, interview with author, October 2010. Author's note: A small portion of this interview also appeared in my Forbes.com piece "The Rich Afterlife of Michael Jackson," May 25, 2010, http://www.forbes.com/2010/10/21/michael-jackson-sony-business-entertainment-dead-celebs-10-jackson.html?boxes=businesschannellighttop.

14. Meryl Natow, "Paul McCartney to Regain Rights to Beatles Songs," The Fader.com, August 11, 2009, http://www.thefader.com/2009/08/11/paul-mccartney-to-regain-rights-to-beatles-songs/.

15. Shirley Halperin, "Sony ATV's Martin Bandier on Acquiring EMI Publishing," *The Hollywood Reporter*, November 11, 2012, http://www.hollywoodreporter.com/news/sony-atvs-martin-bandier-acquiring-389209.

16. Robin Leach, "'Michael Jackson *One*' is Cirque du Soleil's Best," *Las Vegas Sun*, May 24, 2013, http://www.lasvegassun.com/vegasdeluxe/2013/may/24/michael-jackson-one-cirque-du-soleil-best-and-incl/.

17. Author's observation, Las Vegas, Nevada, May 2013.

18. John Branca, interview by author, Beverly Hills, California, May 2013.

19. Author's observation, Gary, Indiana, July 2012.

20. Mayor Karen Freeman-Wilson, interview by author, Gary, Indiana, July 2012.

21. Greg Campbell, interview by author, Gary, Indiana, July 2012.

INDEX

A

"ABC," 30

Abdul-Jabbar, Kareem, 145

Abdullah, Sheikh, 199, 203, 208

Abrams, Mathis, 162–63

Adidas, 145

Aerosmith, 69, 181

Africa, 34–35, 71, 182

Alexenburg, Ron, 40, 43

Altman, Josh, 143

Alwaleed Bin Talal, Prince, 178, 185

    Jackson's partnership with, 172–73

Anschutz Entertainment Group
    (AEG), 214–15

    This Is It and, 217–21

    wrongful death suit against, 230–31

Anti-Defamation League (ADL),
    176–77

Apollo Theater, 9, 22–23, 25, 223

Apple, 108–9

Areheart, Shaye, 139–40

Arvizo, Gavin, 192–93, 195–97

Associated Press, 123

Astaire, Fred, 28, 71

ATV:

    administration of, 108, 131, 157,
    181

    Beatles' catalogue and, 1, 100–102,
    104–6, 108, 131

    Branca and, 166–67

    income and profitability of, 107–8,
    121

    Jackson's acquisition of, 1–2, 5,
    100–109, 125, 174, 252

    selling price of, 2, 104–5

    Sony's attempted acquisition of, 166

    Sony's merger with, 3, 6–7, 173–75

    sound effects library of, 101, 107

    see also Sony/ATV

Australia, 1–2, 34, 132, 139

    Holmes à Court and, 2, 100, 105,
    107

Azoff, Irving, 103–4

B

baby-dangling incident, 190

Bad, 48, 94, 117, 121, 126–31, 139,
    153, 190, 231

    Dangerous and, 155, 158

    sales of, 126, 128, 148, 155

Bad Tour, 114, 129–34, 136, 139

    Jackson's perfectionism and,
    133–34

    Jackson's preparations for, 132–33

    production of, 130–32

    ticket sales of, 2–3, 146

BAD 25, 231–32

Bahrain, 199–200, 202–3, 207–8

Bain, Raymone, 195, 199–200

Baldwin, James, 134

Bandier, Marty, 125

    ATV acquisition and, 100–106, 109

    Sony/ATV and, 52, 96–97, 107–8,
    174

Bank of America, 188, 200, 202, 205

Barnes, John, 127

Barnum, P. T., 5–6, 121–22, 124, 157,
    190–92, 232

Barrack, Tom, 102, 212–15, 224
 Jackson's relationship with, 210,
  212, 214
 and Jackson's search for new home,
  221–22
 Neverland foreclosure and, 211–13
 on Sony/ATV, 212–13
 This Is It and, 218
Barron, Steve, 66
Bashir, Martin, 192–93
Batman Forever, 179
Beach Boys, 1, 53
Beastie Boys, 125
"Beat It," 59–60, 78, 88, 116, 127
 music video to, 5, 7, 68–69, 71, 74,
  86
Beatles, 41, 59
 licensing recordings of, 124–26,
  141–42
 Love! and, 235, 238, 241
 music publishing catalogue of, 1,
  96–98, 100–102, 104–6, 108,
  124–26, 131, 141, 191, 204, 214,
  240
Bel Air, Calif., 221
Ben Ammar, Tarak, 178
Benson, Harry, 190
Bider, Les, 99, 138–39, 141
Bieber, Justin, 183, 233
"Big Boy," 20
Billboard, 29, 89, 136, 142, 175, 181,
  187
 Immortal and, 237
 Thriller and, 64–65, 67
"Billie Jean," 59–60, 127, 134, 159, 164,
  176, 224, 238
 Motown 25 and, 70–71
 music video to, 5, 66–68, 71, 74, 92,
  116, 145
"Black or White," 153, 156, 158–59
blacks, 1, 19, 50, 193, 206
 and backlash over Jackson's success,
  134
 "Billie Jean" video and, 5, 66–67

 exploitation of, 57–58, 72, 188
 Jackson's legacy and, 134
 racism and, 5, 66–67, 137, 188–89, 195
Blackstreet, 155, 176
Blond, Susan, 46, 87
Blood on the Dance Floor, 180–81
BMI, 54, 204
Bon Jovi, Jon, 131–33
Bonner, Erle, 225
Branca, John, 1–2, 52–56, 61–65, 112,
  131, 136–42, 146–50, 169
 E.T. project and, 63–64, 79
 fired by Jackson, 149–50, 157, 189
 Humbug and, 121, 124
 Immortal and, 235, 241–42
 investment suggestions of, 97–98
 Jackson's business acumen and, 77,
  83, 102
 Jackson's death and, 224–27
 Jackson's debts and, 226, 228
 on Jackson's expenditures, 178
 Jackson's motivational speech for,
  72–73
 Jackson's relationship with, 4, 52–53,
  55–56, 62, 64–65, 72–73, 147
 Jackson's royal nickname and,
  137–38
 Jackson's song acquisitions and, 2, 5,
  52–53, 98–104, 106–8, 138–39,
  166, 173–74, 252
 Jackson's will and, 225–26, 228–30
 LeGrand's investigations of, 189–90
 master recordings ownership and,
  73, 79
 Motown 25 and, 70
 One and, 234–35, 238, 241–42
 record deal negotiations and, 52,
  54–55, 72, 184
 rehired by Jackson, 166–67, 218–19
 This Is It and, 8, 227
 Thriller album and, 61–62, 126
 "Thriller" video and, 74–76
 Victory Tour and, 83–84
 Yetnikoff's apology to, 78–79

Branson, Richard, 100, 104, 106, 111
Braun, Scooter, 183
Brown, James, 17, 23, 172, 188
Bruton Music, 107
Bubbles (chimpanzee), 135, 161, 236
 Bad Tour and, 129, 133
Burkle, Ron, 208, 214
 Jackson's debts and, 201–2, 206–7
 Jackson's drug use and, 220
 and Jackson's search for new home,
  221
Bush, Michael, 224
 Bad Tour and, 130
 Captain EO and, 114, 116
 This Is It and, 219, 221
Buxer, Brad, 170–71

C
Calder, Clive, 107
Campbell, Greg, 12, 16, 162, 243
Cannes Film Festival, 179
"Can You Feel It," 57, 65–66
Captain EO, 110–19, 163–64
 budget of, 110, 115–17
 debut of, 117–18
 filming and editing of, 116–18
 Jackson's abandonment of, 117–19
 Jackson's wardrobe in, 114
 music and choreography of, 113
 reviews of, 118
 script and storyline of, 113, 116
 technology for, 114
Cascio, Eddie, 161, 166–67
Cascio, Frank:
 Jackson's drug use and, 166, 186–87
 Jackson's emotional deterioration
  and, 167
 Jackson's marriage and, 172, 179
 and Jackson's relationships with
  children, 161–62, 166
CBS Records, CBS Songs, 46, 63–70,
 82–84, 106–8, 158–59, 173
 Bad and, 128
 "Billie Jean" video and, 66–67, 74

Jackson 5 and, 37
Jacksons and, 40–41, 43–44, 54
Jackson's E.T. project and, 63–64
Jackson's record deals with, 47, 52,
 54–55, 72, 184
Sony's acquisition of, 128–29
Thriller album and, 61, 68, 72, 74, 87
"Thriller" video and, 74–75
Yetnikoff and, 2, 7, 39–40, 44, 51,
 63–65, 67–68, 72, 78, 91, 98, 102,
 106, 129, 141
see also Epic Records
Century City, Calif., 98
Chandler, Evan:
 and child molestation allegations
  against Jackson, 162–63, 168,
  170, 173, 193
 Jackson sued by, 165, 168–69, 173,
  193
Chandler, Jordan, 161–63
 Jackson's alleged molestation of,
  162–63, 165–66, 168–70, 173,
  186, 193
Chicago, Ill., 19–22, 25, 27
Cirque du Soleil, 8, 52
 and *Immortal*, 235–38
 and *One*, 234–35, 238–39, 241
"Climb Ev'ry Mountain," 16
Cline, Patsy, 114
Coca-Cola, 144, 249
Cochran, Johnnie, 167–68, 193, 201
Cohl, Michael, 95, 129
 Victory Tour and, 90, 92–93
Colony Capital, 210, 214
Combs, Sean "Diddy," 175, 215
"Come Together," 1, 100, 141–42
Commodores, 37
Control, 117, 181
Coppola, Francis Ford, 110, 115–17
copyrights:
 ATV and, 100–101, 103, 107–8, 174
 Jackson's father and, 56
 Jackson's song acquisitions and, 1,
  109, 138–39, 174, 181, 186, 240

copyrights (*cont.*)
  losing of, 138
  of McCartney, 97, 240
Corporation, 27, 37
Crow, Sheryl, 3, 133–34
Culkin, Macaulay, 196
Czeisler, Charles, 220

D

Dallas, Tex., 90, 92
Dancing Machine, 34
Dangerous, 153–58, 175
  cover art of, 156–57
  debut of, 156
  Jackson's LA Gear deal and, 147,
    150–51
  promotion of, 188
  reviews of, 156–57
  sales of, 155, 157
Dangerous Tour, 158, 163–64, 166–68,
    219, 238
David, Donald, 202–6, 240
Davis, Clive, 89
Davis, Sammy, Jr., 47, 188
Days of Thunder, 141–42, 148
Dean, Kasseem "Swizz Beatz," 216, 232
Def Jam Records, 5, 71–72
de Passe, Suzanne, 25, 29, 69
Destiny, 43
Detroit, Mich., 24–25
Diana Ross Presents the Jackson 5, 29
"Didn't Mean to Hurt You," 172
Dileo, Frank, 2
  Bad Tour and, 129, 131–32
  fired by Jackson, 148–50, 157
  Humbug and, 121, 124
  Jackson's image and, 120–24, 136
  Jackson's relationship with, 147–48
  rehired by Jackson, 218
  This Is It and, 220
  Thriller and, 74
  Victory Tour and, 82–84
"Dirty Diana," 128, 239
Disney, 3, 111–15, 118–19, 173

Disney, Walt, 112, 115, 217
Disneyland, 110–11, 117, 166
Dodger Stadium, 92
"Don't Stop 'Til You Get Enough,"
    49, 57
"D.S.," 176

E

Eastman, John, 101
Ebert, Roger, 49
Eisner, Michael, 112, 115, 117
Elephant Man (Joseph Merrick), 124,
    128, 134, 160, 190
EMI Records, EMI Music Publishing,
    96, 99, 240
  CBS deals and, 107
  and licensing of "Revolution," 125
  and Sony's merger with ATV, 174
Empire State of Mind (Greenburg), 8
Encino, Calif., *see* Hayvenhurst
Epic Records, 61, 69, 74, 82–83
  Jackson 5 and, 37
  Jacksons and, 40, 43, 46
  see also CBS Records, CBS Songs
E.T. companion audiobook, 63–64, 79

F

Fab 5 Freddy (Fred Brathwaite), 5, 66,
    128
Falcons, 14, 18
Fields, Bert, 167
50 Cent (Curtis Jackson), 3–4
  entrepreneurial ventures of, 3,
    144–45, 151–52, 215–16, 249
  Jackson's writing with, 215–16
Forbes, 8, 39, 80, 223, 251
Forger, Matt:
  Bad and, 126–27
  and *Blood on the Dance Floor*, 181
  Captain EO and, 114, 116
  and changes in recording industry,
    184
  Dangerous and, 156
  Jackson's business education and, 72

Jackson's video game deals and, 171
Thriller and, 59–60, 114, 156
Fortress Investment Group, 200, 202
Barrack and, 213–14
Fox, 158, 192, 227
Foxborough, Mass., 84–85, 88
Foxman, Abraham, 177
France, 33, 203
Freeman-Wilson, Karen, 14, 242–43

G

Gallin, Sandy, 3, 158, 161
Jackson's film career and, 149, 156
Jackson's relationship with, 149–50, 177
Gamble, Kenny, 42–43, 98
Game Creek, 95
Gary, Ind., 9, 16–18, 55
finances of, 242–43
Jackson 5 and, 17–18, 20, 25, 29–30
Jackson's childhood home in, 11–14, 223, 242–43
Jackson's death and, 11, 223
and Jackson's move to Los Angeles, 27–28
Gaye, Marvin, 37, 63
Geffen, David, 1–2, 111
ATV acquisition and, 2, 102
and *Days of Thunder* soundtrack, 141–42, 148
Jackson's relationship with, 141, 148–49, 177, 190
Yetnikoff's relationship with, 140–42, 148
Germany, 33, 182, 190–91, 194, 242
Get Rich or Die Tryin', 144, 152
Giraldi, Bob, 68, 86
"Girl Is Mine, The," 59–61, 64–65
G.I.T.: Get It Together, 34
Globe and Mail, 49
Goin' Places, 42–43
Gongaware, Paul, 219–20
"Good Vibrations," 126

Gordy, Berry, 108
daughter of, 31, 33–34, 37–38
finances of, 28, 33–34, 69, 74
impressed by Jackson, 10, 26, 38
Jackson 5 and, 4, 20, 24–30, 35, 37–38, 40–41, 255*n*
Jackson's artistic freedom and, 32, 35
Jackson's business education and, 4, 32, 44, 54, 70, 72
Jackson's death and, 38
Jackson's relationship with, 4, 25, 28–29, 31, 37–38, 44, 49, 69–70, 189
Jackson's song acquisitions and, 99
Motown and, 4, 20, 24–28, 33, 37, 41, 69, 99, 189, 255*n*
Motown 25 and, 69–70
rules and sayings of, 4, 32
The Wiz and, 44–45, 50
Gore, Tipper, 121
Got to Be There, 32
Greenberg, Robert, 146
Grouse Lodge, 208

H

Harlem, N.Y., 22, 44, 153, 188
"Harmonices Musices Odhecaton" (Petrucci), 36
Hayvenhurst, 31, 42, 70, 72–73, 136, 165, 228
Bad and, 127
Victory Tour and, 83
"Heal the World," 153, 156, 159
"Help Me Make It Through the Night," 99
hip-hop, 72, 94, 128, 144–45, 175, 181, 207
Hirsh, Warren, 93–94
HIStory: Past, Present and Future, Book I, 6, 175–78, 180, 187–88
HIStory Tour, 177–79, 184, 219
Hoefflin, Steven, 123
Holly, Buddy, 97, 125
Hollywood Palace, The, 29

Holmes, Cecil, 82
Holmes à Court, Penny, 105
Holmes à Court, Robert, 2, 100–105, 107
Houston Chronicle, 125
"How to Rob," 144
Hudson, Saul "Slash," 157–58
Huff, Leon, 42–43, 98
"Human Nature," 45, 60, 133–34
Humbug (Harris), 5, 121–22, 124, 191
Huston, Anjelica, 110, 117
hyperbaric oxygen chambers, 122–24,
    134, 161

I

"I Just Can't Stop Loving You," 48, 133
"I'll Be There," 30
Imagineers, 112, 114–15
"I'm Down," 125
Immortal, 235–42
Internal Revenue Service (IRS), 231
"In Da Club," 215
Invincible, 7, 183–88, 217
Iovine, Jimmy, 176, 181
Ireland, 9, 208–9
"Is It Scary," 180
"I Want You Back," 26, 28–29, 32

J

Jackson, Hazel Gordy (sister-in-law),
    31, 33–34, 37–38
Jackson, Jackie (brother), 13–15, 33
    athletic activities of, 19, 23, 31
    Neverland visits of, 142–43
    Victory Tour and, 81–85, 89, 92–93
Jackson, Janet (sister), 13, 181, 225
    brother's drug use and, 186–87
    brother's will and, 228–29
    Captain EO and, 117
    HIStory and, 176
Jackson, Jermaine (brother), 12–15, 19,
    21, 165
    Apollo and, 22–23
    brother's comeback and, 217
    brother's injuries and, 87, 182
    brother's marriage and, 172
    brother's will and, 228–29
    Gordy's daughter and, 31, 33–34,
        37–38
    Jackson 5 and, 17, 20, 22–23, 37, 41,
        255*n*
    Jacksons and, 41–42, 87
    solo career of, 38, 81, 89
    Victory Tour and, 81–85, 88–89,
        91–93
Jackson, Jesse, 195, 200
Jackson, Joe (father), 16, 56, 136, 182, 229
    ATV acquisition and, 101
    Bad and, 126
    children's upbringing and, 4, 15,
        18–19, 21, 41, 71
    employment of, 14–15, 19
    Epic and, 37, 40, 43
    Gordy and, 26–27, 31, 37, 40–41
    Jackson 5 and, 15, 17–22, 25–26,
        29, 37
    Jacksons and, 40–43, 50
    Motown and, 18, 20, 22, 25–26, 40–41
    move to Los Angeles of, 28
    musical talents of, 14–15, 18
    Neverland visits of, 143
    son's age and, 33
    son's childhood and, 4, 13, 15, 19
    son's death and, 224, 230–31
    son's musical talents and, 15, 28
    son's physical appearance and, 34
    son's relationship with, 41, 51, 56, 71
    son's social life and, 45
    This Is It and, 218
    Victory Tour and, 82, 84–85
Jackson, Katherine (mother), 13–14,
    19, 135–36, 143
    disappearance of, 229
    Jackson 5 and, 18, 20
    move to Los Angeles of, 28
    musical talents of, 14
    son's childhood and, 16
    son's death and, 224–26, 230–31
    son's marriage and, 171

son's will and, 225–26, 228–30
Victory Tour and, 82, 84–85
Jackson, Keith (cousin), 12, 19, 49
Jackson 5 and, 30–31
Jackson, La Toya (sister), 12–13, 45
Jackson, Marlon (brother), 13, 22, 41
Victory Tour and, 81–85, 88–89,
92–93
Jackson, Maureen "Rebbie" (sister), 13,
228–29
Jackson, Michael:
adolescence of, 32–34, 42, 44–46
alleged eccentricities of, 122–24,
134, 160–61, 190–91, 232
ambitions and goals of, 10, 50, 57–59,
65, 75, 92, 98–99, 112, 115, 117,
123, 126, 128, 146–47, 149, 152–53,
155–56, 170, 172, 179–80, 216–17,
240
anger of, 58–59, 169, 189, 193
artistic freedom issues of, 32, 35, 37,
91–92, 115, 129–30, 158
autobiography of, 3, 17–18, 45, 47,
51, 57, 61, 91–92, 97, 115, 137,
139–40, 228
awards and honors of, 57, 67, 77–79,
81, 87, 128, 134, 137, 153, 224
birth of, 9, 13, 27
business acumen of, 5–7, 13, 16, 39,
42, 50–51, 77, 83, 86, 93, 97, 102,
109, 118–19, 122, 143
business education of, 4, 29, 32, 36,
44, 54, 70, 72
childhood of, 4, 8–9, 11–19, 21–22,
25, 30, 34, 38, 47, 49, 55, 58, 71,
88, 133, 137, 223, 242–43
childlike qualities of, 31, 46, 51, 162,
165, 206
child molestation allegations
against, 6, 118, 162–70, 173,
175–76, 186, 193–200, 231
children of, 1, 180, 190, 197–99,
201, 208, 211, 216, 225–26, 229,
231, 240

clothing line of, 3, 93–94, 144, 173,
215–16
comebacks of, 121–22, 214–21, 225,
232
comparisons between Greenburg
and, 8–9
controversial business dealings of,
124–26
crying of, 9, 23, 34, 137, 201
dancing of, 7, 9, 18, 46–47, 50,
68, 70–72, 87, 92, 98, 113, 116,
132–33, 136, 139, 142, 150, 159,
175, 232, 238
death of, 2, 6–8, 11, 38, 52, 110, 118,
168, 182, 223–28, 230–33, 238,
240, 243, 250
debts and loans of, 7–8, 10, 107,
173, 186, 188, 200–207, 210–13,
222, 225–28, 230
divorces of, 179–80
drugs taken by, 7, 88, 150, 166–67,
169, 180, 182, 186–87, 197, 206,
212, 217, 220–21, 223, 230
earnings of, 3, 6, 17–18, 26, 52, 54,
72–73, 77, 81, 87, 93–94, 97, 110,
121, 134, 139, 157–58, 166–68,
178, 186, 200, 206, 212–13, 218,
237, 240, 242, 250–51
emotional issues of, 34, 166–68,
202–4, 206, 219–21
estate of, 8, 52, 57, 170, 200, 207,
226–32, 234–40, 250, 252
expenditures of, 6–7, 157, 178,
185–86, 202–3, 207, 212–13
fears of, 23, 207, 217, 219
film career of, 3, 6–9, 44–46, 49–50,
57, 65–66, 110, 112–19, 139,
141, 149, 154, 156, 163–65, 170,
179–80, 192–93, 213, 216–17,
227–28, 231–32
generosity and charitableness of, 6,
16–17, 31, 78, 80–81, 87, 93, 105,
153, 159–60, 182, 187, 201, 219,
226, 249

Jackson, Michael (*cont.*)
heritage of, 180
illnesses of, 6, 17, 128, 160, 219–21
injuries of, 87–88, 150, 181–82
inquisitiveness of, 4, 21, 28, 37, 147
insecurity of, 9–10, 217
instincts and intuition of, 3, 8, 42,
    53, 102, 109, 160, 173, 175
intelligence of, 4, 8, 10, 13, 21, 160,
    212, 214
international audiences of, 33, 71,
    79, 129–31, 133, 146, 158, 164,
    166–67, 178, 215, 217–18, 221,
    223, 225, 242
jackets of, 93, 223–24, 236
lawsuits and trials of, 151, 165,
    168–69, 173, 195–200, 202–6,
    208, 225
legacy of, 7–8, 134, 151, 195, 226,
    231–32, 237, 249
lyrics controversy of, 176–77
marketing and promotion of, 5, 42,
    77, 88, 138
marriages of, 52, 171–72, 178–80
motivational speeches of, 72–73
museum for, 236
musical education of, 18, 21, 28,
    31–32, 42–43
musical talents of, 9, 12, 14–16, 19,
    28, 32, 42, 48–50, 127, 149, 176
perfectionism of, 4, 7, 9, 45, 49,
    70–71, 74, 118, 122, 126, 133–34,
    149–50, 152, 155–56, 160, 171,
    177, 185
physical appearance of, 1, 6–7, 34,
    44, 47, 83, 128, 132, 147, 149–50,
    159–60, 192, 196–98, 209, 219,
    224
popularity and fame of, 3, 7, 30, 35,
    46, 49, 68, 71, 81, 87, 90–91, 113,
    117, 121, 129, 133, 156, 161,
    166, 171, 173, 197, 207, 209–10,
    217–18, 223–24, 232–33, 239,
    242

postmortem recordings of, 227–28,
    231–32
press on, 30, 49–50, 62, 123–25,
    128–29, 156, 158, 165, 171–72,
    176, 187, 190, 194–95, 197, 199,
    217, 223
problems with advisors of, 6, 76,
    148–50, 157–58, 177–78, 189–90,
    192, 194, 199–200, 202, 204–5,
    208, 212, 220, 228, 241
public appearances avoided by, 46,
    117–19, 121, 199
public image and reputation of, 6, 86,
    117, 120–24, 134, 136, 140–41,
    146, 158, 171, 173, 190–92, 212,
    231–32
reading of, 59, 195
recognition denied to, 57–58, 62
relationships between children and,
    142–43, 161–62, 164, 166, 192–93,
    197
religious beliefs of, 45–46, 75–76,
    91, 124
royal nickname acquired by, 136–38
on secrecy, 122
security for, 91–92, 129, 153, 167,
    179, 194, 203, 211
self-confidence of, 10, 32, 133
sense of humor of, 91, 98, 105,
    113–14, 127, 130, 132, 154, 171
shoe line of, 3, 144, 146–47, 149–52,
    173, 215
shoes worn by, 130, 136, 239
showmanship and professionalism
    of, 45, 122, 145
social life of, 45–46
sunglasses worn by, 13, 53–54, 147,
    159, 239
surgeries of, 88, 128, 150, 160, 232
video game deals of, 3, 139, 144,
    170–71, 228
Jackson, Randy (brother), 13
brother's debts and, 200–201, 205–6
brother's drug use and, 186–87, 197

brother's lawsuits and, 204–6
brother's will and, 225–26, 228–29
and child molestation allegations
   against brother, 193–94
Jacksons and, 42–43
songwriting of, 43, 56
Victory Tour and, 81–85, 89, 92–93
Jackson, Tito (brother), 13–15, 172,
   229
   athletic activities of, 31
   brother's drug use and, 186–87
   Jackson 5 and, 17, 22–23
   marriage of, 33
   Victory Tour and, 81–85, 89, 92–93
Jackson, T. J. (nephew), 229
Jackson 5, 49, 58, 132–33, 239
   Apollo and, 22–23, 25
   artistic freedom of, 35–36
   birth of, 15
   earnings of, 21, 26, 31, 40
   Gordy and, 4, 20, 24–30, 35, 37–38,
      40–41, 255n
   international audiences of, 33–35
   Jackson's song acquisitions and, 99
   Motown and, 4, 17–18, 20, 22,
      24–26, 28–31, 37–38, 40–41, 81,
      255n
   move to Los Angeles of, 27–28
   polishing and promoting of, 19–20
   popularity and fame of, 30–31,
      33–35
   press on, 30, 62
   recordings of, 20, 25–30, 32–34, 40
   rehearsing and practicing of, 17–19
   reunions of, 70, 187
   touring of, 4, 18, 21, 30–31, 33–35,
      37
Jacksons (group), 40–46, 50–51, 56–57,
   181
   cartoon show of, 42
   CBS and, 40–41, 43–44, 54
   Motown 25 and, 70, 81
   Pepsi ad of, 86–87
   recordings of, 42–43, 57, 81

relationships between brothers in,
   89, 91–92
reunions of, 80–82
television show of, 42
Victory Tour and, 80, 89–93, 95
Jacksons, The (album), 42
Jagger, Mick, 81, 88, 219
"Jam," 159
Japan, 34, 71, 129–31, 139, 164
Jay Z, 3, 8, 144–45, 170, 215–16, 236
Jehovah's Witnesses, 18, 45–46, 124
   "Thriller" video and, 75–76, 91
Jerkins, Rodney, 183, 186
Jews, 176–77, 206
Jobete, 99
Joel, Billy, 63, 67, 121, 128–29, 185
Johnson, Jack, 195
Johnson, John, 1, 102
Jones, E. Rodney, 19–20
Jones, Quincy, 176
   awards and honors of, 77–78, 141
   Bad and, 126–27
   Bad Tour and, 129
   "Billie Jean" video and, 67
   Jackson's ambitions and, 58–59
   Jackson's relationship with, 47–48,
      153, 268n
   Thriller and, 58–60, 62, 77
   The Wiz and, 47
Jordan, Michael, 3, 145–47

K
Katzenberg, Jeff, 111–12, 114–15
Katzenstein, Andrew, 226, 230
Kawashima, Dale, 108, 131, 157,
   181–82
Keith, Gordon, 20, 27
Kelley, Kitty, 73
Kellogg, John, 68–69
King, Don, 82–85
King, Jamie, 238–39
Kingdom Entertainment, 172
Knight, Gladys, 4, 21–22, 26, 37
Koppelman, Charles, 100–107

Korakuen Stadium, 129, 131
Kraft, Robert, 94

L

Lady Gaga, 97, 233
"Lady in My Life, The," 61
LA Gear, 145–47
　Jackson's shoe deal with, 3, 146–47,
　　149–52
Laliberté, Guy, 235, 241
Landis, John, 74–76
Langford, Karen, 54, 98, 171, 236
Las Vegas, Nev., 9, 13, 191–93, 213
　Immortal and, 236, 241
　Jackson in, 209–12, 216
　Jackson's house in, 211
　Jackson's search for new house in,
　　221–22
　One in, 234–35, 238, 240–41
Leach, Robin, 241
"Leave Me Alone," 128
LeGrand, David, 189–90
LeMarque, Philip, 196
Lemorande, Rusty:
　Captain EO and, 110–19, 163–64
　on Jackson's business acumen, 118–19
　Jackson's film project miniatures
　　and, 163–65
　Jackson's relationship with, 113–15,
　　117
Lennon, John, 96, 100, 108, 240
　and licensing of "Revolution,"
　　124–25
Leno, Jay, 196–97
Levine, Michael, 120–23, 134
licensing, 36, 93, 215
　ATV and, 107–8
　of Beatles' recordings, 124–26,
　　141–42
Like a Virgin, 121
Liles, Kevin, 5, 72
Living with Michael Jackson, 192–93
London, 52, 97, 115, 118, 157, 167,
　215, 223

ATV acquisition and, 102–6
Jackson 5 and, 33
This Is It and, 217–18, 221, 225
Lookin' Through the Windows, 34
Lord, Donny B., 142–43
Loren, Bryan, 131
Lorenzo's Oil, 8–9
Los Angeles, Calif., 9, 35, 47, 58, 68,
　77, 88, 98, 105, 112, 118, 120,
　142, 159, 170, 193, 221
　"Beat It" video and, 68
　Branca and, 52, 55, 157
　and child molestation allegations
　　against Jackson, 162–63, 165,
　　169
　Jackson 5's move to, 27–28
　Jackson's children and, 231
　Jackson's death and, 224, 226
　Jackson's LA Gear deal and, 147
　Motown and, 24, 27
　Victory Tour and, 84, 92
Los Angeles Times, 118, 125, 128, 156,
　171, 194, 223, 237
Love!, 235, 238, 241
"Love You Save, The," 30
Lucas, George, 110, 112–17
Ludacris, 4, 72
Lugosi, Bela, 76, 157
Lumet, Sidney, 44–45

M

McCartney, Paul, 96–97, 160, 240
　ATV and, 100–101, 106, 108
　Jackson's relationship with, 97, 106,
　　125
　songs owned by, 97, 125
　Thriller and, 59–60, 64
McClain, John, 8, 52, 181, 225–30
McGuinness, Paul, 230
Madison Square Garden, 95, 145, 186
Madonna, 85, 121, 160
"Man in the Mirror," 128, 176, 239
Maresca, Ernie, 98
Martin, Tom, 208–9

Marvel Comics, 3, 172–73, 191
master recordings, 36–37, 125
  Jackson's ownership of, 3, 37, 73, 79, 260*n*
MCA Records, 63–64, 103
Mellencamp, John, 125
Mercedes-Benz, 191–92
Mesereau, Tom, 193–98, 200
Mesnick, Michael, 53
Mexico, 52, 167, 224–25
Michael, 215
Michael Jackson's Ghosts, 179
Michael Jackson's This Is It, 8, 227–28, 232
  see also This Is It (concert series)
Michael Jackson The Immortal World Tour, 235–42
Mijac Music, 57, 99, 138, 191, 212, 232
  administration of, 108
  Jackson's lawsuit and, 204
  Jackson's loans and, 228
  and Sony's merger with ATV, 174
Mills, Stephanie, 44–45
Minor, Cynthia, 86, 90–92
Mister Lucky's Lounge, 16–17
MJJ Music, 156, 172
"Monster," 215
Moon, Sun Myung, 143
Moonwalker (film), 139, 154
Moonwalker (video game), 170–71
moonwalking (dance), 70–72, 105, 159, 191, 223, 238, 247
"Morphine," 180
Moslehi, Hamid, 192–93
Motown: The Musical, 24, 38
Motown Records, 24–33, 49, 54, 56
  artistic freedom issues and, 32, 35–37
  Gordy and, 4, 20, 24–28, 33, 37, 41, 69, 99, 189, 255*n*
  Jackson 5 and, 4, 17–18, 20, 22, 24–26, 28–31, 37–38, 40–41, 81, 255*n*
  Jackson's solo recordings for, 43–44
  Knight and, 21–22
  move to Los Angeles of, 24, 27
Motown 25: Yesterday, Today, Forever, 69–71, 81, 260*n*
Mottola, Tommy, 148, 174
  alleged racism of, 188–89
  Jackson's relationship with, 185, 187–89, 226
Moving Violation, 34
MTV, 57, 65, 237
  "Billie Jean" video and, 5, 66–67
  Jackson's royal nickname and, 137–38
  "Thriller" video and, 74–75, 77
Muhammad, Leonard, 194
Murray, Conrad, 7, 220–21, 223, 230
Museum of Natural History, 87
music publishing, 154
  Beatles' catalogue and, *see under* Beatles
  Branca and, 2, 52–53, 56–57, 98–104, 106, 108, 138–39, 166, 173–74, 252
  Jackson's debts and, 200–205, 212–13
  Jackson's song acquisitions and, 1–2, 5, 52–53, 98–109, 121, 125–26, 131, 138–39, 141, 166, 173–75, 181–82, 186, 189, 191, 200–204, 207, 212–14, 240, 252
  see also copyrights; licensing; royalties; *specific music publishers*
music videos, 150
  to *Bad*, 139
  to "Beat It," 5, 7, 68–69, 71, 74, 86
  to "Billie Jean," 5, 66–68, 71, 74, 92, 116, 145
  to "Can You Feel It," 57, 65–66
  Captain EO and, 113, 116
  Jackson's clothing line and, 93–94
  Jackson's impact on, 5, 7, 77, 113, 163
  to "Leave Me Alone," 128
  One and, 239
  to *Thriller* (album), 65–69, 71, 73–77, 91, 112

music videos (*cont.*)
    to "Thriller" (song), 5, 74–77, 91,
        93, 116, 139, 157, 227
My Friend Michael (Cascio), 162
"My Girl," 17–18

N
Nas, 207
Neverland Valley Ranch, 9, 210–14,
        236
    and child molestation allegations
        against Jackson, 165, 176, 193,
        196
    children at, 142–43, 161–62, 185,
        192–93, 196, 198, 201
    Dangerous and, 153–55, 157
    foreclosure of, 211–13
    Jackson family visits to, 142–43, 198
    and Jackson's appearance on
        Winfrey's special, 160–61
    Jackson's death and, 224
    Jackson's debts and, 201, 205–6
    Jackson's expenditures on, 157, 185,
        203
    Jackson's purchase of, 136
    and Jackson's search for new home,
        221–22
    and *Living with Michael Jackson*,
        192–93
    physical appearance of, 135–36
    value of, 5, 143, 207
New Balance, 145
New York Times, 65, 118, 128, 140, 156,
        176, 187, 237
Ne-Yo, 216, 232
Nielsen Company, 40, 160, 224, 249
Nike, 3, 124–26, 145–47
"No Diggity," 176
Notorious B.I.G., 175

O
Obama, Barack, 95, 219
*OFFICIAL MICHAEL JACKSON
    OPUS, THE*, 97

Off the Wall, 43, 48–51, 54–55, 57–59,
        64
Onassis, Jackie Kennedy, 45, 139
One, 234–35, 238–42
O'Neal, Shaquille, 175–76
Ono, Yoko, 100–101, 104, 106, 124–25
Ortega, Kenny, 219–21

P
Parker, Tom, 148
"Penny Lane," 100, 105
Pepsi, 249
    BAD 25 and, 231–32
    Jackson's endorsement deals with,
        2, 68, 86–88, 121, 125, 150, 173,
        182, 231
Perry, Katy, 127–28, 233
Petrucci, Ottaviano, 36
Petty, Tom, 125–26
Phillinganes, Greg, 48, 236–37
Phillips, Randy, 215, 217, 220–21
Picasso, Pablo, 101–2, 185
Pittman, Bob, 66–67
Porcaro, Steve, 60
Prefontaine, Steve, 145
Prescient Acquisition, 200, 202, 205–6
Presley, Elvis, 96, 230
    comparisons between Jackson and,
        115, 136–37, 148, 163
    Jackson's song acquisitions and, 5,
        98, 181, 204
    Viva Elvis and, 235, 241
Presley, Lisa Marie (first wife), 167, 207
    Jackson's divorce from, 179–80
    Jackson's marriage to, 52, 171–72,
        178–79
Prince, 6, 108, 121, 127, 160
Propofol, 220–21, 223, 230
publishing rights, 36–37, 56, 97, 141
Purple Rain, 121

R
Reagan, Nancy, 73
Reagan, Ronald, 78, 224

Regal Theatre, 19, 21–22, 25
"Revolution," 124–26
Richards, Keith, 65
Riley, Teddy, 153–55, 215, 268*n*
    Dangerous and, 153–54
    HIStory and, 176
Roberts, Kenny, 98–99
Robinson, Smokey, 4, 21, 26, 34, 41,
    50, 69
"Rock with You," 49
Rolling Stone, 30, 50, 62, 64, 128, 157
Rolling Stones, 1, 65, 147, 160, 230
    touring of, 95, 213, 241
Rosemount, 208–9
Ross, Diana, 121
    Jackson's relationship with, 28,
        46–47
    Motown and, 24, 29
    The Wiz and, 45–47, 49
Rowe, Debbie (second wife), 180, 197
royalties, 4, 40, 97–99, 146, 172, 215,
    249
    BMI and, 54, 204
    Jackson's debts and, 203–4
    Jackson's Sony deal and, 156
    Motown and, 26
    songwriters and, 36, 54
    Thriller and, 73
Rudin, Mickey, 72–73
Run-D.M.C., 69, 145

S

Saemann, Sandy, 146–47, 150–51
Santa Barbara, Calif., 165, 176, 198
Santa Maria, Calif., 194–96
Schaffel, Marc, 194
Schumacher, Joel, 179–80
    The Wiz and, 7, 44–46, 50, 179
"Scream," 176
Sega, Sega Genesis, 3, 139, 170–71
September 11 attacks, 187, 189
"Shake Your Body (Down to the
    Ground)," 43, 56
Sharpton, Al, 85, 188–89, 195, 226

Sheldon, Dom, 176
"She's Out of My Life," 49
Shields, Brooke, 87, 160
Sinatra, Frank, 72–73, 136, 147
Sinclair, Catherine, 18
SK Energy, 152, 249
Skywriter, 34
Sly and the Family Stone, 5, 98–99,
    126
"Smooth Criminal," 128, 130
Sneddon, Tom, 176
songs, songwriters, songwriting, 48, 97
    Bad and, 127–28
    and *Blood on the Dance Floor*, 181
    controversial lyrics in, 176–77
    Dangerous and, 153, 155
    Gordy and, 32, 37
    of Jackson, 37, 40, 43–44, 49, 54,
        56–60, 81–82, 116, 121, 127–28,
        135, 149, 153, 155, 170, 176–77,
        180–81, 215–16, 232
    Jacksons and, 40, 42–43
    monetary value of, 36, 56
    royalties and, 36, 54
    Thriller and, 58–61
    see also music publishing; *specific*
        music publishers
Sonic the Hedgehog 3, 170–71
Sony, Sony Music, 8, 172
    in attempt to acquire ATV, 166
    ATV's merger with, 3, 6–7, 173–75
    CBS acquired by, 128–29
    Invincible and, 184–86, 188
    Jackson's feud with, 188–89
    Jackson's record deals with, 156,
        177, 184, 187
    Yetnikoff and, 140, 148, 150
Sony/ATV, 107, 188–89, 211–13, 232,
    251
    Barrack on, 212–13
    and child molestation allegations
        against Jackson, 195–96
    creation of, 174
    EMI acquired by, 240

Sony/ATV (*cont.*)
  Jackson's death and, 226–27
  and Jackson's loans and debts, 186,
    188, 200–202, 212–13, 228, 230
  songs owned and administered by,
    52–53, 57, 96, 108, 181, 204
  value of, 6–7, 97, 108–9, 175, 195,
    207, 212, 227, 252
Spann, Pervis, 19–20
Spielberg, Steven, 63, 111, 115, 177, 190
Springsteen, Bruce, 63, 67, 108, 121,
    128–29, 160, 185
Stabler, Donald, 200–202, 205–6
"State of Shock," 81, 88
Steeltown Records, 20, 25, 27
Stiffelman, Gary, 102, 149
"Stranger in Moscow," 170, 176, 239
Sullivan, Charles:
    background of, 80, 84–85
    Jackson's clothing line and, 93–94
    physical appearance of, 80, 84, 92
    Victory Tour and, 80–81, 84–86, 88,
      90–91, 93–95
Sullivan, John Jeremiah, 180
Sullivan, Pat, 95
Super Bowl, 89, 94
    Jackson's halftime show at, 158–60
Swedien, Bea, 48, 127, 129
Swedien, Bruce, 88, 127, 129, 153,
      268*n*
    Invincible and, 185
    Jackson's relationship with, 48–49
    Thriller and, 60–62
Swift, Taylor, 7, 97, 228, 233, 237

T

Taylor, Elizabeth, 160
    and child molestation allegations
      against Jackson, 167–68
    Jackson's relationship with, 137, 142,
      167
"Tell Me I'm Not Dreamin' (Too
    Good to Be True)," 88–89
Temperton, Rod, 48, 58–61

Temptations, 12, 17, 37
"They Don't Care About Us," 176
This Is It (album), 227–28
This Is It (concert series), 217–21, 232
    Jackson's death and, 225
    Jackson's health problems and,
      219–21
    rehearsals for, 8, 127, 218–21, 227
This Is It (film), 8, 227–28, 232
"Thoughts on Work and Secrecy"
    (Jackson), 122
3T, 172
Thriller (album), 7, 46, 58–69, 71–80,
      84, 114, 137, 149, 152
    awards and honors of, 71, 77–78,
      87, 141
    Bad and, 126–28
    Dangerous and, 156, 158
    music videos to, 65–69, 71, 73–77,
      91, 112
    profitability of, 121
    promotion of, 65, 67–68, 73
    recording technology and, 60–61, 184
    reviews of, 64–65, 77
    sales of, 2, 4, 33, 64–65, 71, 73, 79,
      81, 87, 121, 148
    Victory Tour and, 80, 89, 92
"Thriller" (song), 159, 215, 218–19
    budget of, 74–77
    Jehovah's Witnesses and, 75–76, 91
    music video to, 5, 74–77, 91, 93,
      116, 139, 157, 227
TimeOut, 49
Tohme, Tohme, 210–11
Tokyo, 129, 131, 157, 164
Tompkins, Dennis, 114, 130
"Torture," 81
Tree of Hope, 22–23
Triumph, 81
Tucker, Chris, 196–97

U

United Kingdom, 33, 79, 99, 192,
    218–19

V

Van Halen, Eddie, 60
Vanity Fair, 190
Victory, 81, 88
Victory Tour, 80–86, 88–95, 103,
    129–30, 143
    fans' reactions to, 89–90
    financing of, 80–82, 84–85, 90,
        93–94
    gross earnings of, 80, 92
    Jackson's disappointment with,
        91–92
    merchandizing for, 84, 90, 92
    promotion and marketing of, 85–86,
        88, 94
    staging shows in, 88–89, 92–93
    threatened boycotts and protests
        on, 85–86
    ticket sales of, 81–82, 84, 86, 90,
        92–93
Viva Elvis, 235, 241
Vogel, Joe, 121, 126
voodoo story, 190

W

Warner, Warner Music, 67, 99, 138,
    227
"We Are the World," 121, 159
Weinberg, Neil, 35
Wenner, Jann, 62
Westlake Recording Studios, 58–59,
    126–27
"What More Can I Give," 187
White, Barry, 41, 131
White, Chris, 226
"Who Is It," 170
Wiener, Jon, 125
Wiesner, Dieter, 178, 181, 191–92, 194,
    271*n*

Williams, Pharrell, 4, 216
Winfrey, Oprah, 95, 137, 162, 172, 207,
    219
    Jackson's appearance on special of,
        9, 34, 70, 137, 158, 160–62, 192
Wiz, The, 7, 44–47, 49–50, 57, 65–66,
    112, 179
Wonder, Stevie, 24–25, 35
World Food Programme (WFP), 249

Y

"Yesterday," 1, 100, 108
Yetnikoff, Walter, 41, 50, 71, 89, 117,
    217
    apology to Branca of, 78–79
    ATV acquisition and, 102, 109
    "Billie Jean" video and, 66–67, 73
    CBS and, 2, 7, 39–40, 44, 51, 63–65,
        67–68, 72, 78, 91, 98, 102, 106,
        129, 141
    and *Days of Thunder* soundtrack,
        141–42
    firing of, 148, 150, 157
    Geffen's relationship with, 140–42,
        148
    Jacksons and, 40, 91
    Jackson's awards and, 77–78
    Jackson's business acumen and, 39,
        42, 51, 109
    Jackson's E.T. project and, 63–64,
        79
    Jackson's master recordings
        ownership and, 79, 260*n*
    Jackson's relationship with, 7, 43–44,
        73, 77–79, 184–85
    Thriller and, 61–62, 65, 67–68, 73–74,
        77, 79
"You Are Not Alone," 176
Yu, Susan, 194–95, 198, 200

ABOUT THE AUTHOR

Zack O'Malley Greenburg is a senior editor at *Forbes* and author of the Jay Z biography *Empire State of Mind* (2011), which Bloomberg News called "one of the year's best rock books." A child star, Zack played the title role in the film *Lorenzo's Oil* alongside Nick Nolte and Susan Sarandon. He graduated from Yale with a degree in American Studies in 2007 and immediately joined the staff at *Forbes*, where he has since chronicled pension-fund scandals, investigated the tourism business in post-conflict Sierra Leone, and written cover stories on the business of Justin Bieber and Toby Keith. Zack's work has also appeared in *The Washington Post*, *Sports Illustrated*, *Vibe*, and *McSweeney's*, among others; he has served as a guest on television programs including *Good Day New York*, *Entertainment Tonight*, and *60 Minutes*. He lives in New York with his soon-to-be wife, Danielle. For more, follow Zack on Twitter (@zogblog) and visit his website (www.zogreenburg.com).

ABOUT THE COVER

To capture Michael Jackson as he'd never been captured before, Simon & Schuster commissioned contemporary pop artist Borbay. He used his signature medium—acrylic paint over a collage of *New York Post* headlines—to interpret the author's words and the King of Pop's career in a single, arresting image. Borbay, dubbed the Big Apple's most creative resident by *Time Out New York*, has been recognized by publications from *BBC World* to *Wall Street Journal Japan*. His subjects range from Kanye West to the Guggenheim Museum, earning him comparisons to Andy Warhol for his deft manipulation of pop imagery. He lives in Manhattan with his gorgeous wife, Erin, and their daughter, Coraline. For more on Borbay, visit his website (www.borbay.com). For more on the cover, head over to www.michaeljacksoninc.com/cover.